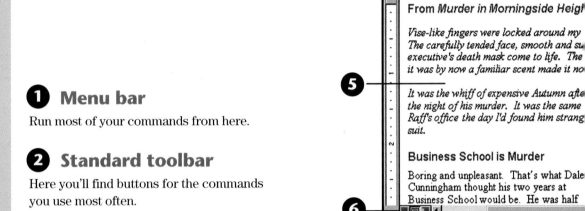

❶ Menu bar

Run most of your commands from here.

❷ Standard toolbar

Here you'll find buttons for the commands you use most often.

❸ Formatting toolbar

Here you'll find buttons for commands that change the look of your text and page.

❹ TipWizard

Check here for tips on how to use Word more effectively.

❺ Document window

This is where you type your document.

❻ View buttons

Use these buttons to control how your document is displayed.

❼ Ruler

Margin boundaries and tab stops are shown here.

❽ Scroll arrows

Use these arrows to scroll the page one line at a time.

❾ Scroll box

Drag here to scroll quickly through your document.

Formatting Paragraphs	Shortcut
Decrease hanging indent by tab	Ctrl+◆Shift+T
Single space between lines	Ctrl+1
1.5 spaces between lines	Ctrl+5
Double space between lines	Ctrl+2
Add/remove 12 points of space before a paragraph	Ctrl+0
Remove paragraph formats	Ctrl+Q
Display/hide nonprinting characters	Ctrl+*

Other Important Actions	Shortcut
To Get help	F1
To Find text	Ctrl+F
To Find and replace text	Ctrl+H
To Go to a page	Ctrl+G, F5
To Run spell checker	F7
To Run thesaurus	◆Shift+F7

Changing your Word options

To change any of the following options, choose <u>T</u>ools, <u>O</u>ptions and click the tab listed in the second column.

To Do This...	Choose This Tab
AutoFormat as you type	AutoFormat
Automatic save	Save
Automatic spell checking	Spelling
Automatic word selection	Edit
Background repagination	General
Backup copy	Save
Beep on error actions	General
Blue background, white text	General
Compatibility options for other software	Compatibility
Custom dictionaries	Spelling
Drag-and-drop text editing	Edit
Embed TrueType fonts	Save
Fast saves	Save
File locations	File locations
Grammar and style rules	Grammar
Mailing address	User Info
Measurement units	General
Name	User Info
Overtype mode	Edit
Password protection	Save
Printing: Annotations	Print

To Do This...	Choose This Tab
Printing: Background printing	Print
Printing: Default tray	Print
Printing: Drawing objects	Print
Printing: Hidden text	Print
Printing: Summary info	Print
Replace special characters with symbols	AutoFormat
Replace straight quotes with smart quotes	AutoFormat
Show tab characters	View
Show bookmarks	View
Show hidden text	View
Show scroll bars	View
Show highlight	View
Show paragraph marks	View
Show spaces	View
Show status bar	View
Spell checking	Spelling
TipWizard active	General
Typing replaces selection	Edit
Use smart cut and paste	Edit

Word's Best Keyboard Shortcuts

Managing Files	Shortcut
Start new document	Ctrl+N
Save current document	Ctrl+S
Close current document	Ctrl+W
Open document from disk	Ctrl+O
Print current document	Ctrl+P

Selecting Text	Shortcut
Select to end of word	Ctrl+⬆Shift+→
Select to start of word	Ctrl+⬆Shift+←
Select to end of line	Ctrl+End
Select to start of line	Ctrl+Home
Select to end of paragraph	Ctrl+⬆Shift+↓
Select to start of paragraph	Ctrl+⬆Shift+↑
Select document	Ctrl+A
Select to end of document	Ctrl+⬆Shift+End
Select to start of document	Ctrl+⬆Shift+Home

Editing Text	Shortcut
Delete selected text	Del
Delete character before insertion point	⬅Backspace
Delete character after insertion point	Del
Delete to end of word	Ctrl+Del
Delete to start of word	Ctrl+⬅Backspace
Cut selected text to Clipboard	Ctrl+X
Copy selected text to Clipboard	Ctrl+C
Paste selected text from Clipboard	Ctrl+V

Moving the Insertion Point	Shortcut
Move to next character	→
Move to previous character	←
Move one line up	↑
Move one line down	↓
Move to start of next word	Ctrl+→
Move to start of previous word	Ctrl+←
Move to start of line	Home
Move to end of line	End
Move to start of next paragraph	Ctrl+↓

Moving the Insertion Point	Shortcut
Move to start of current paragraph	Ctrl+↑
Move to top of screen	Ctrl+PgUp
Move to bottom of screen	Ctrl+PgDn
Move up one screen	PgUp
Move down one screen	PgDn
Move to top of document	Ctrl+Home
Move to bottom of document	Ctrl+End

Formatting Text	Shortcut
Turn boldface on/off	Ctrl+B
Turn italics on/off	Ctrl+I
Turn underline on/off	Ctrl+U
Underline words only on/off	Ctrl+⬆Shift+W
Double underline on/off	Ctrl+⬆Shift+D
Turn subscript on/off	Ctrl+=
Turn small caps on/off	Ctrl+⬆Shift+K
Turn all caps on/off	Ctrl+⬆Shift+A
Change case	⬆Shift+F3
Turn superscript on/off	Ctrl+⬆Shift+=
Hide/Show text	Ctrl+⬆Shift+H
Copy formats	Ctrl+⬆Shift+C
Paste formats	Ctrl+⬆Shift+V
Remove formats	Ctrl+Spacebar
Change point size	Ctrl+⬆Shift+P
Next larger point size	Ctrl+>
Next smaller point size	Ctrl+<
Up one point size	Ctrl+]
Down one point size	Ctrl+[
Change font	Ctrl+⬆Shift+F

Formatting Paragraphs	Shortcut
Left-align text	Ctrl+L
Right-align text	Ctrl+R
Center text	Ctrl+E
Justify text	Ctrl+J
Indent one tab from left margin	Ctrl+M
Decrease indent by one tab	Ctrl+⬆Shift+M
Create one-tab hanging indent	Ctrl+T

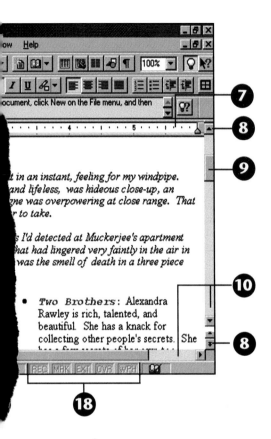

QUE®

201 W. 103rd Street Indianapolis, IN 46290
(317) 581-3500
Copyright© 1995 Que Corporation

13 ## Section number

Shows the current section.

14 ## Page number/ number of pages

Shows the current page number and the number of pages in the document.

15 ## Insertion point location

Shows the distance of the insertion point from the top of the image.

10 ## Scroll bars

Click above or below the scroll box on the vertical scroll bar to scroll your document one page at a time.

16 ## Line number

Shows the current line of the insertion point.

17 ## Column

Shows the character position of the insertion point within the line of text.

11 ## Status bar

Check here for information about your document, current action, toolbar buttons, and menu commands.

18 ## Mode indicators

Appear when modes such as Overstrike and Mark Revisions are active.

12 ## Page number

Shows the current page.

Using

Word for Windows 95

Using
Word for Windows 95

Eric Maloney

and

Joshua C. Nossiter

Using Word for Windows 95

Library of Congress Catalog Number: 95-78876

ISBN: 0-7897-0085-9

97 96 95   6 5 4 3 2

Interpretation of the printing code: The rightmost double-digit number is the year of the book's printing; the rightmost single-digit number, the number of the book's printing. For example, a printing code of 95-1 shows that the first printing of the book occurred in 1995.

Screen reproductions in this book were created using Collage Plus from Inner Media, Inc., Hollis, NH.

Credits

President
Roland Elgey

Vice President and Publisher
Marie Butler-Knight

Associate Publisher
Don Roche, Jr.

Editorial Services Director
Elizabeth Keaffaber

Director of Marketing
Lynn E. Zingraf

Managing Editor
Michael Cunningham

Senior Series Editor
Chris Nelson

Acquisitions Editors
Deborah Abshier
Jenny L. Watson

Product Director
Kathie-Jo Arnoff

Product Development Specialists
Robin Drake
Lorna Gentry
Lisa D. Wagner

Editor
Lynn Northrup

Assistant Product Marketing Manager
Kim Margolius

Technical Editor
Gregory A. Dew

Technical Specialist
Cari Skaggs

Acquisitions Assistant
Tracy M. Williams

Editorial Assistants
Jill Byus
Carmen Phelps

Novice Reviewer
Angela Kozlowski

Book Designer
Dan Armstrong

Cover Designer
Dan Armstrong

Production Team
Angela D. Bannan, Claudia Bell,
Chad Dressler, DiMonique Ford,
Karen Gregor-York, Daryl Kessler,
Julie Quinn, Kaylene Riemen,
Bobbi Satterfield, Michael Thomas,
Scott Tullis, Kelly Warner

Indexer
Mary Jane Frisby

Composed in *ITC Century*, *ITC Highlander*, and *MCPdigital* by Que Corporation.

For Miles Maloney and his faithful companion,
Hermie the Wonder Crab.

Eric Maloney

For Andrew and Eric Nossiter, who are never at a
loss for words.

Joshua C. Nossiter

About the Authors

Eric Maloney, a journalism instructor at Keene (NH) State College, is also a contributing editor for *Maximize* and *DOS World* magazines. Eric has been an editor and writer in the computer field since 1980 when he joined the staff of *Kilobaud Microcomputing* magazine. He later served as editor-in-chief of *80 Micro*, *PC Resource*, and *LAN Technology* magazines before becoming a freelance writer.

Joshua C. Nossiter received a BA in English from Dartmouth College and an MBA in Finance from Columbia University. He has worked in broadcasting in California and in public finance on Wall Street. His interest in computers dates back to the 1970s, when he first began using the Dartmouth mainframe system. Josh now lives in San Francisco with his two children, where he writes about software, among other things.

Acknowledgments

This book was a team effort from start to finish. Thanks to all the tireless editorial and production staff at Que for their usual heroics.

Acquisitions Editors Jenny Watson and Debbie Abshier got us afloat, and kept us there through many weeks of toil.

Product Development Specialists Kathie-Jo Arnoff, Robin Drake, Lorna Gentry, and Lisa Wagner performed the routine miracle of their trade: transforming a mass of words and pictures into the book in your hands.

The peerless Lynn Northrup, Editor, left no comma unturned in her quest for authorial clarity.

Technical Editor Greg Dew contributed many valuable suggestions and corrections.

Thanks to Lisa Bucki for her contribution to this book.

Thanks also to Don Roche, Jr., Associate Publisher, for providing us with a truly great group of colleagues.

We'd like to hear from you!

As part of our continuing effort to produce books of the highest possible quality, Que would like to hear your comments. To stay competitive, we *really* want you, as a computer book reader and user, to let us know what you like or dislike most about this book or other Que products.

You can mail comments, ideas, or suggestions for improving future editions to the address below, or send us a fax at (317) 581-4663. For the on-line inclined, Macmillan Computer Publishing has a forum on CompuServe (type **GO QUEBOOKS** at any prompt) through which our staff and authors are available for questions and comments. The address of our Internet site is **http://www.mcp.com** (World Wide Web).

In addition to exploring our forum, please feel free to contact me personally to discuss your opinions of this book: on CompuServe, I'm at 76507,2715 and on the Internet, I'm **karnoff@que.mcp.com**.

Thanks in advance—your comments will help us to continue publishing the best books available on computer topics in today's market.

Kathie-Jo Arnoff
Product Director
Que Corporation
201 W. 103rd Street
Indianapolis, Indiana 46290
USA

Contents at a Glance

Expert Topics for Non-Experts 351

Troubleshooting 431

Table of Contents

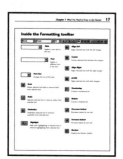

*Inside the Formatting
toolbar
see page 17*

Part I: What's the Good Word?

1 What You Need to Know to Get Started

2 Creating a Document: First Steps

"How do I move around in this document?"

see page 34

*Selecting
big chunks
of text*

see page 86

Part II: Editing Your Text

5 How to Delete, Move, Copy, and Change Your Text

*All about
AutoText*

see page 89

Spell checking made easy!

see page 102

6 My Grammar and Speling Ain't So Good

Let Word fix errors as you type

see page 108

7 Prepare to Print!

Inside the Print dialog box
see page 129

Fun with fonts
see page 135

Part III: Live Fast, Die Young, and Leave a Good-Looking Document

8 Character Sketches: Formatting Your Type

Alignment tricks you should know
see page 165

9 Formatting Paragraphs and Blocks

Inserting page and section breaks

see page 188

10 Formatting Your Page

Close-Up: the Header and Footer toolbar
see page 197

*"How can I
use tables
to create
interesting
effects?"*

see page 204

Part IV: Be Your Own Publisher

13 Columns, the Pillars of Sturdy Documents

14 Borders, Colors, and Typographical Tweaks

15 Picture This! Documents with Graphics

Shading and color make paragraphs jump off the page

see page 272

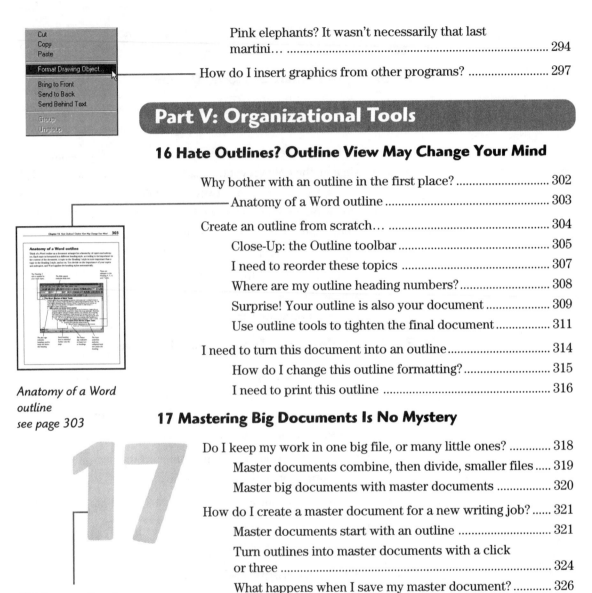

Part V: Organizational Tools

16 Hate Outlines? Outline View May Change Your Mind

Anatomy of a Word outline
see page 303

17 Mastering Big Documents Is No Mystery

"How do I create a master document"

see page 321

18 Running a Tight Ship: Managing Your Files

Create a list of the folders you use the most!

see page 338

Part VI: Expert Topics for Non-Experts

19 Document Signposts: Tables of Contents and Indexes

*Close-Up: the
WordArt toolbar
see page 371*

*Customize
Word to
work the
way you do*

23

*"Can I copy
my Excel
table to a
Word
document?"*

see page 426

Part VII: Troubleshooting

Troubleshooting Word for Windows 95

*Find the
answers
to your
questions
here!*

Index

Introduction

In the early days of personal computers, a word processor wasn't much more than a souped-up typewriter. Its main attraction was that you could edit your documents and save them for later use. Frills such as spell checkers, fonts, macros, and even simple menus were kept to a minimum to preserve the computer's valuable but scant resources.

Alas, the golden age of simplicity is over. No longer are word processors content to let you just sit down and start writing. They've become massive and complex pieces of software that challenge you to conquer them.

Take Word, for example. Its tantalizing arrays of shiny buttons and blinking lights are endless. Menus have commands that have dialog boxes with options that have icons that lead to more menus. Word does everything but feed the cat and put out the milk bottles.

The problem is not with Word itself. In the world of computers, power usually begets complexity. The problem is that most of us don't have the need (or the time) to learn about everything Word offers. We're too busy with our everyday work. All we want to do is produce attractive documents with a minimum of fuss. Leave the vari-dimensional, hyperlinked, multi-matrixed composition generators to the software gurus.

What this book is all about

The goal of *Using Word for Windows 95* is to return simplicity to word processing. We show you the easiest way to handle your most common tasks. We'll help you pick through Word's flea market of features to find only the items you really need.

We won't beat you blind with endless lists of commands you'll never use. We won't waste your time with dozens of obscure keyboard combinations that you'll never remember. And we won't wear you out with descriptions of every option in every menu and dialog box. We'll give you only the best, leaving the rest for you to investigate on a rainy day.

Exploring the unknown

When we refer to Word's most important features, we don't just mean the obvious ones. Naturally, we've got plenty on how to manage files, edit documents, and format type. But we're also going to explore some of Word's lesser-known features that, while they might not jump out at you as day-glo icons, can be invaluable writing tools.

For example, Word's grammar checker produces readability statistics. The information these obscure numbers provide can be a powerful aid in helping you to improve your writing skills. Word's documentation doesn't tell you how to use these statistics, but we do.

Something old, something new

This book pays special attention to Word's most important new features and commands. While Word for Windows 95 strongly resembles its predecessor, Word 6, many of its new features are notable. Specifically, we'll show you:

- How to use Word's new long file names

- When *not* to use Word's long file names

- How to use new file management features that let you easily move, copy, and delete documents

- How to use Windows 95's new system of folders for saving your Word documents

- How to use Word's feature-packed new dialog boxes

- How to use Word's enhanced and improved table maker

The solution finder

Many computer books provide solutions in search of a problem. Our strategy is the opposite. We identify common problems and then give you the simplest solutions. You'll discover two major advantages to this approach.

First, getting the information you need is easier. You don't have to wade through lots of material that doesn't apply directly to the task at hand.

Second, you don't need to read the book sequentially. You can learn how to check your spelling in Chapter 6 without reading all of Chapters 1 through 5.

If you're the inquisitive type, you'll also find that the book's design lends itself to indiscriminate browsing. Just pick a page at random, and there's a good chance you'll learn a new trick or technique.

What's inside

Here's what you'll learn from this book.

Part I: What's the Good Word?

Chapters 1 through 4 show you the easiest way to start writing in Word. Here is where you'll learn how to find your way around the screen; how to create a document; how to name, save, and open documents; and how to use Word's extensive on-line Help files.

Part II: Editing Your Text

What's the easiest way to delete, move, and copy text? We'll show you in Chapters 5 through 7, along with how to use the spelling and grammar checkers and how to prepare your documents for printing.

Part III: Live Fast, Die Young, and Leave a Good-Looking Document

Chapters 8 through 12 cover what you need to know to make your documents more attractive. Topics include how to create simple and attractive tables, how to use styles to automate your formatting, and how to format type, paragraphs, and blocks.

Part IV: Be Your Own Publisher

Here's where we get to the sizzle: creating fancy documents such as brochures and newsletters. Chapters 13 through 15 show you how to put text in columns, how to choose and use type and borders, and how to insert pictures and objects into your documents.

Part V: Organizational Tools

Chapters 16 and 17 cover outlines and how to deal with large documents more efficiently, while Chapter 18 tells you all about Word's new file management features.

Part VI: Expert Topics for Non-Experts

When you get bored with the easy material, turn to Chapters 19 through 23 to find out how to use Word's graphics makers; make your own toolbars, menus, and macros; and use form letters and mail merge. You'll also learn how to share files with other Windows programs.

Part VII: Troubleshooting

This part of the book is dedicated to helping you find the answers to your questions. Here you'll find a comprehensive listing of typical problems you may encounter in Word, along with their solutions.

Nuggets of information

Throughout this book, you'll find a variety of special devices that we use to give you special information.

 TIP   **Tips describe shortcuts and secrets that show you the best way** to get a job done, and point out information often overlooked in the documentation.

 CAUTION   Cautions warn you about potential problems, such as loss or corruption of data, that might arise from a particular action.

Q&A *Do you have a question?*

We try to anticipate and answer questions or problems you might have about Word's features and procedures.

Plain English, please!

Here we translate **computer terms** and **jargon** into English.

In addition, you'll run across text that is in a different typeface:

A `special typeface` indicates what you see on your screen.

Bold is for new terms or text that you type.

When you see an underlined letter in a command, press the Alt key plus that letter to execute the command. For example, press Alt+F to display the File menu.

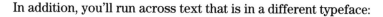

Sidebars: entertainment and information

Sidebars are detours from the main text. They usually provide background or interesting information that is relevant but not essential reading.

Part I: What's the Good Word?

1

What You Need to Know to Get Started

● **In this chapter:**

- **In the beginning: how to create a new document**

- **Open sesame! Getting a file from your disk**

- **What's in a document name?**

- **Exiting Word**

You don't need to be a computer genius to use Word. Learn these basics, and you'll be producing simple documents before you even finish this chapter . . . . ➤

I t seems like every computer book has a chapter titled, "What You Need to Know to Get Started." Then it proceeds to detail everything you *don't* need to know about IRQs, file allocation tables, upper memory blocks, and other technical arcana. You'd probably have more fun memorizing tax tables.

This chapter is different. For starters, we don't know any technical arcana. But even if we did, you wouldn't need it to get Word running. While Word *looks* imposing, it's pretty much designed for human consumption.

Setting up Word for Windows

When you install Word, Setup adds Microsoft Word to Windows' Start Programs menu. You run Word by clicking the Start button, choosing Programs, and choosing Microsoft Word, as shown in figure 1.1.

Fig. 1.1
Click Microsoft Word to run the program.

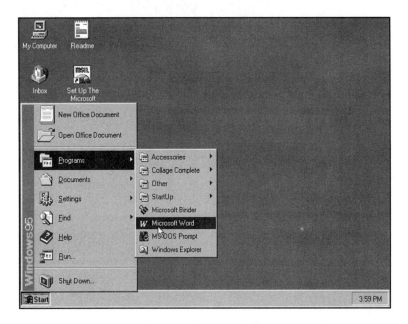

If you're using Word as part of the Office suite, you can open Word by choosing New Office Document or Open Office Document from the Start menu (refer to fig. 1.1). New Office Document displays the New dialog box, from which you can open a new blank document. Open Office Document displays the Open dialog box, which lets you open a document you've already saved to disk.

To use these options, you first need to know how to use the New and Open dialog boxes. You'll find information on the New dialog box in Chapter 2, while Chapter 4 discusses the Open dialog box.

TIP   **Run Setup if you find that Word is missing a component. Make** sure you have your installation disks or CD-ROM ready.

The Word screen

You'll need some time to become familiar with the basic Word screen. There's a lot to learn. Perhaps more important, there's a lot *not* to learn. Mastering Word depends on how well you can filter nonessential features and focus on the relatively few features you'll need to get started.

The following page, entitled "What's what in Word," shows the main areas of the screen. Let's take a quick look at each of these areas so you have an idea of where to go for what.

The menu bar

The menu bar gives you access to your essential commands. You display a menu by clicking once on the option, or by pressing the Alt key plus the underlined letter (for example, press Alt+F for the File menu).

 Plain English, please!

Throughout this book, you'll find references to the **Alt** and **Ctrl** keys. These labels stand for **alternate** and **control**, respectively. Alt and Ctrl don't do anything by themselves; you use them in combination with other keys (and sometimes with each other) to run commands or perform other actions. For example, you can press Alt+E to view the Edit menu, or Ctrl+S to save a file.

When you use the Alt key, you can press and release it and then press the second key, or you can press Alt and the second key together. However, when you use the Ctrl key, you must hold it down while you press the second key. 99

What's what in Word

The Word screen is divided into three basic areas: the bars above the document window, the document window, and the bar below the document window.

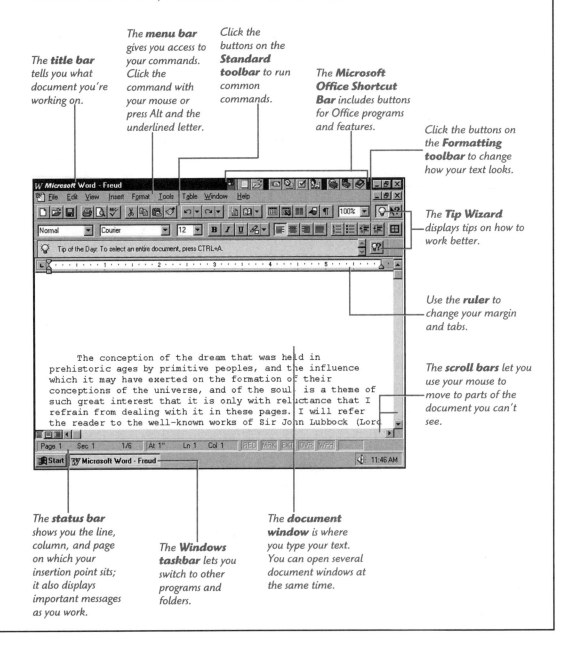

*The **menu bar** gives you access to your commands. Click the command with your mouse or press Alt and the underlined letter.*

*Click the buttons on the **Standard toolbar** to run common commands.*

*The **title bar** tells you what document you're working on.*

*The **Microsoft Office Shortcut Bar** includes buttons for Office programs and features.*

*Click the buttons on the **Formatting toolbar** to change how your text looks.*

*The **Tip Wizard** displays tips on how to work better.*

*Use the **ruler** to change your margin and tabs.*

*The **scroll bars** let you use your mouse to move to parts of the document you can't see.*

*The **status bar** shows you the line, column, and page on which your insertion point sits; it also displays important messages as you work.*

*The **Windows taskbar** lets you switch to other programs and folders.*

*The **document window** is where you type your text. You can open several document windows at the same time.*

Figure 1.2 shows the results of choosing the File menu.

Fig. 1.2

Drop down a menu from the menu bar by clicking the menu item once with the mouse, or by pressing Alt plus the underlined letter (in this case, Alt+F).

To run a command from a menu, slide the bar insertion point to the command and click once with your mouse button. If you're using the keyboard, press the underlined letter (for example, press O for Open).

TIP Some menu commands are followed by a key combination; for example, Ctrl+O for Open. These are keyboard shortcuts that let you bypass the menu. Take a few minutes to learn them; they'll save you a lot of time.

The shortcut menu

You can save trips to the menu bar by clicking your right mouse button and calling up a shortcut menu, like the one shown in figure 1.3. The shortcut menu changes depending on what part of the window you click and what you're doing at the time. The menu in figure 1.3, which appears when you're working on text in the document window, includes selected commands from the Edit and Format menus.

Fig. 1.3
Click the right mouse button to get a shortcut menu. This is the one you get when you click selected text in the document window. Other types of shortcut menus appear when you click other parts of the screen.

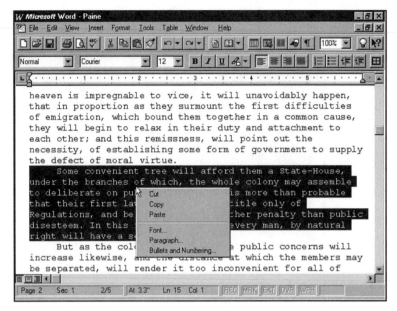

 Some of my menus have options that are grayed out, and nothing happens when I click them. Are they unavailable in my version of Word?

They're available, they're just not active because they can't be used at the moment. For example, if you're not working in a table, most of the commands on the T<u>a</u>ble menu are dormant and therefore grayed out.

The Standard toolbar

The Standard toolbar is the first row of buttons directly beneath the menu bar. It gives you mouse-powered shortcuts to common commands. For example, instead of choosing <u>F</u>ile, <u>O</u>pen from the menu bar to start a new document, click the Open icon (which looks like an open file folder) on the Standard toolbar.

When you become more familiar with Word, you can remove the buttons you seldom use and replace them with others of your choosing.

Some of the icons are self-explanatory, but others are somewhat inscrutable. For example, what's that curved backward arrow under T<u>a</u>ble? To find out, just touch the icon with your pointer, and a little box (called a **ToolTip**) pops up with the word Undo. And at the bottom of the screen, you'll see a description: Reverses the last action.

The following page, entitled "Inside the Standard toolbar," briefly explains what the Standard toolbar buttons do.

Questions? Get help fast!

 The Standard toolbar does include one special feature that you'll probably use from the start: the Help button on the far right end. This button gives you immediate and specific help on items in Word's window.

To use the Help button, click it once. Move the mouse pointer (which now includes a question mark) to the part of the screen on which you want help (you don't need to hold down the mouse button). Click the mouse button again. Word gives you a full screen of information from its Help files.

You can use the Help button to get information on menu commands, too: just click the Help button, open the menu, and click the command again. If you click text in your document, Help gives you information about your paragraph and font formatting. And you can click the Help button to call up the Help Topics dialog box.

To cancel Help, press the Esc key.

 TIP   **Click the TipWizard button (it looks like a light bulb) next** to the help arrow to have Word display or turn off the TipWizard toolbar beneath the Formatting toolbar. Here, Word gives you suggestions on how to use its features more effectively. Magically, the TipWizard provides help on whatever you happen to be doing in your document.

The Formatting toolbar

The Formatting toolbar gives you easy access to commands that change the appearance of your document. The page entitled "Inside the Formatting toolbar" gives you a quick look at the toolbar buttons and what they do.

Inside the Standard toolbar

New
Starts a new document.

Open
Opens a saved document.

Save
Saves the current document.

Print
Prints the current document.

Print Preview
Previews a document before printing.

Spelling
Checks the spelling of a document or selected text.

Cut
Removes text or an object to the Windows Clipboard.

Copy
Copies selected text or an object to the Windows Clipboard.

Paste
Pastes text or an object from the Windows Clipboard.

Format Painter
Copies a format to another part of the open document.

Undo
Reverses an action.

Redo
Repeats an action.

AutoFormat
Automatically formats a document.

Address
Inserts an address from the Address Book.

Insert Table
Inserts an empty table into a document or converts selected text into a table.

Insert Microsoft Excel Worksheet
Inserts an Excel worksheet into a document (Excel must be installed).

Columns
Puts text into columns.

Drawing
Shows or hides the Drawing Bar.

Show/Hide Paragraph Marks
Shows or hides nonprinting characters in a document, such as paragraph marks and tabs.

Zoom Control
Scales the size of an open document.

TipWizard
Shows or hides the TipWizard toolbar.

Help
Gets help. One click lets you point to and get help on an item on the screen; two clicks calls the Help Topics dialog box.

Inside the Formatting toolbar

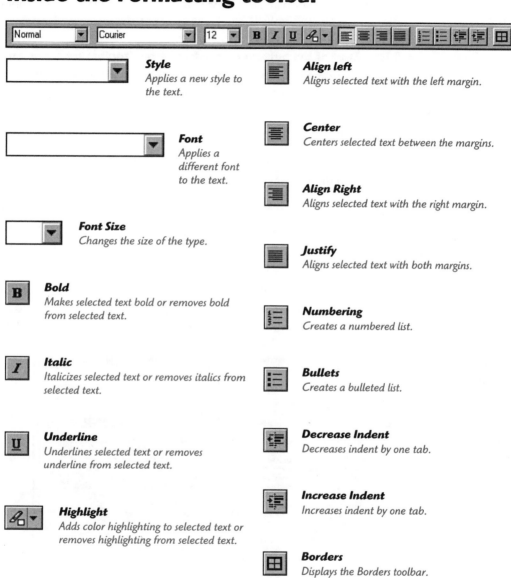

Style
Applies a new style to the text.

Align left
Aligns selected text with the left margin.

Font
Applies a different font to the text.

Center
Centers selected text between the margins.

Align Right
Aligns selected text with the right margin.

Font Size
Changes the size of the type.

Justify
Aligns selected text with both margins.

Bold
Makes selected text bold or removes bold from selected text.

Numbering
Creates a numbered list.

Italic
Italicizes selected text or removes italics from selected text.

Bullets
Creates a bulleted list.

Underline
Underlines selected text or removes underline from selected text.

Decrease Indent
Decreases indent by one tab.

Increase Indent
Increases indent by one tab.

Highlight
Adds color highlighting to selected text or removes highlighting from selected text.

Borders
Displays the Borders toolbar.

You'll spend a lot of time with the Formatting toolbar after you've learned how to create documents and want to spiff them up. But you can learn quite a few tricks on your own right now simply by clicking the various toolbar buttons, typing some text, and watching what happens.

TIP **Most of the buttons on the Formatting toolbar toggle on and off.** For example, if you want boldface, click the Bold button and start typing. When you want to revert to regular text, just click the Bold button again.

The roving toolbar

Your toolbars don't have to be at the top of the screen. You can put them anywhere in the Word window.

To move the toolbar to either side of the document window or to the bottom of the window, click any space between two buttons. Hold down the mouse button. The toolbar becomes bordered by a dotted line. Drag the toolbar to where you want it, then release the mouse button.

To move the toolbar inside the document window, use the same drag-and-drop method or click twice on an empty space. The toolbar becomes a floating object that you can drag to any spot on the screen (see fig. 1.4).

Fig. 1.4
Click twice on the space between two icons to float a toolbar in your document window.

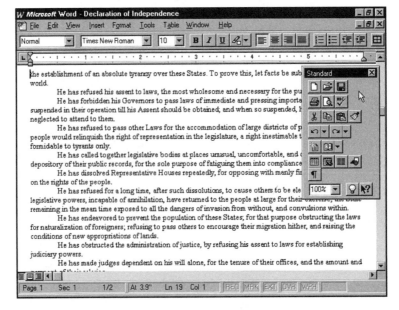

To change the shape of the toolbar, click and drag the borders. To put the toolbar back up on top, double-click a space.

You'll probably want to keep the toolbars where they are until you've become familiar with them. But eventually, you'll find that for some jobs, a floating toolbar makes the toolbar more accessible and the document window larger.

 Q&A *These toolbar buttons look awfully small. Can I make them bigger?*

Sure. Choose <u>V</u>iew, <u>T</u>oolbars from the main menu. Choose <u>L</u>arge Buttons at the bottom of the Toolbars dialog box, then click OK.

Tons of toolbars

For the sake of simplicity, most of the sample screens in this book show only the Standard and Formatting toolbars. But Word has many other toolbars, including the TipWizard toolbar, Borders toolbar, and Drawing toolbar.

You can display or hide these toolbars as you need them. Choose <u>V</u>iew, <u>T</u>oolbar from the main menu and click the appropriate buttons in the list under <u>T</u>oolbars. You can put these toolbars above the ruler or float them in the document window.

The ruler

If you're old enough to remember using a typewriter in typing class, the ruler should be familiar. It looks and acts a lot like the margin scale that sits behind a typewriter's platen. You use it for much the same thing—to set margins, tabs, and indents.

The view buttons

Moving to the bottom of the page, we have the view buttons, which are to the far left of the horizontal scroll bar (the gray bar just beneath the document window). These give you one-click access to three different ways of viewing your document (Normal, Page Layout, and Outline). They're the same as the first three commands on the menu bar's <u>V</u>iew menu. Stick with Normal view unless you have a specific reason to choose one of the others.

The status bar

Next, we come to the status bar near the bottom of the screen (see fig. 1.5). Don't be fooled by its location; you'll find yourself referring often to this bar for important information about the current document.

Fig. 1.5
The status bar gives you basic information about the current document.

The status bar shown in figure 1.5 displays this information:

- Page 2: The current page number.

- Sec 1: The section you're in. This only becomes important when you start dividing large documents into sections. Until then, it will always say Sec 1.

- 2/5: The first number is the current page; the second is the number of pages in the document.

- At 1.4": Where your insertion point is, in inches, from the top of the page.

- Ln 4: Where your insertion point is, in lines, from the first line on the page.

- Col 1: Where your insertion point is, in characters, from the beginning of the line.

A word about modes

The five abbreviations at the right end of the status bar are called **mode indicators**. These indicators usually appear as gray buttons with chiseled gray lettering.

These buttons tell you when certain Word features are turned on or off. For example, if you press the Insert key, you change from Insert mode to Overstrike mode, and the letters OVR (Overstrike) turn black. If the Help for WordPerfect feature is turned on, the letters WPH (WordPerfect Help) are black.

The REC (Recorder), MRK (Revision Marking), and EXT (Extend Selection) buttons are for advanced uses, and you can ignore them for now.

TIP **To move from Insert to Overstrike mode or vice versa, double-**
click the OVR button on the status bar. Similarly, double-clicking the other
mode buttons either switches modes or calls up a dialog box that lets you
set options for that mode.

And now, a message from your status bar

We're not done with the status bar. In addition to the information we've
already described, the status bar gives you important messages and instructions as you work.

For example, if you click Format on the menu bar, Word displays the
message Format text and graphics in the status bar. As you move the
pointer down the list of format commands, the status bar describes each
one. The descriptions disappear when you return to your document.

You'll see other messages displayed here as you select items from the
toolbar and execute commands.

The Windows taskbar

The Windows taskbar shown beneath the Word window on page 12 is a part
of Windows, not Word. It gives you one-click access to other programs you
have running at the same time, as well as to the Start button.

Whether the taskbar appears on your screen depends on how you've got
Windows set up. If the taskbar is not visible, you can make it so by moving
the mouse pointer to the border at the bottom of the Word window until it
turns into a two-headed arrow, clicking your mouse button, and pulling the
border up like a window shade. To hide the taskbar, do the opposite.

If you can't find the taskbar at the bottom of the Word window, try looking
at the sides and the top. The taskbar is movable, so it won't be in the same
place on all computers.

Most of the screens in this book do not show the taskbar.

Insertion points and other moving objects

The two most important moving objects on the screen are the **insertion
point** and the **mouse pointer**.

Word's insertion point is a blinking vertical bar that marks the spot where you're typing. When you press a key, Word inserts the character after the insertion point.

You can move the insertion point around the document using the arrow keys and the Page keys, or with the mouse. More on navigating your document in a moment.

The mouse pointer

The mouse pointer is a bit of a shape-shifter; it changes shape and function depending on where you are on the screen and what you're doing. Inside the document window, it looks like an I-beam. If you click the mouse button in your text, the insertion point moves to where the I-beam is located.

The mouse pointer changes to the familiar arrow when you move parts of the screen other than the document window. The pointer can also assume other guises for special tasks, such as when you're dragging text or moving borders. You'll learn more about these other shapes as we go along. Table 1.1 lists some of the more common pointers you're likely to encounter.

Table 1.1 Some well-appointed pointers

Pointer shape	What it means
	You can move the insertion point to a new place in the text or select text and graphics. This **I-beam** marks the point where the insertion point will be placed.
	You can select objects outside the document window, such as toolbar icons, menu items, and dialog box buttons.
	You can select blocks of text from the space to the left of the left margin; you can also select a table cell from the space between the left border and the cell text.
	You can click and drag in the direction the arrow is pointing to stretch or shrink an object.
	You can drag and drop selected text.

The end-of-document marker

When you're in Normal view, you'll see what looks like an insertion point lying on its back underneath the last line of the document. The only time this end-of-document marker has any real use is when you need to see how many blank lines you've got between the last line of your text and the end of the document.

Choose your weapon!

Some people like using the mouse, while others prefer the keyboard. Each method has its advantages.

The mouse is easier to use because you don't have to remember a sequence of instructions or key combinations; you just point and click. On the other hand, key combinations are sometimes quicker because you don't have to take your hands off the keyboard when you're typing.

Recognizing that we live in a multifarious culture, the people at Microsoft generously accommodate both preferences. In fact, they give you four ways to handle Word's most common and important tasks:

- You can click the toolbar button.
- You can click the menu bar.
- You can press the Alt key plus the underlined letter of the menu item and then the underlined letter of the command.
- You can use a keyboard combination.

The following table gives you the four options for Word's most-used commands. If you want to be a truly adroit Word whacker, learn them all. With practice, you'll instinctively use the method that's quickest and easiest, depending on what you're doing.

To do this...	Click this icon	Or choose this command	Or press these keys	Or use these keyboard shortcuts
Get new file		File, New	Alt+F, N	Ctrl+F
Open file		File, Open	Alt+F, O	Ctrl+O
Save file		File, Save	Alt+F, S	Ctrl+S

continues

To do this...	Click this icon	Or choose this command	Or press these keys	Or use these keyboard shortcuts
Print file		File, Print	Alt+F, P	Ctrl+P
Undo		Edit, Undo	Alt+E, U	Ctrl+Z
Cut		Edit, Cut	Alt+E, T	Ctrl+X
Copy		Edit, Copy	Alt+E, C	Ctrl+C
Paste		Edit, Paste	Alt+E, P	Ctrl+V
Spelling		Tools, Spelling	Alt+T, S	Ctrl+F7

Word to the max

Let's take a look at how to manipulate the window itself. After all, windows wouldn't be windows if you couldn't expand, shrink, move, size, dematerialize, and otherwise bend them to your will (see fig. 1.6).

Fig. 1.6
The screen elements that you'll work with most are shown here.

When you click the Word Control Menu button, Word pops up a menu you can use to manipulate the window from the keyboard. For a quick shortcut, double-click to exit Word altogether.

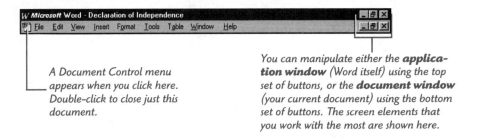

A Document Control menu appears when you click here. Double-click to close just this document.

You can manipulate either the **application window** (Word itself) using the top set of buttons, or the **document window** (your current document) using the bottom set of buttons. The screen elements that you work with the most are shown here.

Let's take a closer look at the buttons you use to manipulate the window:

Word Control
Click this button or press Alt+spacebar for a menu that gives you options for sizing and moving the Word window.

Document Control
Click this button to open the Document Control menu, which lets you move or resize the window for just that document.

Minimize Word
What happens when you Minimize depends on how you have Windows 95 set up. If your taskbar is visible, your Word window disappears, but Word remains as a button on the taskbar. You restore Word by clicking the taskbar button.

If your taskbar is not visible, Word simply vanishes. You can recall it by pressing Alt+Tab.

Minimize Document
Same deal. Click the Minimize Document button to tuck just this document away until you're ready for it; Word itself (and any other open documents) stay put.

Maximize Word
If Word is not maximized (that is, it doesn't fill your entire screen), this button is a **Maximize button**. Click it to make Word fill the entire screen and cover any other open windows.

Maximize Document
If your document is not maximized, click this button to make the document fill the entire Word window (whether or not Word itself if maximized).

Restore Word
If Word *is* maximized, click this button to return the Word window to its previous size and shape. For example, if Word had been sized to take half a screen but now takes the entire screen, click the Restore Word button to return Word to half a screen.

Restore Document
The Restore Document button returns the document window to whatever size it was before it was maximized.

Close Word

Click the Close Word button to exit Word and any open documents.

Close Document

If you want to close this document but leave Word running for later use, click the lower X button.

Changing your document window

You can manipulate your document window separately from your Word window.

Your document window has its own Control menu box, at the far left of the menu bar. When you click it, you get a menu from which you can size and move the document window.

You can also click the Maximize/Restore button at the other end of the menu bar.

Figure 1.7 gives you an idea of how you can organize your open documents. The one on top has been resized to take a smaller portion of the screen. Meanwhile, the Common Sense document has been minimized to a mini-title bar and can be recalled with a mouse click.

Fig. 1.7

This window contains three documents: the Declaration of Independence (foreground), the U.S. Constitution (background), and Common Sense (minimized to a title bar).

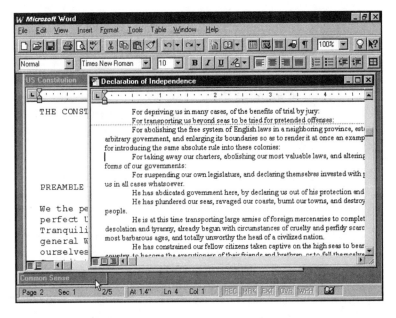

Notice that the document window now has its own title bar and Minimize, Maximize, and Close buttons. These buttons work the same as the Word buttons.

Naming your document

Working with an untitled document is a dangerous practice. If the power should go out or if someone trips over the cord and unplugs your computer, you could lose your document. Get in the habit of naming and saving your file immediately.

We'll examine file-saving and file-naming options in Chapter 4. For now, though, let's look at the quick-and-dirty way to name your file.

Press Ctrl+S to pop up the Save As dialog box (see fig. 1.8). Word suggests a file name in the File Name text box.

Fig. 1.8

Press Ctrl+S for the Save As dialog box. Word automatically gives a new file a file name based on the first characters of text.

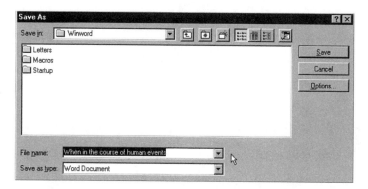

If the document is empty, the suggested file name is Doc1. If Doc1 already exists, Word suggests the next default name, Doc2, and so on.

If the document contains text, the suggested file name consists of the first 234 characters of the document, unless Word first encounters an invalid character or an end-of-paragraph marker.

In figure 1.8, for example, the file name is made up of the characters up to the comma following the word "events."

Click Save to accept the suggested file name. If you want a different file name, just type it into the File Name text box. The suggested file name disappears when you begin typing.

Bailing out

When you and Word have had enough of each other, close it either by clicking twice on the Control menu box at the far left of the title bar, clicking the Close button in the upper-right corner, or pressing Ctrl+F4. Word asks you if you want to save your open documents. Choose Yes to save them, and No to exit Word.

2

Creating a Document: First Steps

● In this chapter:

- **Doing the write thing: rules for typing and formatting**

- **On the move with arrow keys, scroll bars, and other navigational tools**

- **If you've got to go, Go To**

- **How do I get more of my document on the screen?**

- **Inserting and deleting text— the basics**

- **Let Word format your document using templates and wizards**

Starting a new document in Word isn't much more complicated than starting one with a typewriter and paper ·

Anew word processor is easier to learn than just about any other type of program you can buy. You don't need to know any special codes, languages, conventions, or rules to get going; you just start typing. A word followed by a word followed by another word eventually leads you to sentences, paragraphs, and yes, entire documents.

Of course, you do need to learn at least a few rules if you want attractively formatted text. But the basics are rooted so much in common sense that you'll probably understand most of them intuitively. If you've ever laid hands on a keyboard, you've won half the battle.

The basic rules of typing and formatting

Your first document doesn't have to be anything fancy—perhaps a letter to Mom or a list of this weekend's errands. Feel free to experiment with the keyboard. Try typing short sentences, long paragraphs, lines of characters without spaces, and lines of spaces without characters.

For now, stay away from the Ctrl, Alt, and function keys (F1 through F12). Word uses many of these keys to run commands and open dialog boxes, some of which you might not understand how to use yet. We'll discuss these special keys throughout this book.

 Q&A   *Oops! I accidentally pressed some keys that took me out of my document and someplace strange. How do I get back to my document?*

If you happened to open a dialog box, just click the Cancel button or press the Esc key. If you're in a menu or a text box (such as the ones on the Standard toolbar), press the Esc key.

If you press a bunch of keys and the computer beeps at you when you press the Enter key, just press the Esc key a couple of times. You should be able to regain control of your keyboard.

As you fill your screen with text, pay special attention to the behavior of your keyboard. Note what keys result in what action. Then read the following information about the keyboard and see how much you found out for yourself.

The Enter key: the end of paragraphs as we know them

The Enter key (or Return key on some keyboards) is the same as the carriage return on a manual typewriter, only without the sound of the little bell and the "ka-chunk" of the carriage-return lever. In figure 2.1, the Enter key is indicated by the paragraph mark (¶).

On a typewriter, you have to return the carriage after every line. Not so with Word. When Word can't fit any more text on a line, it automatically drops subsequent text to the next line. (This is called **word wrap** in word processing parlance.) You need to press Enter only at the end of a complete paragraph, as shown in the body of the letter in figure 2.1.

Fig. 2.1

Press the Enter key, represented in this document by the paragraph mark (¶), to end a paragraph or each item in a list, and to insert blank lines.

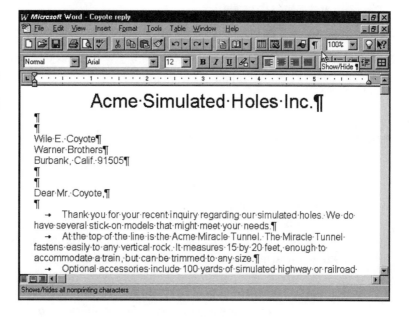

You press the Enter key for two other reasons: to end a short line, such as those in the address in figure 2.1, and to insert a line space, such as between the address and the salutation.

CAUTION **Don't press the Enter key at the end of each line in a paragraph. If** you insert carriage returns manually, you will be unable to properly format and edit your document later.

The Tab key: new paragraphs and text alignment

The Tab key works like the one on a typewriter and serves much the same purpose. The tabs in figure 2.1 are represented by bold right arrows (→). The Tab key has two main uses:

- To start a new paragraph, as in the body of the memo shown in figure 2.1

- To align text in a simple table

When you begin a new document, Word gives you tab stops at half-inch intervals. They're marked with dots on the ruler. You'll learn later how to set and clear tab stops.

 TIP ¶ **To display the paragraph, tab, and space symbols you see in** the document in figure 2.1, click the Show/Hide Paragraph Marks button on the Standard toolbar.

The basic rules of moving around the screen

You'll undoubtedly want to make corrections, changes, and additions as you type, which means that you need to move your insertion point around the screen. The arrow keys are the most obvious tools, but by themselves they can only move the insertion point one character or line at a time. You'll find it far more efficient to use Word's many shortcuts that let you leap over text to get to where you want to go more quickly.

 TIP **You should practice using the arrow keys automatically and** without peeking, even if you're a confirmed mouser. The mouse has lots of uses, but the arrow keys are better for moving short distances.

 Q&A *The keys on the number pad have arrows, but when I press them, all I get are numbers. How do I make the arrows work?*

Press the Num Lock key. This also activates the keys that have labels, such as Home, End, Ins, and Del. Press the Num Lock key again to reactivate the number pad.

Ctrling your destiny

The arrow keys begin to shine when you combine them with the Ctrl key. Try moving your insertion point with the keyboard shortcuts shown in the following table.

To move...	Press these keys
One word forward	Ctrl+right arrow
One word back	Ctrl+left arrow
To start of paragraph	Ctrl+up arrow
To start of next paragraph	Ctrl+down arrow

The Home and End keys

The Home and End keys take you to the beginning and end of a line, respectively. *Learn these keys.* Their functions might seem trivial now, but you'll be surprised at how often you need to go from one side of your document to the other.

The Home and End keys become doubly important when you learn to combine them with the Ctrl keys. Use the combinations shown in the following table.

To move...	Press these keys
To top of document	Ctrl+Home
To bottom of document	Ctrl+End

Pinpoint accuracy with the mouse

The mouse pointer is a good tool for moving to a place in the middle of your document. Just position the pointer where you want to put the insertion point and click the mouse button.

Moving around in big documents

Arrow keys and simple key combinations are effective ways of moving around the part of the document you can see. But they're not so great for documents that are longer than a page or two.

How do you move quickly through three or four pages? Go from page 2 to page 20 in a single bound? Or find that elusive heading somewhere between pages 12 and 18 without hitting the down arrow line after tedious line?

Word gives you a variety of rapid-transit options. For convenience, we'll divide them into two categories: browsers and pointers.

Browsers are like the arrow buttons on your TV remote control, letting you surf through pages of text at a time.

Pointers, on the other hand, are like the remote's number pad, letting you go directly to a specific spot in your document.

Browsing your document

Use the keyboard's Page Up and Page Down keys to move up or down one screen, less one line. (That is, when you press Page Down, the bottom line of the current screen becomes the top line of the next screen.)

The insertion point stays in the same position relative to the top of the screen. If it's on the fifth line from the top on the current screen, it'll be on the fifth line from the top on the next one.

In addition, you can use the Ctrl and Page keys to move your insertion point to the top or bottom of the document window. Use the combinations shown in the following table.

To move...	Press these keys
To top of screen	Ctrl+Page Up
To bottom of screen	Ctrl+Page Down

Using the mouse to browse

When you use the Page keys, the insertion point moves with you. If you want to keep your insertion point where it is while you browse, use the **vertical scroll bar**.

The vertical scroll bar is the long gray bar to the right of your document window (see fig. 2.2). Inside is a sliding box called a **scroll box**. Click anywhere above the scroll box to move up one screen and anywhere below the box to move down one screen. The text moves through your document window while your insertion point stays where you left it.

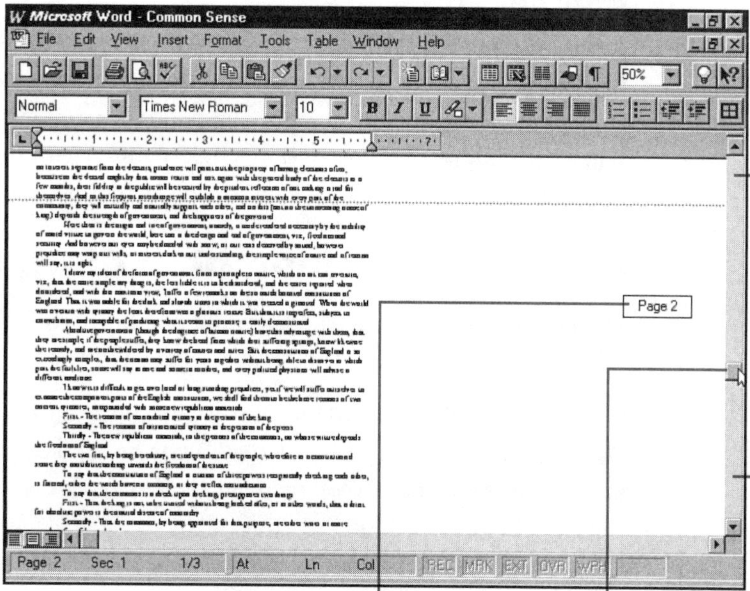

Click once above or below the scroll box to scroll your document one screen at a time.

Fig. 2.2

The vertical scroll bar lets you use your mouse to move lines or screens at a time.

Word shows the page number when you drag the scroll box.

Click and drag the scroll box to move rapidly through your document.

Click the scroll bar arrows to move one line at a time. These are the same as the up and down arrow keys on the keyboard. To return to your insertion point, press one of the arrow keys. To move to a new spot on the current screen, point and click with your mouse.

TIP **To move quickly through your document, click the scroll box and** drag it. Word displays the current page number as you scroll through your document.

Q&A *Why is there a scroll bar on the bottom of my screen?* *When would I need to scroll a document horizontally?*

You use the horizontal scroll bar for extra-wide documents. For example, you might have a document that you're printing lengthwise whose right margin is out of view. Or if you enlarge your document view with Zoom Control on the Standard toolbar, your text might become too big to fit in the document window. You use the horizontal scroll bar the same way you do the vertical scroll bar.

Another mouse trick

Here's another way to move quickly through your document with the mouse. Place your mouse pointer in your document, hold down the mouse button, and drag up or down the screen. The text you scan becomes highlighted. When you reach your destination, click the mouse button or press the right or down arrow. To return to where you started, press the left or up arrow.

Pointers: stopping on a dime with Go To

The larger the document, the less effective the scroll bars and keyboard. What you need is Word's transporter beam, Go To.

The <u>E</u>dit, <u>G</u>o To command lets you go directly to any part of the document. You execute Go To by pressing the F5 key or Ctrl+G, or by clicking the page area of the status bar. Word displays the Go To dialog box (see fig. 2.3).

Fig. 2.3
The Go To dialog box lets you beam directly to any place in your document. Here, selecting Go To moves the insertion point to the top of page 4.

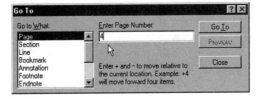

Type the number of the page you want to go to in the <u>E</u>nter Page Number box. The Ne<u>x</u>t button changes into a Go <u>T</u>o button. Click this button, and Word takes you to the top of the target page.

TIP   **You can use Go To to move to a specified line in your document.** For example, if you choose Line in the Go To <u>W</u>hat box and type **188** in the <u>E</u>nter Line Number box, Word takes you to line 188 of the document. This feature is useful for documents that include long lists.

Labeling parts of a document with bookmarks

Remember the college professor who lectured from a text that had about fifty bookmarks sticking out of it? Word has an electronic equivalent,

appropriately called a **bookmark**. Like their little paper counterparts, you use Word's bookmarks to quickly flip to parts of your document.

You can use a bookmark to name a piece of text—a heading, table, or page, for example. You then use the Go To command to move your insertion point to that bookmark. In figure 2.4, choosing the bookmark article12 moves the insertion point to the location with that name.

Fig. 2.4

In this Go To dialog box, choosing Go To moves the insertion point to a section of the document named *article12*.

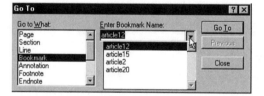

Creating a bookmark in your document is easy. Go to the place in your document where you want the bookmark. Choose <u>E</u>dit, <u>B</u>ookmark from the menu bar. In the Bookmark dialog box, type a label in the <u>B</u>ookmark Name text box and click <u>A</u>dd (see fig. 2.5). (Word won't accept spaces in a bookmark name.)

Use your bookmarks to:

- Mark your place when you close a document.

- Mark text that you want to revise later.

- Mark tables and text that you need to get to quickly.

Fig. 2.5
Create a bookmark
by choosing Edit,
Bookmark and typing a
label in the Bookmark
Name text box.

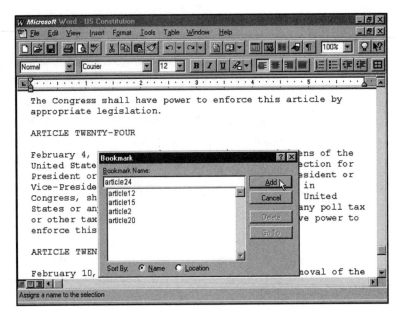

Panoramic screens: how to get a larger view of your document

If typewriters have an advantage (besides the compelling aroma of ribbon ink), it's that you can see the entire page of a document. In contrast, scanning a page in Word is a little like watching a big-screen movie one-eyed through a toilet paper tube. You can focus on detail, but it's tough to get an idea of what the particulars will look like when they're combined into one image.

Word has a couple of tools that can help you overcome this tunnel vision. You can increase the size of your document window and decrease the size of your type. Do both, and you can nearly triple the number of lines on your screen.

Fill the screen with your document window

To expand your document window, choose View, Full Screen from the menu bar. All of your menus and bars disappear (see fig. 2.6). A button labeled Full appears in the lower right-hand corner. Click this button once to return to your previous screen setup.

Fig. 2.6

If you choose View, Full Screen, you hide everything except your document. Click the Full button to bring it all back.

```
Representatives in Congress to which the District would be
entitled if it were a State, but in no event more than the
least populous State; they shall be in addition to those
appointed by the States, but they shall be considered, for
the purposes of the election of President and Vice-
President, to be electors appointed by a State; and they
shall meet in the district and perform such duties as
provided by the twelfth article of amendment. - Section 2.
The Congress shall have power to enforce this article by
appropriate legislation.

ARTICLE TWENTY-FOUR

February 4, 1964 - Section 1. The right of citizens of the
United States to vote in any primary or other election for
President or Vice-President, for electors for President or
Vice-President, or for Senator or Representative in
Congress, shall not be denied or abridged by the United
States or any State by reason of failure to pay any poll tax
or other tax. - Section 2. The Congress shall have power to
enforce this article by appropriate legislation.

ARTICLE TWENTY-FIVE

February 10, 1967 - Section 1. In case of the removal of the
President from office or of his death or resignation, the
```

Click here to return to your previous screen setup.

Q&A *When I'm in a full screen, how am I supposed to access my menu?*

Even though the main menu disappears, you can open a menu by clicking the top of the screen at the spot where you'd normally find the menu. For instance, if you click a little bit in from the upper left-hand corner, the File menu drops down. You can move from one menu to the next with your arrow keys. The menus are also available from the keyboard—Alt+F for the File menu, for example.

Reduce the size of the page

You can reduce the size of the page to as little as ten percent of the original. Of course, this much shrinking will cause your document to nearly disappear. But a more modest reduction is readable for short periods of time. This trick is useful when you need to move blocks of type around or if you want to view a large table or picture.

On the Standard toolbar at the far right, you'll see a box called Zoom Control, usually with 100% in it (refer to fig. 2.5). Click this box, and type a smaller percentage or choose one from the list.

Figure 2.7 combines Full Screen view with Zoom Control set to 75 percent. In this case, the type is 12-point Courier. The percentage by which you can reduce the page and still read it changes, depending on the typeface and point size.

Fig. 2.7
By combining Full Screen view with a reduced page, you can get nearly a full page on the screen.

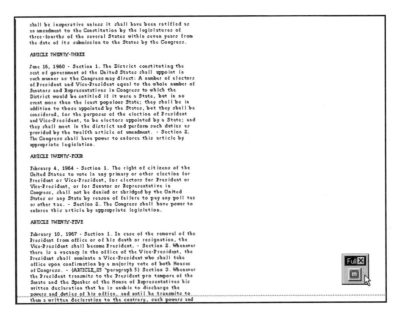

    TIP   **Using Zoom Control to change the view of a page doesn't affect** how the printed document will look.

Deleting and inserting text made easy

Somewhere, there's a parallel dimension in which people always write perfect sentences and never make typing errors. Words like "fix" and "correct" don't exist. But in our flawed universe, changing what we've written is a fact of life.

Word includes a variety of editing tools for those of us with fumbling fingers and stammering brains. For now, we'll concern ourselves with the most basic methods for deleting and inserting text. We'll discuss alternative and advanced techniques in Chapter 5.

Deleting characters

The two keys you use most often to delete a few characters at a time are Backspace and Delete.

The **Backspace** key erases the character you just typed. It also erases tabs and paragraph markers.

The **Delete** key erases the character that follows the insertion point, if there is one. It, too, erases tabs and paragraph markers.

We'll talk about key combinations that delete words, lines, and blocks of text in Chapter 5.

The Insert key and the Overstrike mode

The Insert key moves you between Insert and Overstrike modes. When you're in Insert mode and press a key, Word inserts the character to the left of the insertion point. When you're in Overstrike mode and press a key, Word *replaces* the character that follows the insertion point with the new character.

You can move between the two modes by clicking the mode indicator on the status bar, although pressing the Insert key is usually faster.

You can tell which mode you're in by the OVR mode indicator on right end of the status bar. When the letters OVR are gray, you're inserting; when they're black, you're overstriking.

 TIP **Use the Insert mode and switch to Overstrike mode when you** need to. You're less likely to accidentally erase text.

Starting a second document

Today's compact-disc players are changers that can hold many CDs, any of which you can play at any time. Similarly, Word can hold many documents, all available when you need them.

 The easiest way to start a new document is to click the New button on the Standard toolbar or press Ctrl+N. A fresh page opens immediately.

You can also choose File, New from the menu bar. This is a bit trickier, but offers more options. When you choose File, New, Word presents you with the New dialog box shown in figure 2.8. The icon labeled Blank Document in this dialog box represents a generic document. Clicking it is the same as clicking the New button on the Standard toolbar.

Fig. 2.8
The New dialog box lets you start a new document, even if you already have one open.

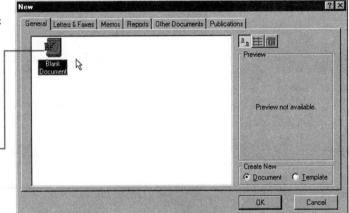

Click here for a new document.

> **TIP**   **When you open a new document, the first one tucks itself away** until you recall it. You move between the two documents by pressing Ctrl+F6. You can also choose Window from the menu bar and press the number that precedes the document you want.

Formatting documents with templates and wizardry

Word can't do your writing for you. But it does give you a variety of pre-formatted forms that can save you the trouble of formatting generic documents such as letters and resumes. You don't have to worry about setting your margins, where to put your text, or what typeface you want. Just click and type; Word does the grunt work.

You open a form from the New dialog box. For example, if you click the Other Documents tab, you can choose from among the forms shown in figure 2.9.

Word gives you two types of forms—templates and wizards.

Fig. 2.9
Word gives you a
variety of preformatted
forms that spare you
the drudgery of
preparing documents
from scratch.

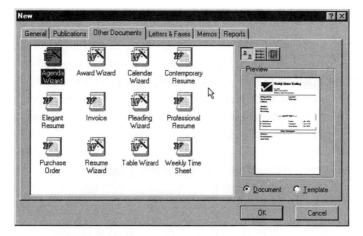

Templates

A **template** is a preformatted document in which you fill in blanks or
replace dummy text. For example, if you choose the Contemporary Resume
template, Word presents you with the resume for someone named Deborah
Greer (see fig. 2.10). Word tells you where to type your address and career
objective, and you replace the rest of the information with your own (unless,
of course, you *are* Deborah Greer).

Fig. 2.10
The Contemporary
Resume template. Fill
in the blanks and insert
your own text to
create a resume that's
formatted and ready to
print.

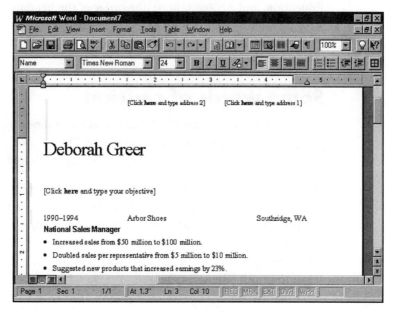

Wizards

A **wizard** is a bit more complicated. Essentially, a wizard lets you make your own template by asking you a series of questions about what you want the template to include. For example, if you choose the Resume Wizard, Word starts by asking you to choose from among four types of resumes (see fig. 2.11). It gives you descriptions of each type of resume and tells you for whom each type might be appropriate.

Fig. 2.11
The Resume Wizard creates a resume template that includes only the features and formats you want.

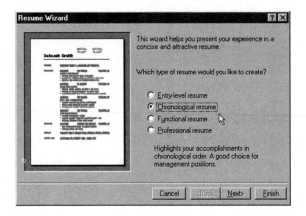

Word then asks you to choose the headings (for example, Work Experience, Education, and Accreditation), the order of the headings, and the overall style (Professional, Contemporary, or Elegant). When you're done, Word gives you a template that you complete as you would the one shown in figure 2.10.

Some words of caution

Some of Word's templates and wizards, such as those for creating resumes, letters, and press releases, are easy to use. They're also great teachers, giving you examples of interesting formatting tricks and techniques.

However, even the simple ones require you to know the basics of creating, formatting, editing, and saving documents. Read at least the rest of Part I in this book before you start using templates seriously. Other templates and wizards, particularly those for publications and reports, are for advanced users only. Don't tackle these until you're thoroughly familiar with Word's formatting and editing commands.

The following section describes Word's templates and wizards and indicates their degree of difficulty. You'll get a chance to experiment with some of the more difficult ones later in this book.

Word's templates and wizards, from a to z

Templates and wizards give you preformatted forms for common types of documents, both personal and professional. Here's a brief description of the ones that come with Word.

To give you an idea of which templates and wizards to tackle first, we've identified each as "Easy," "Fairly easy," "Fairly difficult," or "Advanced." Templates and wizards that are easy require only a basic knowledge of Word's formatting and editing commands. Those that are advanced are for users with a thorough knowledge of page- and text-formatting techniques.

General

Blank Document. The template that loads automatically when you start a new document. *Easy.*

Letters & Faxes

Fax (Contemporary, Elegant, and Professional). Three fax transmission forms that use different formats and typefaces. *Easy.*

Fax Wizard. Similar to fax templates, but prompts you for information and automatically fills in the sheet. *Easy.*

Letter (Contemporary, Elegant, and Professional). Three letter forms that use different formats and typefaces. *Easy.*

Letter Wizard. Gives a variety of several business and personal letters to use as templates. Includes such letters as a returned check notice, a request for a credit report, and an order cancellation. *Easy.*

Memos

(Contemporary, Elegant, and Professional). Three memo templates that use different formats and typefaces. *Easy.*

Memo Wizard. Lets you create a memo with a heading or on your own memo paper. Prompts you for items to include in memo (for example, CC and Priority). Creates headers and footers for multi-page memos. *Easy.*

Reports

Report (Contemporary, Elegant, and Professional). Creates business reports, proposals, and plans that use different formats and typefaces. *Advanced.*

Other Documents

Agenda Wizard. Creates meeting agendas. *Fairly easy.*

Award Wizard. Creates award certificates in four styles. *Easy.*

Calendar Wizard. Creates a one-year calendar for any 12-month period. *Easy.*

Resume (Contemporary, Elegant, and Professional). Three press release forms that use different formats and typefaces. *Fairly easy.*

Invoice. Creates an invoice; automatically calculates subtotals and totals. *Fairly easy.*

Pleading Wizard. Creates legal pleading paper. *Fairly easy* (assuming you have a background in law).

Purchase Order. Creates a purchase order. Automatically calculates subtotals and totals. *Fairly easy.*

Table Wizard. Creates tables in a variety of formats. *Advanced.*

Weekly Time Sheet. Creates employee time sheets or time sheet blanks. *Fairly easy.*

Publications

Brochure. Creates a two-sided, tri-panel, 8.5 × 11 brochure. *Fairly difficult.*

Press Release (Contemporary, Elegant, and Professional). Three press release forms that use different formats and typefaces. *Easy.*

Directory. Lets you create a phone and address directory, with a cover page. *Fairly difficult.*

Manual. Template for manuals, user's guides, and computer documentation, with table of contents and index. *Advanced.*

Newsletter. Basic newsletter template. *Advanced.*

Newsletter Wizard. Choose between classic and modern styles. *Advanced.*

Thesis. Template for academic dissertations. Includes examples of a bibliography and index. *Fairly easy.*

3

Need Help?
Click Here!

● In this chapter:

- ● I need help, and I need it now!

- ● What's context-sensitive Help, and how can it help me?

- ● Tracking down information in Word's Help files

- ● How do I get around in Word's Help screens?

- ● In your own words: adding comments to Help

Word's Help system won't tell you the meaning of life, but it will make your life easier by showing you how to use Word's many commands and features . . . . ▶

Many years ago, devoting an entire chapter to a program's Help command would have been overkill. In fact, for some minimalist software, it wouldn't have been possible—there were no Help files. Not any more. Word's Help is practically a full-blown database program, and you need to learn how to use it to partake of its riches.

When Microsoft started supplementing its manuals with on-line Help, the company wasn't doing it just to save money. On-line Help has many advantages. Most notably, you can get help without knowing the exact term to look for. This feature is called **context-sensitive Help**. You just point at the part of the screen you need help with and ask, "What's this?"

When context-sensitive Help isn't enough, you can use Help's searching and indexing tools to search Help's extensive files for detailed information. You get to these files with the Help command at the far end of the menu bar.

But the quickest way to get help while you're working is context-sensitive Help, and that's where we'll begin.

Why use context–sensitive Help?

Context-sensitive Help lets you get concise information that relates specifically to whatever you're doing at the moment. For example, if you're working in the Save dialog box, you get help on saving files. If you want to change your font, you get help on fonts.

Context-sensitive Help is a real time-saver. You don't have to wade through lists and menus looking for the specific item you need help with. And you avoid the frustration that comes when you can't remember the exact term under which the item is listed in Help's (or the manual's) index.

Help on objects in the Word window

To get a description of any object on the screen, click once on the question mark at the far right of the Standard toolbar. Point the question mark at the object and click again.

In figure 3.1, the question mark has been pointed at the Save button. Clicking the button again displays the Help screen shown in figure 3.2.

Fig. 3.1

To get help on a toolbar button, click once on the Help button and aim the pointer at the button with which you need help...

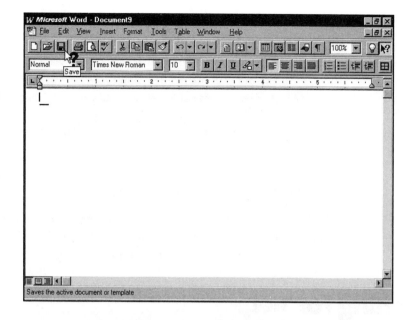

Fig. 3.2

...and click again. Word displays a window that describes the button.

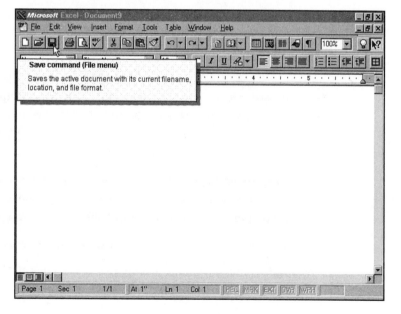

Q&A *How do I keep a Help screen from overlapping the part of the document I want to see?*

You can size the Help window any way you want by dragging the borders in and out with the mouse pointer. The new size becomes a permanent part of your Word configuration until you resize it again.

Or you can move a Help window by clicking its title bar and dragging it to another part of the screen.

Help on menu commands

The F1 function key is an easy way to get help on menu commands. For example, for help on using the thesaurus, choose Tools from the menu bar, place your pointer on Thesaurus, and press F1.

Searching for help

Context-sensitive Help is the quickest solution when you know the command or button that you need help with. But if you want to do a task and have no idea where to begin, or if you need more comprehensive instructions, it's better to use one of Help's search features.

You start a search by choosing Help, Microsoft Word Help Topics from the menu bar, or by double-clicking the Help button. From the Help Topics dialog box, choose from among four ways to look for information (see figs. 3.3A, 3.3B, 3.3C, and 3.3D on the following page).

- **Contents** gives you a table of contents, much like the one you'd find in a book, that groups topics by major category. You can browse through the contents to get an overview of subjects covered in the Help files.

- **Index** lets you search through a list of alphabetical topics.

- **Find** is similar to Index, except that it searches all Help files for any instance of a selected word or partial word.

- **Answer Wizard** lets you ask Word for help using plain-English sentences. You can also access Answer Wizard directly by choosing Help, Answer Wizard from the main menu.

We'll start with Index, which is the easiest to use.

Four ways to get help

When you choose Help from the menu bar, Word lets you choose from among four ways to search for help. In this case, the search is for how to insert a page break in a document.

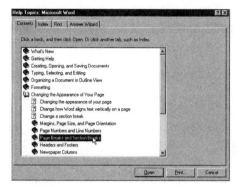

Fig. 3.3A
Browsing through the Contents yields the chapter "Page Breaks and Section Breaks" in the book titled "Changing the Appearance of Your Page."

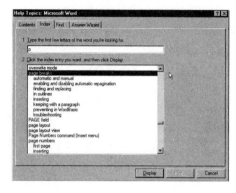

Fig. 3.3B
Searching for the topic "page break" in the alphabetical Index takes you to the "page breaks" as soon as you press the "p."

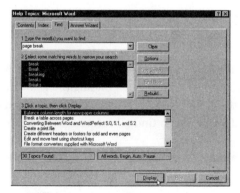

Fig. 3.3C
Searching for the words "page break" under the Find tab brings up a number of topics that include the words "page" and "break."

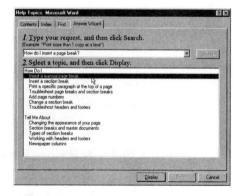

Fig. 3.3D
Asking the Answer Wizard "How do I insert a page break?" also produces a number of topics, including "Insert a manual page break," which takes you step by step through the process.

Q&A   ***I don't quite understand how the Help files are orga-***
nized. Does each of the dialog boxes shown on the
previous page have its own Help files?

All of Word's search features use the same Help files to get their information; they just give you different ways to search. For example, choosing
"troubleshooting" in figure 3.3B and "Troubleshoot page breaks and
section breaks" in figure 3.3D would take you to the same Help screen.

Index

Let's say you want to learn how to insert a page break. The fastest way is to
search the Index for the topic "page break" (refer to fig. 3.3B).

In the <u>T</u>ype The First Few Letters... text box, start typing the word **page**.
When you type **p**, the list box takes you to the first entry beginning with "p,"
which happens to be "page break." Underneath is a list of subtopics. Click
"inserting" twice to retrieve the Help screen.

Find

Find is similar to Index, except that it looks for words and phrases rather
than for topics. It identifies all occurrences of the search term in all Help
files (refer to fig. 3.3C).

For example, the <u>C</u>lick A Topic... text box lists all entries that include the
words "page" and "break."

Find has its drawbacks. As figure 3.3C shows, you'll get a lot of help on
topics you may not be interested in, and sometimes finding the right Help
page is tedious. But Find is better than Index if you have only a general idea
of what you're looking for, or if you want to find all references to a topic.

 Q&A   ***Is it possible to search for entries that include either***
"page" or "break"?

Yes. Under the Find tab, choose <u>O</u>ptions. Then, in the Find Options dialog
box that appears, click the option called At Least <u>O</u>ne Of The Words You
Typed.

Q&A ***When I click the Find tab, I get a Find Setup Wizard dialog box that tells me I have to create a database first. What's going on here?***

Not to worry. Find needs to create a word list from Word's Help files before it can do its job. This is a no-muss, no-fuss procedure. Choose the recommended Minimize Database Size. Word gives you on-screen instructions on what to do next. (You can choose Rebuild from the Find tab if you want to choose another option later.) Building a database is a one-time-only deal; you won't have to do it again unless you have to reinstall Word.

Answer Wizard

Like Index and Find, Answer Wizard lets you enter the topic you need help with (refer to fig. 3.3D). You can use plain-English sentences, such as "Check my spelling," "How do I check my spelling?" or even, if it's late and you're tired, "I command you to tell me how to check my blankity-blank spelling!" Answer Wizard divides its finds into two categories: "How Do I" and "Tell Me About." "How Do I" topics either give you detailed instructions on how to do a task, or actually step you through it. "Tell Me About" topics provide general information.

Let Answer Wizard do the walking

A guitar instructor can help a student learn chords by manually positioning the student's fingers on the strings. Similarly, Word can teach you a task by positioning you in the correct dialog box.

For example, if you choose "Insert a manual page break" in figure 3.3D, Answer Wizard displays the dialog box shown in figure 3.4. After you position your insertion point and click Next, Answer Wizard displays the Break dialog box and instructs you to click the Page Break button. Click it, then click OK, and Word inserts the break.

Fig. 3.4

The Answer Wizard can handle many common tasks automatically. Position your insertion point where you want a page break and click Next, and Word takes you to the Break dialog box.

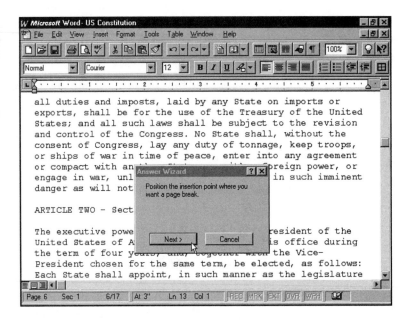

Step-by-step instructions

When Word doesn't step you through a procedure, it gives you a screen with instructions on how to do the task. For example, if you choose "Add page numbers" under the "How Do I" heading in figure 3.3D, Windows displays the screen shown in figure 3.5. Click Start Page Numbering Where You Want to display the step-by-step instructions shown in figure 3.6.

Fig. 3.5

This Help screen gives you a list of topics on which you can get step-by-step instructions.

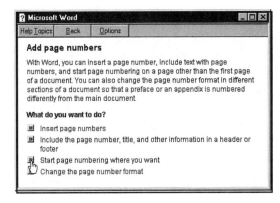

Fig. 3.6
Choosing Start Page Numbering Where You Want in figure 3.5 displays these easy-to-follow instructions.

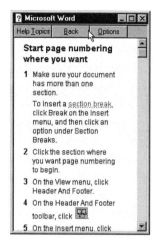

We'll look at the Help screen's menu and buttons in a moment.

Tell me about...

Word provides many graphics screens that lead you to general information on a topic. For example, if you click "Changing the appearance of your page" in figure 3.3D, Word displays the screen shown in figure 3.7. Clicking a topic displays a window like the one shown in figure 3.8.

Fig. 3.7
A graphical Help screen. Touch a topic with the pointer until the pointer turns into a hand, then click.

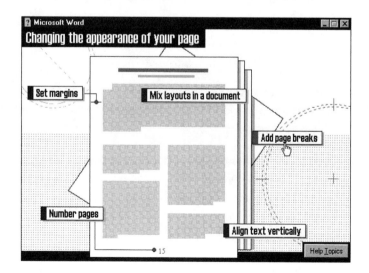

Fig. 3.8

Here's the information you get if you click *Add page breaks* in figure 3.7.

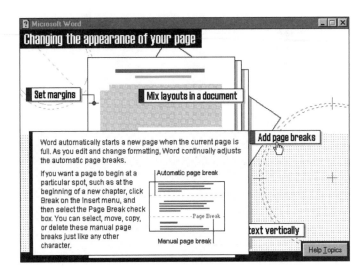

Contents

Contents is our final stop in the Help Topics dialog box (refer to fig. 3.3A). Here, Word takes a more traditional approach to providing information.

Contents presents a list of general Help subjects, called **books**, each of which is preceded by a closed-book icon. Click a book twice to open it. A table of contents drops down from the title.

The table of contents can include books, topics (which are preceded by question marks), or both. Double-click a book to get another table of contents, or double-click a topic to get a Help screen.

For example, in figure 3.3A, the table of contents for the book titled "Changing the Appearance of Your Page" includes three topics and five other books.

TIP   **If you've been using a previous version of Word, make sure you** open the "What's New" book under the Contents tab to find out about improvements and additions.

Inside the Help screen

Getting help doesn't have to stop with reading the information and returning to your document. Word's Help screen has several features that you might find useful. For instance, you can print a Help screen, copy the information into a document, and even add your own notes (see the following page entitled "Taking a closer look at the Word Help screen"). Many Help screens also include links to other Help screens that have related information.

 Q&A *Can I return to my document without closing the Help window?*

Yes. Click the Help window's Minimize button, click anywhere in the document window, or press Alt+Tab. The Help window will remain in the background. You can bring it back by pressing Alt+Tab.

Options galore

Don't overlook the Options menu, which you get by clicking the <u>O</u>ptions button or the right mouse button. From here, you can print, save, and add notes to a Help screen.

Printing a Help screen

Often, it's more convenient to have a printout of a Help topic so you can tape it to your forehead until you've got the material memorized. <u>O</u>ptions, <u>P</u>rint Topic takes you to the Print dialog box, from which you can send the active Help screen to your printer. (For more information on printing, see Chapter 7.)

Copying a Help screen

Perhaps you'd like to select Help topics for a personal or office manual. You can do it easily with <u>C</u>opy, which lets you copy the contents of a Help screen into a Word file.

Taking a closer look at the Word Help screen

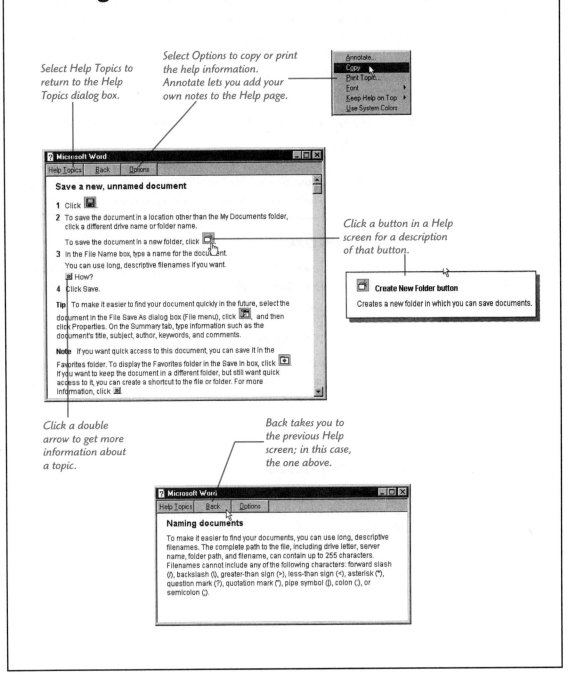

Select Help Topics to return to the Help Topics dialog box.

Select Options to copy or print the help information. Annotate lets you add your own notes to the Help page.

Annotate...
Copy
Print Topic...
Font
Keep Help on Top
Use System Colors

Microsoft Word

Help Topics   Back   Options

Save a new, unnamed document

1 Click .

2 To save the document in a location other than the My Documents folder, click a different drive name or folder name.

   To save the document in a new folder, click .

3 In the File Name box, type a name for the document.

   You can use long, descriptive filenames if you want.

   How?

4 Click Save.

Tip To make it easier to find your document quickly in the future, select the document in the File Save As dialog box (File menu), click , and then click Properties. On the Summary tab, type information such as the document's title, subject, author, keywords, and comments.

Note If you want quick access to this document, you can save it in the Favorites folder. To display the Favorites folder in the Save In box, click . If you want to keep the document in a different folder, but still want quick access to it, you can create a shortcut to the file or folder. For more information, click .

Click a button in a Help screen for a description of that button.

 Create New Folder button

Creates a new folder in which you can save documents.

Click a double arrow to get more information about a topic.

Back takes you to the previous Help screen; in this case, the one above.

Microsoft Word

Help Topics   Back   Options

Naming documents

To make it easier to find your documents, you can use long, descriptive filenames. The complete path to the file, including drive letter, server name, folder path, and filename, can contain up to 255 characters. Filenames cannot include any of the following characters: forward slash (/), backslash (\), greater-than sign (>), less-than sign (<), asterisk (*), question mark (?), quotation mark ("), pipe symbol (|), colon (:), or semicolon (;).

Before you undertake such a project, you'll probably want to read about copying text (see Chapter 5) and formatting documents (see Part III). But here are the basic steps:

1 In the Help screen, choose Options, Copy (nothing apparent will happen, but that's OK).

2 Close the Help screen and start a new Word document.

3 Choose Edit, Paste from the menu or press Ctrl+V.

The text of the Help screen, minus icons and formats, appears in your document.

Adding comments to a Help screen

The Annotate command lets you include your own notes in a Help screen. This is useful for adding reminders or emphasizing important information.

Choose Annotate from the Options menu. The Annotate dialog box pops up, like the one shown in figure 3.9. Type your note in the Current Annotation text box, then click Save.

Fig. 3.9

You can add your own comments to a Help screen using the Annotate command on the Options menu.

Click the paper clip to see your annotation.

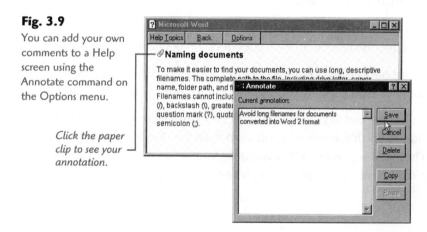

A small paper clip appears at the beginning of the Help screen's text. Click the paper clip to recall the Annotate dialog box.

Q&A *Whenever I move from a Help screen to my document, the Help screen disappears. How to I keep it visible, so I can refer to it while I'm in the document?*

Simple. From the Options menu in any Help window, select Keep Help On Top, On Top. Thereafter, you can move between the Help window and your document window by clicking inside one or the other, or by pressing Alt+Tab.

Other helpful Help features

The Help system is far too extensive to describe fully in a few pages. Many of the Help options are best suited to browsing, and the best way to find out what's there is to explore. Here are a few key menu items you might want to check out:

- To find out how to get technical help from Microsoft, go to the Contents tab, open the "Getting Help" book, and choose "Technical Support." Among other services, you'll get an 800 number that you can use for recorded or faxed replies.

- To get a list of WordPerfect commands and their Word equivalents, open the "Switching from WordPerfect" book under the Contents tab.

- To get information about your hardware, operating system, memory, and disk storage, choose Help, About Microsoft Word, System Info.

- To learn about keyboard shortcuts, go to the Contents tab, open the "Reference Information" book, then open the "Keyboard Guide" book. The list of topics includes everything you need to know, and much more, about how to use the keyboard.

4

Saving and Opening Your Documents

In this chapter:

- **Save your documents early and often!**

- **The name game: using Word's new long file names**

- **Saving documents automatically with AutoSave**

- **And the password is...**

- **Backup files: Word's safety net**

- **Can I look at a file before I open it?**

Word knows more ways to save than a traveling preacher. Use as many of them as you can; they're your best protection against system crashes . . . . ▶

Most of us learn how to open and close Word documents before the installation disks are cold. Unfortunately, in our zeal to start writing, we often neglect important lessons on other aspects of document management.

There's far more to saving a document than clicking the Save button. How do you protect your open files from system failures? Word lets you save files in ways that minimize your risk. What do you call the file? Using names to organize your files is practically an art. Where do you put the file? Surely, you don't want to put it where you can't find it later.

Word gives you buttons and keyboard shortcuts for many file management tasks, but you should start by learning the File menu (see fig. 4.1). You'll gain a thorough and systematic understanding of Word's many file management options.

Fig. 4.1

When you choose File from the menu bar, you get this pull-down menu of file management commands.

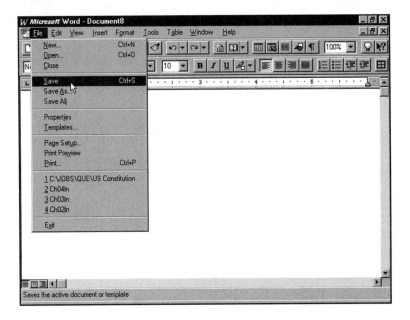

The file menu contains two options for saving: Save and Save As. You'll need both of them. Let's look at Save first.

Saving files: the basics

Word is designed to let you save files easily and often—and you should. Nothing's more depressing than watching four hours of work disappear because a squirrel jumped on a live wire and brought down the power grid.

So how complicated can saving a file be? Don't you just give the sucker a name and well, *save* it? It's more involved than you might think.

If you're new to computers, here are a few guidelines for happy file-saving:

- Give your document a name and save it immediately—before you even start typing.

- Save your file often. Work under the theory that a meteor is going to hit your house sometime in the next five minutes.

- Copy your documents to floppy disks at least once a day, more often when you're making frequent and substantial changes.

- Use Word's AutoSave feature to automatically save your file at regular intervals.

- Close your document when you're away from your computer for more than a few minutes.

- *Always* close all files, exit Word, and exit Windows before turning off your computer!

 Plain English, please!

A **file name** is the name you give a document when you save it to disk. A file name consists of a **base name** and an **extension**, which for Word documents is .DOC. The base name and the extension are separated by a period. For example, in the file name BUDGET.DOC, the base name is BUDGET and the extension is .DOC.

If your file name has more than one period, the extension is made up of the characters after the last period. For example, in the file name BUDGET.95.ACTUAL.DOC, the base name is BUDGET.95.ACTUAL and the extension is .DOC. In all, a file name and extension can be 255 characters long, although the extension can't be more than three characters long. (More on Word's long file names in a moment.) You don't need to type the extension; Word adds it automatically.

When you load Word, the title bar shows the name of the file as Document1. If you start a second new file, Word calls it Document2, and so on. These are not file names, and you should give your file a real name before starting work on your document.

Choose File, Save to pop up the Save As dialog box shown in figure 4.2. The suggested file name—in this example, Doc10—is highlighted in the File Name text box. Type the new file name (the suggested file name disappears when you start typing) and click OK. The file is now stored on disk.

Fig. 4.2
The Save As dialog box. To replace Word's suggested file name, *Doc10*, type the new file name into the File Name text box.

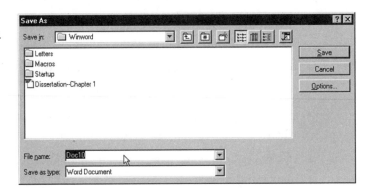

TIP **When you're naming your document for the first time, you** can go directly to the Save As dialog box by pressing Ctrl+S or by clicking the Save button on the Standard toolbar.

The keys to valid file names

Your file names can include any letter or number. You can also use all characters *except* an asterisk (*), forward slash (/), backslash (\), greater-than sign (>), less-than sign (<), question mark (?), quotation mark ("), vertical bar (|), colon (:), or semicolon (;). Word accepts spaces in a file name, too.

Experienced PC users take note: Windows 95 accepts a variety of characters that were not valid in Windows 3.1 and its ancestors. These are the period (.), plus sign (+), comma (,), equal sign (=), and brackets ([]). But despite Word's willingness to let you use all sorts of character combinations, your best plan is to stick with letters and numbers. Use symbols only if you have a good reason to, such as to separate elements in your file name.

Q&A *What if I want an extension other than .DOC?*

Put the entire file name in quotation marks; for example, "REPORT.PRN."

TIP You name folders following the same rules you use to name files.

Saving a document to an existing file name

What if you want to replace a file on your disk with a document you've just created? That's easy. When you're in the Save As dialog box, click the file name in the list box directly below Save <u>I</u>n, then click <u>S</u>ave. You can tell which files are word documents by the Word icon to the left of the file name (Dissertation—Chapter 1 in fig. 4.2).

Word asks you if you want to replace the existing file. Click Yes to save, No to return to the Save As dialog box, and Cancel to return to the document.

The file to which you've saved the document becomes the default file name.

CAUTION When you save a document to an existing file name, you irrevocably destroy the file you're replacing. It is gone forever. Never overwrite a file unless you're certain you don't need it!

Resaving a file

Once you've saved a document, you can resave it without returning to the Save As dialog box. Click the Save button on the Standard toolbar or press Ctrl+S. Word lets you know it's saving the file by changing the mouse pointer to an hourglass and displaying a horizontal meter in the status bar. Both of these displays mean, "Hold on a minute, I'm busy doing something."

Saving to another file name

When you want to save a document but give it a new name, choose <u>F</u>ile, Save <u>A</u>s. You get the same Save As dialog box shown in figure 4.2. The current file name appears in the File <u>N</u>ame text box. Just type the new name and click <u>S</u>ave.

Saving to another file type

"I need a copy of the Hopper report," says Smithers. "Oh—and can you give it to me in Windows Write 3.0 format?"

Gulp. You've just learned how to create Word for Windows documents, and now you're supposed to make Windows Write documents too?

Not to worry. You don't need to know a thing about Write to meet Smithers' request. Word can save a document to a file that's Write-ready. It can also save documents for WordPerfect and other versions of Word. You can even save a document in a universal format that nearly any other word processor on the planet can open.

 Plain English, please!

When Word saves a file, it doesn't simply store your text. The file also includes instruction codes that control how your document looks. For example, one code might say, "We want bold text here," another, "Let's change the type size to 10 points," and so on. Together, these codes are called Word's **format**.

A file that contains text but no codes goes by a variety of names, including **text**, **unformatted text**, and **plain text**.

Occasionally, you'll hear a technically oriented user refer to **ASCII files**. (ASCII stands for American Standard Code for Information Interchange.) Don't be fooled by the jargon; the person probably wants a text file.

File types for the millions

You save a file in another format using the Save As <u>T</u>ype drop-down box in the Save As dialog box (see fig. 4.3).

The text box probably reads Word Document, which is the option for Word for Windows 95 documents. Click the text box, choose the new file type, and click <u>S</u>ave.

TIP Chapter 22 tells you more about how to save files for use by database managers and by other types of software.

Fig. 4.3

The Save As Type drop-down box lets you save a file to other formats, including ones that other versions of Word can use.

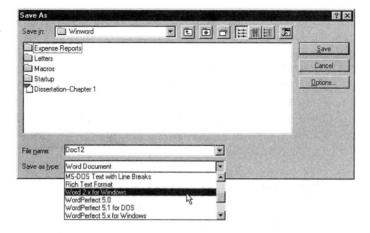

Saving to a floppy disk

Networks have become a force in the workplace, but the floppy disk is still a popular vehicle for moving files from one computer to another.

To save a Word document to a floppy disk, make sure you have a disk in the floppy drive, then click the Save In box. A tree drops down, similar to the one shown in figure 4.4. Move the insertion point to the floppy drive (in this case, A:) and click it. Name the file and save it.

Fig. 4.4

To save to a floppy disk, click the Save In box and select the floppy drive. Make sure you have a disk in the drive!

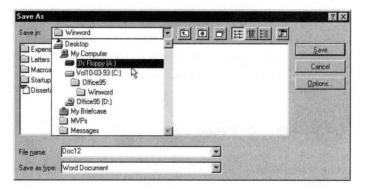

AutoSave: Word's crash-protection air bag

It's happened to all of us. You've just finished three inspired pages of brilliant prose. Exhilarated but exhausted, you leave your desk for a glass of water. Suddenly, the building goes dark—a power failure. As you stand dumbfounded at the cooler, the company wit says, "Sure hope everybody saved their files!" Of course you saved your document—or did you?

No matter how fanatical you are about saving files, the day may come when you'll simply forget. Why take the risk? Word can save your document automatically with a great feature called AutoSave. AutoSave puts your document in a temporary file at intervals you specify. If your computer crashes before you've saved your document, Word tries to recover the AutoSaved file when you run Word again.

 TIP   **AutoSave does not save the document to the actual file, so your** changes to the document don't become permanent until you manually save the document to its file name.

To use AutoSave, click <u>O</u>ptions from the Save As dialog box (refer to fig. 4.3). Find the check box for Automatic <u>S</u>ave Every and make sure it contains an x. In the text box to the right, enter the interval in minutes (that is, how often you want to AutoSave the file), then click OK.

Word suggests an AutoSave interval of ten minutes—fine for most documents. The shorter the interval, the better, but keep in mind that long documents take time to save, and an AutoSave every few minutes can become intrusive.

 TIP   **AutoSave saves all open documents. If the documents are long** and the interval you've set is short, your keyboard might seem to freeze whenever AutoSave kicks in. You can minimize these delays by closing any documents you're not using.

How to use long file names

If you've used Windows 3.1 and its predecessors, you've probably been frustrated with the fact that you could only use 11 characters in a file name (up to eight in the base name and three in an optional extension, such as LETRTOJM.DOC). Did you name that memo to Ed EDREP821.DOC or RPTEDFIN.DOC? What does the cryptic IV05NSJL.DOC stand for, and what's in the file?

Word's rules for naming files are much more liberal, but with freedom comes added responsibility. If you start typing 50-word file names based on whatever pops into your mind, you're going to have major headaches managing your documents.

The war of the Words

Let's say you get a call from Smudgley, asking for the same Hopper report you sent to Smithers as a Write 3.0 file. Armed with your new-found knowledge of file types, you ask Smudgley what word processor he uses. "Word," he says. "Great," you say, and send him the file through office e-mail.

A few hours later, Smudgley calls again. He says he opened the file and got several screens full of garbage characters. "I asked for a Word file," he says. "I gave you a Word file," you protest. "What version are you using?" he asks. "Version?" you answer.

Welcome to the Version Zone, a cockeyed world in which Word on one computer is apparently something else on another.

Actually, there's a simple, if not entirely satisfactory, explanation. Different versions of Word save in different formats. While Word for Windows 95 can translate all the other formats, the other versions of Word might not be able to translate the Word for Windows 95 format.

So how can you make sure you're saving your Word files in a format your officemates can use? Here are a few helpful hints:

- Make sure you know which version of Word the recipient of the file is using. If she says Word 6, find out if it's Word 6 for Windows or Word 6 for DOS; they're different formats.

- People using Word 6 for Windows can read your files in Word for Windows 95 format. Also, Windows 95's WordPad word processor will open your Word for Windows 95 documents.

- If you're not sure what version the other person has, save in Word 3.x-5.x for MS-DOS format. This is a sort of protoformat that all other versions of Word understand.

- Choose the matching version in the Save File As <u>T</u>ype box.

- The file name should not have more than eight characters; earlier versions of Word won't recognize a long file name.

- If you're not sure the other person is even using Word, provide a plain-text file as well (the Text Only option). The document's formatting instructions will be removed, but at least your colleague will be able to read the file.

One caveat: even though you've saved a file in the correct Word format, you can't be sure that document will look the same on the other person's screen. It might have type- and page-formatting instructions that other versions can't use. Word discards these instructions when it saves to an earlier format.

Smart file-naming strategies

The best way to exploit long file names is to use them to organize your files. Follow the same logic you would for manila folder tabs, starting with the general and moving to the specific.

For example, let's say you're planning a product promotion and have written three related documents: a list of promotion ideas, schedule, and summary of expenses. You might name the files:

> PROMO.FALL.IDEAS
>
> PROMO.FALL.SCHEDULE
>
> PROMO.FALL.EXPENSES

Try to keep your file names as short as possible. The longer the file name, the more cluttered your Open and Save As dialog boxes. Also, you lessen the chance of typos when you save a new file that has an existing base (such as PROMO.FALL in the above example).

Q&A *Does it matter if I use upper- or lowercase letters in a file name?*

No. MYDOC.doc, myDoc.doc, and MyDoc.doc are all the same to Word. You can't create two files with the same name, regardless of their case, unless you put them in separate folders.

When to avoid long file names

On the surface, long file names seem to have nothing but advantages. But if you share documents with people who use earlier versions of Word and Windows, your long file names could become someone else's headache.

Most PCs on this planet do not run Windows 95. Their operating system is MS-DOS, usually version 6.x, often coupled with Windows 3.1. File names on these computers are limited to 11 characters—an eight-character base and three-character extension. These older systems do not recognize long file names.

To make Windows 95 files compatible with older machines, Windows 95 automatically converts a long file name into an 11-character **alias**. For example, if you save a file as "Actual Expenses for June," Windows gives it the alias ACTUAL~1.DOC.

I am Sparta~1!

This alias becomes the file name when the disk it's on is read by software written for older systems. Thus, when you pass your document to a person using, say, Word 6 and Windows 3.1, he'll see a file called ACTUAL~1, not "Actual Expenses for June."

You don't need a vivid imagination to see the potential problems. The file names that your friends and colleagues see will often bear little resemblance to the ones you created, nor will they always make sense.

Of course, you want to use Windows 95's special features as much as possible. But when you create a document that someone else might open in an earlier version of Windows, you'll do that person a favor by sticking with an 11-character file name.

Play it safe with password protection

You can give your file a password to protect it from the curious. Select Options from the Save As dialog box. In the lower left-hand corner of the Options dialog box that appears, you'll see two text boxes: Protection Password and Write Reservation Password (see fig. 4.5).

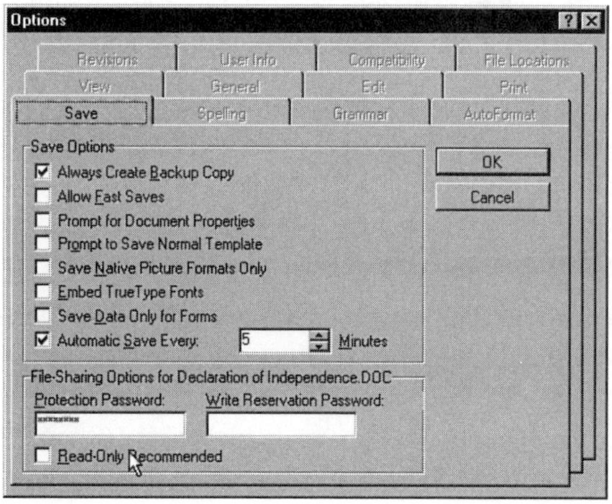

Fig. 4.5

A protection password locks the file from anyone who doesn't know the password. A write reservation password lets other people read the file but not change it.

If you enter a protection password, only those who know the password can open the file.

If you enter a write reservation password, someone who doesn't know the password can open and read the document, but can't resave it with the same name to the same folder. This gives other people access to the document but prevents them from making changes.

TIP **We slothful types tend to use passwords that we can remember** easily, such as the name of our dog, our phone number, or (if we're really feeling lazy) "password." These happen to be passwords that virtually any sentient file-cracker will guess. If you're serious about your password, use a nonsense string of letters and numbers at least five characters long (the names of Icelandic cities do nicely, unless you named your dog "Reykjavik").

CAUTION **Once you've protected a file, you won't be able to open that file** without the password. Write down your password and store it in a secure place (and remember where you put it!).

Backing up your documents

You can instruct Word to automatically save the previous version of your document to a backup file whenever you save the current version.

A backup can be a godsend if you accidentally save a file with unwanted changes. It also gives you extra protection against file corruption woes. If your hard disk acts up and you can't open the main file, you can often retrieve most of your work by opening the backup.

To make an automatic backup active, select Options from the Save As dialog box and put a check mark in the box next to Always Create Backup Copy under Save Options (refer to fig. 4.5).

Opening a backup file

Because backup files have the extension .WBK instead of .DOC, you won't see them listed in the Open dialog box. To list your backups, either choose All Files in the Files Of Type list box, or type ***.WBK** in the File Name text box and click Open. You can easily identify a backup file because it is named "Backup of" followed by the name of the original file.

Q&A *How do I print my document?*

 You can get a printout quickly by clicking the Print button on the Standard toolbar. Make sure your printer is turned on. Word bypasses the Print dialog box and sends your document straight to the printer. Chapter 7 gives you details on printing, including how to preview a document, set your margins, and print envelopes and labels.

Closing a document

Once you're finished with a document, there's no point letting it hang around taking up memory and slowing AutoSaves. To clear it from your screen, choose File, Close.

If you've made changes to the document since the last time you saved it, Word gives you the option of saving your document before closing it. Closing a document does not close Word or affect other active documents.

Opening a file

You've learned how to create a new file and save it. Now let's talk about how you get it back.

The easiest way to open a file is to click the Open button on the Standard toolbar. You can also choose File, Open or press Ctrl+O.

Either way, you'll get the Open dialog box shown in figure 4.6. It looks like the Save As dialog box, except that Save In becomes Look In and Save As Type becomes Files Of Type.

Fig. 4.6
The Open dialog box shows you the Word documents available in the selected folder.

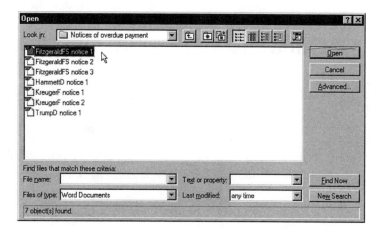

You select a file to open by clicking the file name twice, or by typing the file name in the File Name box.

Narrowing your list of files

If your folder begins to fill with documents and other types of files, you can limit which files Word lists in one of several ways.

If you type a string of characters in the File Name text box, Word displays only those files that include those characters. For example, typing **WRI** lists Wright.invoice, Tax.writeoffs, and Orders.wri.

If you want only those files that start with WRI, use the asterisk as a wildcard, like this: **WRI***.

To list files that have a .WRI extension, type ***WRI**.

 Plain English, please!

Just as a wildcard in poker can represent any card in the deck, a **wildcard** in a file name stands in for any valid file name characters. Word's two wildcards are the asterisk (*) and the question mark (?). The difference is that the asterisk can represent any number of characters, while the question mark can represent only a single character.

For example, the file name REP*5.DOC could represent REP95.DOC, REPORTFOR1995.DOC, or REP5.DOC. The file name REP?5.DOC, on the other hand, can represent only REP95.DOC.

Calling all file types!

If you work exclusively with Word for Windows 95 files, they have the .DOC extension, and the Open dialog box shows you all Word documents in the selected directory. But if you want to see files created with other word processors, you have to change the file type.

For example, suppose a coworker gives you a floppy disk that contains a report he wrote in Windows Notepad. You put the disk in your floppy drive, go to the Open dialog box, click the Look In drop-down box, and select drive A:. The list box comes up empty. Did your colleague forget to save the file before handing you the disk?

Probably not. Notepad saves documents with a .TXT extension. Word displays the file name if you click the Files Of Type drop-down box and select Text Only Files (*.txt).

TIP   **If you don't know the extension of the file you're looking for,** choose All Files (*.*) in the Files Of Type drop-down box. Click the Details button if you're not sure which are documents and which are other types of files.

Opening several files at once

Word lets you open several documents in a folder at the same time. To select individual files scattered throughout the list, click each separate file while holding down the Ctrl key. Each file becomes highlighted, as shown in figure 4.7. Then click Open.

Fig. 4.7
You can open more than one file at the same time by clicking each file while holding down the Ctrl key.

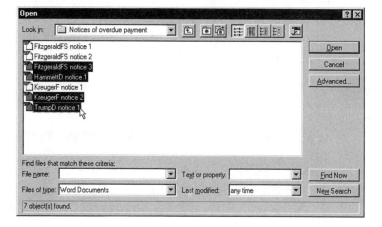

To select contiguous files, click the first file; then, holding down the Shift key, click the last file. Word highlights both files and all files in between.

Opening recent files

Word lets you open documents you've worked on recently without going to the Open dialog box. Choose from the list that appears at the bottom of the File menu.

You can change the number of files that appear on this list. Choose Tools, Options from the menu bar and click the General tab. Type a number from between 0 and 9 in the Entries box.

Opening a new file

You've seen how Word creates a new empty file when you first start Word. You can create a file at any time by selecting File, New from the menu bar. Choose the General tab in the New dialog box and click the Blank Document icon to open a generic, unformatted document.

You can bypass the New dialog box by clicking the New button on the Standard toolbar or by pressing Ctrl+N.

Previewing a file

It's not unusual to maintain three or four files that contain different versions of the same document. For example, you might keep several resumes—each one geared toward a slightly different type of job. Rather than open each document until you find the right one, you can use the Preview button in the Open dialog box to peek at them first.

In the Open dialog box, click the name of the file you want to look at and click the Preview button. Figure 4.8 shows Preview in action.

Fig. 4.8
Click the Preview button to peek at the selected file.

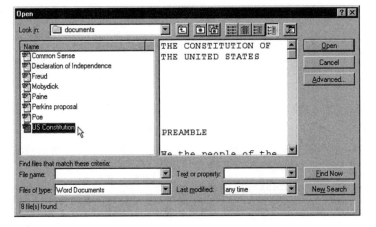

Or use Quick View to take a peek

Quick View works a little like the Preview button, letting you get a glimpse of a file before you open it. But Quick View has some important advantages:

- Quick View gives you a bigger picture of the file so you can see what it'll look like when you open it.

- Quick View can preview files in other formats. For example, in figure 4.9, Quick View shows a Lotus 1-2-3 spreadsheet. The Preview window (behind the Quick View window in fig. 4.9) shows the spreadsheet as a bunch of garbage characters.

- Quick View is a Windows 95 program, not a part of Word. You can close your Open dialog box and keep the Quick View window active. This lets you move between your document and the Quick View window (using Alt+Tab). You can also keep the window on top of your document, a useful feature when you want to compare an open document with one on disk.

Fig. 4.9
Quick View lets you preview files in a variety of formats. Here, the viewer sneaks a peek at a Lotus 1-2-3 spreadsheet.

	A	B	C	D	E	F	G	
1				----240 Months----			----360 Months----	
2				Monthly	Min.		Monthly	
3	Amount	Rate		Payment	Salary		Payment	
4	70000	8		585.51	25093.20		513.64	2
5	70000	8.5		607.48	26034.70		538.24	2
6	70000	9		629.81	26991.78		563.24	2
7	70000	9.5		652.49	27963.94		588.60	2
8	70000	10		675.52	28950.65		614.30	2
9	70000	10.5		698.87	29951.40		640.32	2
10	70000	11		722.53	30965.65		666.63	2

payments.wk1 - Quick View — File View Help

Display details may be inaccurate.

Q&A ***I can't find Quick View where you said it would be!***

If Quick View is not on your shortcut menu, it's for one of two reasons:

- Quick View isn't installed on your system. Refer to the Windows 95 Help files or manual for information on how to install it.

- You're trying to look at a file whose format Quick View doesn't recognize. For example, Quick View won't appear on the shortcut menu if you've selected a program file.

Part II: Editing Your Text

5

How to Delete, Move, Copy, and Change Your Text

● **In this chapter:**

- **How do I select text?**

- **Quick and easy ways to delete, move, and copy text**

- **Save time with text libraries**

- **How to replace text, formats, and special characters**

- **Oops! I didn't mean to do that!**

- **cHANGING the CASE of Words And leTTers**

From hammers to polish, Word has the editing tools that let you pound and buff your document until it's a work of art . . . .

Many of us do not use our word processor's editing functions very efficiently. Walk into any office; odds are most people won't know, for example, how to use shortcut keys to move text.

If you're new to word processing, train yourself properly from the start. Learn the best techniques for deleting, copying, and moving text—whether it's with the keyboard or mouse—and do each task the right way until it becomes instinctive.

If, like a self-trained hunt-and-peck typist, you've developed bad habits, now is the time to retool your skills. While you might feel like a wobbly toddler as you pause to ponder your every keystroke and mouse move, you'll soon wow the Word warriors in your office with your flickering fingers and pyrophoric pointer.

You have to select something before you can do anything with it

The key to efficient editing is knowing how to select text. Once you learn the quickest way to choose the words, paragraphs, or blocks you want to edit, the actual editing becomes easy.

To get an idea of how efficient you can be, take a look at figure 5.1 and imagine that you want to delete the highlighted paragraph.

How would you do this? Well, you can:

1 Click at the start of the paragraph.

2 Hold down the Shift key.

3 Press the right arrow key about 1,000 times until you get to the end of the paragraph.

4 Choose Edit, Cut.

Or you can just click twice to the left of the paragraph and press Delete.

Fig. 5.1

Deleting a paragraph requires only two mouse clicks and a keystroke.

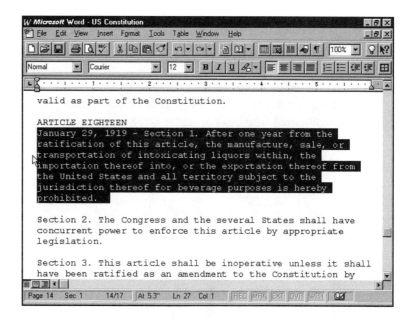

Word lets you select text by the word, line, sentence, paragraph, screen, or document. You can select to the beginning or end of a document. And in most cases, you can use the keyboard or the mouse.

The Word manual includes more than two dozen keyboard and mouse operations, but there's not much point in trying to memorize them. You'll only remember the ones you need, and the odds are you'll need just a few. Once you learn the most important tricks, you can add to your repertoire.

Selecting blocks

You can **mark**, or select, any block of text in one of three ways:

- If you're at the beginning of the block you want to select, put the mouse pointer at the end of the block, hold down the Shift key, and click the mouse button.

- The mouse-only technique is to click at the beginning of the block, and drag the mouse pointer to the end of the block. Move across the screen to select text character by character; move up or down to select text line by line.

- If you prefer the keyboard, place the insertion point at the beginning of the text. Hold down the Shift key and press the appropriate arrow key. For larger blocks, you can press the Page Up or Page Down key.

Vertical blocks—a slice is nice

One of Word's more interesting editing features is vertical select, which lets you select text in vertical columns. This feature is a great time-saver when you want to format single letters aligned vertically. In figure 5.2, for example, the vertical letters spelling "Chuck Berry" are selected and can be highlighted with bold or made a different font or size.

Fig. 5.2

You can select vertically aligned text for formatting, such as with bold or italics.

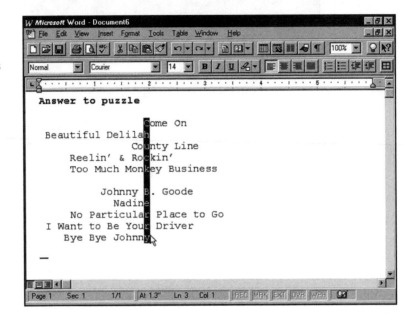

You can also use vertical select to delete or format columns in tabular material.

To select text vertically, place the insertion point at the top of the column, hold down the Alt key, and drag down with the mouse. You can also drag the mouse left or right to include more columns.

Vertical select works best with the Courier font. Other fonts might not realign your text properly after you've formatted the column. Check out Chapter 8 for more information on formatting type.

Selecting words

The previous methods are best for large blocks, but they're overkill if you just want to select a word or two. It's easier to use these techniques:

- To select a word, click twice anywhere on the word. If you prefer the keyboard, put the insertion point at the beginning of the word and press Ctrl+Shift+right arrow.

- To select several words, click twice on the first word. Hold down the mouse button on the second click and drag across the next words. With the keyboard, put the insertion point at the beginning of the word, press Ctrl+Shift, and repeat the arrow as many times as you need to.

- To select from the middle of a word to the end, put the insertion point where you want to start the selection and press Ctrl+Shift+right arrow. To select to the beginning of a word, use Ctrl+Shift+left arrow.

Selecting lines

A line of text is one that occupies a single line in your document, regardless of punctuation or length. Use these techniques to select lines:

- Select a line by clicking the space to the left of the line. At the keyboard, place the insertion point at the beginning of the line, and press Shift+End.

- Select multiple lines by clicking the space to the left of the line and dragging the mouse pointer up or down.

- Select to the end of a line by pressing Shift+End. Select to the beginning of a line by pressing Shift+Home.

Selecting sentences

You can select a sentence by clicking twice on the first word and dragging the mouse to the end, but there's an easier way: hold down the Ctrl key and click the sentence.

Selecting paragraphs

A paragraph is all text between two paragraph marks. A paragraph can consist of a single word, a line, or a thousand lines. The techniques for selecting paragraphs are:

- Select a paragraph by double-clicking the space next to the paragraph, or triple-clicking inside the paragraph.

- Select multiple paragraphs by double-clicking the space next to the paragraph and dragging the mouse pointer.

Selecting big chunks of text

Sometimes, selecting a few measly sentences or paragraphs isn't enough; you need to cover large expanses of document fast. Here are a couple of helpful shortcuts:

- Select to the end of your document by pressing Ctrl+Shift+End.

- Select to the beginning of your document by pressing Ctrl+Shift+Home.

- Select the entire document by triple-clicking the space next to your text or by pressing Ctrl+A.

 TIP **You can cancel your selected text by clicking anywhere in the text** or by pressing an arrow key.

Okay, my text is selected. Now what?

Once you've got your text selected, you're ready to delete, copy, or move it.

Get rid of it

You delete, or clear, selected text by pressing the Delete or Backspace key.

You can restore deleted text by immediately choosing <u>E</u>dit, <u>U</u>ndo Clear from the menu bar or by pressing Ctrl+Z.

 TIP **You can delete a word by putting the insertion point at the** beginning of the word and pressing Ctrl+Delete. To delete a word that's behind your insertion point, press Ctrl+Backspace.

Moving text with the mouse

Like what you wrote, but decided it would work better somewhere else? Word gives you two ways to move text with the mouse. The first method uses two buttons on the Standard toolbar: Cut and Paste.

 Select your text and click the Cut button. The text disappears, but don't worry—you haven't lost it. Word has stashed the text in a storage bin for later use. Removing text in this manner is called **cutting**, and the storage bin is called the **Clipboard**. The Clipboard, which is a part of Windows, is an important tool for moving text and graphics within a document, among documents, and even among different programs.

 Next, position the insertion point where you want to move the text and click the Paste button. Word takes the text out of storage and inserts or **pastes** it at the position of your insertion point.

You can also paste the block by clicking the right mouse button and choosing <u>P</u>aste from the shortcut menu.

 Q&A *I cut a block of text I didn't want to cut! How do I restore it?*

If you haven't moved your insertion point, simply click the Paste button or press Ctrl+V. If you've moved to somewhere else in the document, click the Undo button or press Ctrl+Z to undo the cut. Word restores the cut text to its original location. This second method works only if you haven't made any editing or formatting changes since the cut.

Drag-and-drop moving

You can move selected text to any place in your document by pointing to the highlighted block and holding down the mouse button. A small checkered box attaches itself to the pointer as you move the block. Drag the block to its destination and release the button. Word drops the block into its new location.

Dragging and dropping text is effective if you're traveling no farther than the visible document. It's less practical if you have to go to another part of the document. The window sometimes scrolls too fast to let you accurately position your pointer, especially if the selected block is large. The better alternative in such cases is to use the buttons on the toolbar.

TIP   **If you start dragging your selected text and decide you don't want** to move it after all, move the mouse pointer outside the document window. When it turns into a circle with a line through it, release the button.

Some people prefer the keyboard

To move a block of text with the keyboard, cut it by pressing Ctrl+X, move the insertion point to the point of insertion, and press Ctrl+V.

Can I swap these paragraphs?

You can switch the order of two paragraphs without cutting and pasting. This trick is particularly useful when you want to reorder items in a list.

Put the insertion point anywhere inside the paragraph you want to move (it doesn't have to be highlighted). Press Alt+Shift+up arrow to move it before the previous paragraph. Press Alt+Shift+down arrow to move it after the next paragraph.

Copying with the mouse

Copying text is almost the same as moving it, except that you keep the selected block where it is.

Click the Copy button on the Standard toolbar instead of the Cut button. Like cutting, copying puts the text on the Clipboard, but Word doesn't delete the selected text.

Move the insertion point to where you want to copy the block. Click the Paste button or choose Paste from the shortcut menu.

To copy text with the drag-and-drop method, first hold down the Ctrl key, then point to the selected block, hold down the mouse button, and drag the block to its destination.

Copying with the keyboard

Press Ctrl+C. Move the insertion point to where you want to copy the text and press Ctrl+V.

TIP **When you put a block of text on the Clipboard, you can paste that** text as often as you like. This is a time-saving trick if you have a line of text that you want to repeat several times.

CAUTION **When you cut or copy a block of text to the Clipboard, it replaces** and permanently deletes any text that is already on the Clipboard. If you want to store the block for later use, use AutoText, described below.

I want something else here instead

You can delete text and replace it with new text in two steps. Select the text you want to replace; then:

- Start typing new text, or

- Paste text from the Clipboard

What is AutoText?

The Clipboard is great for simple moves and copies, but what if you want to save a block of text permanently? Something you can insert into a document whenever you need it, such as a greeting in a form letter?

Enter AutoText. This <u>E</u>dit menu command lets you create a library of commonly used text. You can insert the text in any document, at any time, until you remove it from the library. (Word 2 users: AutoText is the same as the Glossary.)

Create the entry first

Let's say you've got an opening paragraph that you want to use in a series of letters. Select the paragraph and choose <u>E</u>dit, AutoTe<u>x</u>t from the main menu. You'll get the AutoText dialog box shown in figure 5.3.

AutoText gives you an entry name based on the first few words of the text, or you can create your own. Short names are better because they're easier to remember and faster to type. For example, the name of the text in figure 5.3 could be so instead of soldout.

When you're done, click <u>A</u>dd to store the entry.

Fig. 5.3
AutoText lets you create a permanent library of text blocks that are available to all of your documents.

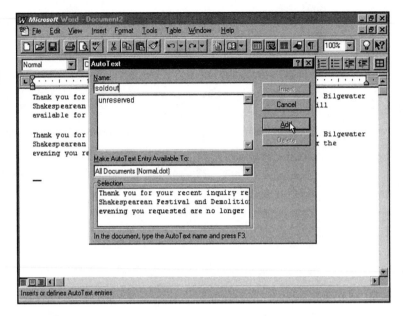

How do I insert an entry?

To insert an AutoText entry, type the name of the entry and press F3. Word replaces the entry name with the text.

If you don't remember the name of the entry, go to the AutoText dialog box. You can look at any entry in the Preview box by highlighting its name. Double-click the name to insert it.

AutoText tips

Here are a few other ways to get more out of AutoText:

- You can type only the first few characters of an entry name when you insert the entry, as long as no other entry name starts with the same characters. For example, type **Ret** to insert the entry "Return Address" and **Res** to insert "Response."

- If you want to keep font and paragraph formatting—for example, italics, special fonts, and type size—you must include the paragraph marker when you select the block. If you're not sure where the marker is, click the Show/Hide Paragraph Marks button on the Standard toolbar.

- If you want the format of an entry to be the same as the text into which you're inserting the entry, go to the AutoText dialog box, select the Plain Text option button, and choose Insert. For example, if your Auto-Text entry is in Courier but your document is in Times New Roman, selecting Plain Text will convert the entry into Times New Roman.

- You can change an AutoText entry by inserting it in a document, editing it, selecting it, and then selecting the original entry name in the Auto-Text dialog box. Click Add and choose Yes when Word asks you if you want to redefine the entry.

Easy Undoes it

We've already seen how you can use Edit, Undo to reverse a deletion. But Undo has several other valuable uses.

You can reverse almost any typing or editing—including deletes, cuts, copies, and pastes. The Undo command on the Edit menu changes to tell you what action you've just taken. For example, if you've just deleted selected text, the command on the Edit menu is Undo Clear. If you pasted text, the command is Undo Paste.

 Word lets you undo up to 98 actions. Click the down arrow next to the Undo button on the Standard toolbar. You'll see a drop-down list box similar to the one shown in figure 5.4. Select as many actions as you want undone.

 CAUTION   **You can't undo file commands such as Open, Close, and Save.**

Undoing Undo

 Every once in a while, you'll undo an action or series of actions that you didn't want undone. To reverse the undo, press Ctrl+Y or click the Redo button on the Standard toolbar.

To redo several undos, click the down arrow next to the Redo button. You'll get a drop-down list box similar to the one for Undo.

Fig. 5.4

Word's multiple Undo lets you undo up to the last 98 actions, including deletes, cuts, copies, and pastes.

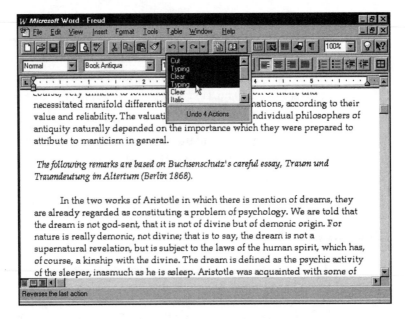

I need to make the same change in a bunch of different places

You've just written a long proposal pitching your company's services to Berwick Manufacturing Co. when a colleague points out that the correct spelling is "Berwyck." You go about the tedious task of scrolling through your document and correcting each misspelling manually. You then spend the rest of the day wondering if you caught every error, comforted by the knowledge that a $3.2 million account is at stake.

Why not let the Replace command do the work for you? Just tell Word to replace every instance of "Berwick" with "Berwyck."

Select Edit, Replace or press Ctrl+H to display the Replace dialog box. The following page, entitled "Instant Replace," gives you a detailed look at how Replace works.

Instant Replace

Word's Replace command lets you replace or delete text, formats, and special characters, either one at a time or *en masse*.

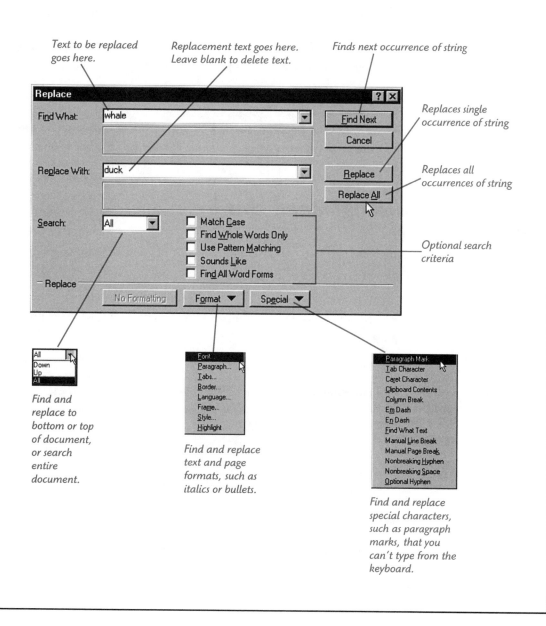

Text to be replaced goes here.

Replacement text goes here. Leave blank to delete text.

Finds next occurrence of string

Replaces single occurrence of string

Replaces all occurrences of string

Optional search criteria

Find and replace to bottom or top of document, or search entire document.

Find and replace text and page formats, such as italics or bullets.

Find and replace special characters, such as paragraph marks, that you can't type from the keyboard.

Type the text you want to replace in the Fi<u>n</u>d What text box and the replacement text in the Re<u>p</u>lace With text box.

Click <u>F</u>ind Next or <u>R</u>eplace. Word finds the first occurrence of the string in your document and highlights it. To replace the string, click <u>R</u>eplace. To skip the string and go to the next occurrence, click <u>F</u>ind Next.

To replace all instances of the text in the document, click Replace <u>A</u>ll.

 Don't use Replace <u>A</u>ll unless you're sure of the results. Replacing strings one at a time is slow and sometimes tedious, but it's safer.

 To move the Replace dialog box out of the way so you can see more of your document, click the title bar and drag the box to another part of the screen.

Warning! Read this first

<u>R</u>eplace is a dangerous command that can lead to unpredictable and distressing results. If you're not careful, you'll find yourself mangling words without even knowing it.

In particular, you need to be careful of capitalization and strings of text inside words. When you plan a find-and-replace, ask yourself these important questions:

Am I looking for whole words only?

Am I looking for a word that is capitalized?

Whole words vs. strings

By default, Word searches for *all* instances of a text string, whether it's a whole word or embedded in a larger string. That is, if you look for the abbreviation mph, Word also finds emphatic and camphor. Replacing mph with miles per hour also changes emphatic to emiles per houratic and camphor to camiles per houror!

To avoid such accidents, check Find <u>W</u>hole Words Only in the Replace dialog box.

How to match case

Replace also ignores capitalization. For example, Bill will find Bill Clinton and please send me the bill. And if you change Bill to President, you also change bill to president.

If you want to find and replace only Bill, put a check next to Match Case. When you match case, you must type the replacement text in the proper case.

Form-fitting searches

Word has an interesting new option called Find All Word Forms that lets you replace all forms of a noun or verb, not just the form you put into the Find What box. For example, if you replace goose with duck, Word also replaces geese with ducks. Or, if you replace go with drive, Word changes these sentences:

    I went to the store.

    She goes to the store.

    We have gone to the store.

to these sentences:

    I drove to the store.

    She drives to the store.

    We have driven to the store.

Neat, huh? Note, however, that the above will also replace the sentence I'm going out of my mind with I'm driving out of my mind. To be on the safe side, replace each occurrence of the word separately with Replace.

Replace as a shortcut for deleting text

You can use Replace to delete all instances of a word. Leave the Replace With text box blank.

Botching such a surgical strike can result in serious damage to your document. Make doubly sure you've checked the appropriate search criteria in the Replace dialog box, and use the Find Next and Replace buttons to replace each instance of the string individually.

TIP You can reverse a bungled replace with Undo.

TIP Word lets you move between your document and the Replace dialog box, so you can edit text without interrupting a search or replace. If you're in the dialog box, click the document; if you're in the document, click the dialog box. You can also move between the two by pressing Alt+F6.

Can I replace fonts and formats, too?

Word gives you lots of options when it comes to replacing fonts, font styles, and type sizes. While we haven't discussed formatting yet, this simple example should give you an idea of what you can do.

Let's say that you want to change all italicized text in your document to bold italics. Here's what to do:

1 In the Replace dialog box, place the insertion point in the Find What text box.

2 Click Format, and choose Font from the drop-down menu. The Find Font dialog box shown in figure 5.5 appears.

Fig. 5.5
Word is being instructed to look for all instances of italicized words, and to replace the italics with bold italics.

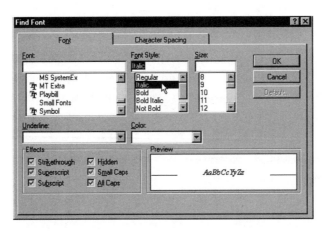

3 Choose Italic from the list under F_o_nt Style and click OK.

4 Move the insertion point to the Re_p_lace With text box.

5 Repeat steps 2 and 3, only choose Bold Italic instead of Italic.

6 Click OK.

7 Click Replace A_l_l.

Replacing special characters and codes

As you can replace formats, so you can replace special characters that you can't type from the keyboard, including paragraph marks and tabs.

Figure 5.6 shows you the list box you get when you click Spe_c_ial in the Replace dialog box. In this case, a tab, represented by ^t, has already been placed in the Fi_n_d What text box. Choosing _P_aragraph Mark puts ^p in the Re_p_lace With text box. The subsequent replace changes all tabs to paragraph marks.

Fig. 5.6

Use Replace to replace special characters that you can't type into the Find What and Replace With text boxes.

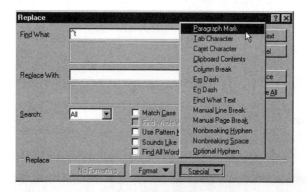

Here are the some instances in which these special characters are useful:

- *Paragraph Mark.* If you get text from another word processor that has a paragraph mark at the end of each line, you can replace the paragraph marks with spaces. You can also add paragraph indents by changing each paragraph mark to a paragraph mark and a tab.

- *Tab.* You can get rid of paragraph indents by replacing paragraph mark+Tab with a paragraph mark. These appear as ^p^t and ^p in the Fi_n_d What and Re_p_lace With text boxes, respectively.

- *Any Character, Any Digit, and Any Letter.* These are wildcards. Imagine, for example, that an instructor wants to replace all test scores between 80 and 89 in a grade report with the letter grade B. He enters **8,** followed by Any Digit in the Find What text box. The characters appear as ^#. He then enters a **B** in the Replace With text box, and clicks Replace All.

Finding a string

You can use the Replace dialog box to find strings without replacing them. Leave the Replace With text box open and use Find Next.

You can also find text with the Find command on the Edit menu. Find doesn't do anything Replace can't, but using it eliminates the chance that you might accidentally replace or delete text.

If you use the Find dialog box and decide that you want to change a string, Find has a Replace button that transfers you to the Replace dialog box.

Changing case

You can change the case of selected text by pressing Shift+F3. Word loops you through different combinations of upper- and lowercase letters. For example, if you were to select you don't have to shout, Shift+F3 would give you the results in the following table.

Do this...	To change the text to this
Press Shift+F3	You Don't Have To Shout
Press Shift+F3 again	YOU DON'T HAVE TO SHOUT
Press Shift+F3 again	you don't have to shout

You can also choose Change Case from the Format menu and choose from the options shown in this table:

Format	Example
Sentence	Fire in the theater!
Lowercase	fire in the theater!
Uppercase	FIRE IN THE THEATER!
Title	Fire In The Theater!

In addition, the Change Case dialog box has a Toggle Case option that changes all uppercase letters in your selected text to lowercase, and vice versa. For example, "Upper and Lower" becomes "uPPER AND lOWER."

 TIP **To change the case of a word, you don't need to select the word.** Just put the insertion point anywhere in the word and press Shift+F3.

How to edit a document

Editing a document with a word processor gives you unbridled flexibility—and that's exactly the problem. Word makes it so easy to tweak your copy that you can spend too much time editing and not enough time writing.

To edit your own material effectively, you can't let the computer control your work habits. Here are a few guidelines to help ensure that Word works for you and not the other way around:

Think before you write.

Unless your goal is to write stream-of-consciousness prose, compose each sentence in your mind before you write it.

Word processors are seductive. They seem to assure you that you can write down any half-formed idea and then hone it into an articulate thought. But that's not what editing is for. Half-formed ideas will stay half formed, and trying to give them flesh through editing is a waste of valuable time.

Also, the more you organize your material before you write it, the less editing you need to do when a deadline is closing in and the document has the freshness of week-old whipped cream.

Word has some valuable tools for outlining that can help you organize yourself before you start; these are covered in Chapter 16.

Write first, revise later.

Curb your impulse to make every minor change as you go along. So what if a word isn't quite the right one or you catch a redundancy in the previous paragraph? These are the sorts of trivial problems you can catch in a second read—if you notice them at all when you return to them.

When you have an immediate fix, then by all means use it. Otherwise, there's no reason to interrupt your flow just so you can spend five minutes trying to find a perfect synonym for "egregious."

Give your document time to cool before you edit it.

If you can, put your document aside for as long as possible before you look at it again. Even a few hours helps. You'll see the document with fresh eyes and find problems you otherwise might miss.

Edit your document at least once on paper.

A document looks, feels, and reads differently on paper than it does on the screen. You'll catch problems with transitions, continuity, and style that you will overlook if you read the document only by scrolling through it.

Accept imperfection as a fact of life.

Just because you're using a computer doesn't mean that you must now produce flawless documents. Do the best job you can, save the file, and get on with your other work.

My Grammar and Speling Ain't So Good

● **In this chapter:**

- **Did I spell that rite?**

- **Create your own dictionaries**

- **AutoCorrect: Word's automatic spell-fixer**

- **Use the grammar checker to improve your writing skills**

- **How to use (and *not* use) the thesaurus**

Can't spell? Forgotten what passive voice is? Let Word's spelling and grammar checkers show you the errors of your ways. . . . . ●

Nothing undermines the credibility of a letter or report faster than spelling errors, grammatical blunders, and typos. Most of us know this. But few of us are able to exercise complete command of the English language's many anomalies. No matter how carefully you edit and proofread a document, chances are something will slip past your guard.

Word provides three lines of defense: the spelling checker, AutoCorrect, and the grammar checker. They aren't perfect (they have their own problems handling the language's vagaries), and you should never rely on them alone to check your documents. But they can give you an extra measure of quality control, catching mistakes you overlook and pointing out subtle problems of style and word use.

With previous versions of Word, you usually used the checkers on a finished document. Word for Windows 95 includes a new feature that catches mistakes as you make them and lets you make on-the-spot corrections.

Casting a magic spell check

Nearly every first-time Word user heads straight for the spelling checker as soon as he or she learns how to create a document. Even good spellers find the spelling checker a welcome addition to their arsenal of writing tools.

Word lets you check your entire document, any selected part of a document, or even a single word. Word also lets you modify the spell checker. You can add words to the dictionary as you go, and you can create special dictionaries for documents that include unusual words and jargon.

Spell checking made easy

Word for Windows 95 has a new feature that conveniently checks your spelling as you type. When you misspell a word, Word highlights the word with a wavy line, as shown in figure 6.1.

Fig. 6.1

When Automatic Spell Checking is turned on, Word highlights words that aren't in its dictionary. Click the right mouse button to correct misspelled words.

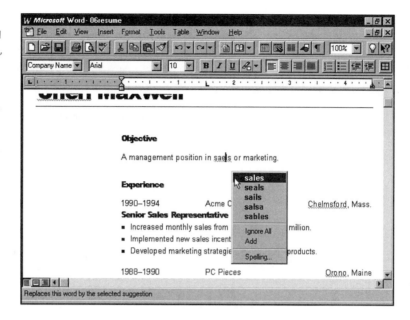

To fix the error, click the word with the right mouse button. A shortcut menu appears with a list of possible replacements. Click the correct spelling.

The shortcut menu also lets you add the word to a supplemental Custom dictionary. For example, in figure 6.1, right-clicking the word "Chelmsford" and then choosing Add tells the spell checker that Chelmsford is correct and to no longer highlight it. (You'll learn more about the Custom dictionary and how to create your own special dictionaries later in this chapter.)

If you want the checker to ignore the word for the rest of the document, whether it's right or wrong, choose Ignore All. Word won't try to correct the word, but it won't bug you about it either.

You turn on the spell checking feature by choosing Tools, Options from the main menu, clicking the Spelling tab, and clicking the box next to Automatic Spell Checking.

 TIP **You can reverse a spelling change with the Edit, Undo command.** To reverse all changes, click the arrow next to the Undo button on the Standard toolbar, then click the last Spelling action listed in the drop-down list box.

Running the spelling checker

You've just received a lengthy report that you need to print and photocopy for a meeting in 20 minutes. "Maybe you should proof this first," the department head suggests. "You know how bad my spelling is."

You could turn on AutoCorrect and spend 20 stressful minutes fixing the mistakes manually. Or you could spell check the document in one fell swoop with Word's spelling checker. Word finds all potential misspellings and presents them to you one by one for correction. (You might also suggest that your department head use AutoCorrect from now on.)

To run a spell check, press F7 or click the Spelling button on the Standard toolbar. You can start anywhere in the document. Word checks everything from the insertion point to the end of the document. When it's done, Word gives you the option of checking the beginning of the document.

I just need to check this part

To spell check just a portion of your document, select the text and run the checker. Word spell checks only the text in the defined block.

You can check words, paragraphs, and lines quickly with simple keyboard and mouse combinations. The following table lists the most common types of spell checks.

To spell check...	Do this
Whole document	Press F7 or click the Spell button.
Single word	Double-click the word and press F7, or press Ctrl+Shift+left arrow and press F7.
Single line	Click once next to the line and press F7, or press Shift+End and press F7.
Paragraph	Double-click next to the paragraph and press F7.

TIP **If you want to return to where you began your spell check, create** a bookmark with Edit, Bookmark before you start your check. When Word finishes the check, choose Edit, Bookmark, Go To. For more information on bookmarks, see Chapter 2.

Using the Spelling Checker dialog box

When you start a spell check, Word finds the first word it doesn't recognize and displays the Spelling dialog box shown in figure 6.2.

Fig. 6.2

When the spell checker finds a misspelled word, it gives you a list of potential corrections to choose from.

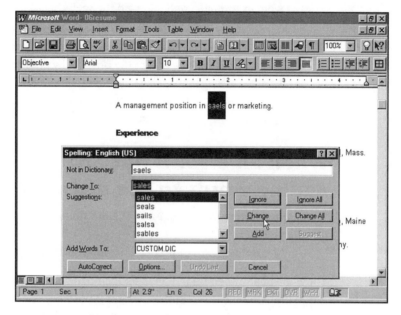

The unrecognized word appears in the Not In Dictionary box. If the dictionary includes possible replacements, it lists them in the Suggestions list box and puts the most likely one in the Change To box.

You'll be surprised at how often the spell checker puts the correct word in the Change To box. For example, in figure 6.2, the dictionary correctly decided that "saels" was supposed to be "sales" and not "salsa."

To accept the suggested change, click the Change button. If you want another word on the list, double-click it. To replace the word with one that is not in the Suggestions box, type the new word and click Change.

At any point, you can click Change All to change all instances of the word in the document or selected text.

To add the word to your dictionary, click Add.

To keep the word as is, click Ignore. However, the checker will query you on the word if it reappears. If you want the checker to accept the word for the entire document, click Ignore All.

Q&A *What do I do if I want to delete the word?*

Press the Delete key. This deletes the highlighted word in the Change To text box. The Change and Change All buttons turn into Delete and Delete All buttons, respectively. Click the button you want; Word deletes the word in text and continues with the spell check.

TIP **You can move between the Spelling dialog box and your** document by clicking one or the other or by pressing Alt+F6. This lets you keep the dialog box open while you work. You can use this technique to check several blocks of text without constantly opening and closing the dialog box.

When an error is not an error: adding words to the dictionary

When you add a word that's not in the dictionary, you're actually adding it to a special dictionary called Custom. Word refers to both the regular and Custom dictionaries when it spell checks a document.

You can speed up your spell checks by putting names, acronyms, and special terms that you use often in the Custom dictionary. The simplest way is to add your words one by one as the spelling checker flags them. But you can also add words *en masse* by opening and editing the Custom dictionary.

Open Custom by clicking the Add button in the Custom Dictionaries dialog box (see fig. 6.3). Make your additions, then save the file and close it.

Word turns off Automatic Spell Checking when you open Custom. Don't forget to turn it back on after you've closed Custom.

Fig. 6.3

The Custom Dictionaries dialog box lets you add entries to Word's Custom dictionary or create and modify your own special dictionaries.

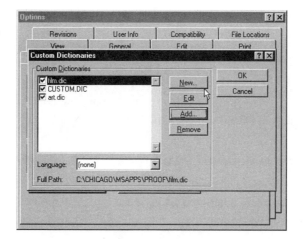

 Q&A *The Add button in my Spelling dialog box is grayed out. Am I missing my Custom dictionary?*

Probably not. It's more likely that the dictionary isn't active. To fix the problem, choose Options in the Spelling dialog box and Custom Dictionaries in the next Spelling dialog box. If CUSTOM.DIC appears in the Custom Dictionaries list box, make sure it has a check in the box, then click OK. If CUSTOM.DIC doesn't appear, click the Add button. Then choose CUSTOM.DIC from the Add Custom Dictionary dialog box.

Create your own dictionaries

Imagine that you're a film critic (aren't we all?) and you're tired of Word suggesting you change "Meryl Streep" to "Merrily Strap." Sure, you could put "Meryl" and "Streep" in your Custom dictionary. But here's an alternative: create a dictionary called Film that includes only actors' names and other film-related terms.

You can use this technique to build a dictionary for any vocation or avocation that has its own lexicon. You can then make that dictionary active only when you need it. Here's how:

1 Click the Options button on the Spelling dialog box.

2 Click Custom Dictionaries. Word displays the Custom Dictionaries dialog box shown in figure 6.3.

3 Click <u>N</u>ew. Word displays a Create Custom Dictionary dialog box that looks like the Open dialog box. If you're not already in it, find the Proof subfolder that contains your dictionaries.

4 Type the name of the new dictionary in the File <u>N</u>ame text box and click <u>S</u>ave. Word creates the dictionary file and returns you to the Custom Dictionaries dialog box.

Adding words to your special dictionary

You need to activate and select your special dictionary before you can add to it. Otherwise, when you add a word during a spell check, Word puts it in the Custom dictionary.

To activate your dictionary, put a check next to it in the Custom <u>D</u>ictionaries list box (refer to fig. 6.3). You can activate up to ten dictionaries, including Custom.

To select the dictionary during a spell check, choose it from the Add <u>W</u>ords To drop-down box in the Spelling dialog box (refer to fig. 6.2).

Let Word fix errors as you type

Do you sometimes feel as if you have a mental block about the spelling of particular words? One that prevents you from ever remembering how to spell words like "relevant," "harass," and "embarrass"?

You're not alone. We all have our little orthographic obstacles. "Relevant" or "relevent"—no matter which one you type, it looks wrong. The more you look at the word, the more your brain hurts, until small objects start flying off your desk and your dog flees the room.

And then there's the disconnect between your brain's language center and your fingers. Certain words never come out the way they're supposed to. "Character" comes out as "characater" and "information" as "inforamtion." It's as if your fingers have been cursed by the Voodoo Priest of Annoying Typos.

What spell check won't do—and how to fix it

The spell checker takes a lot of the work out of spell checking, but don't throw away your Webster's dictionary just yet. The spell checker isn't perfect. In fact, if you're fastidious about your spelling, you might miss more mistakes than you do with a manual spell check.

The spell checker has three main drawbacks:

- It can't distinguish between homonyms. For example, it will not correct "affect" when you should have used "effect" or "their" when you meant "there." You need to use the grammar checker to catch such slips.

- Similarly, it won't correct you if you get similar words confused: For example, if you use "loose" instead of "lose."

- It won't catch typos that result in valid words. For example, it won't correct you when you type "form" instead of "from" or "I supposes he will" instead of "I suppose he will."

There is a solution—at least, a partial one. You can tell Word to flag words that you consistently have problems with, by creating an Exclude dictionary.

This dictionary is a special list of words that the spell checker will query you on, even if the word is in the main dictionary. For example, if you put "affect" in the Exclude dictionary, Word shows you "affect" whenever it appears.

You create the dictionary as a document in Word. It's a bit tricky to set up, but you only have to do it once.

1 Open a new document and create your word list. Press the Enter key after each word.

2 Open the Save As dialog box (File, Save or press Ctrl+S).

3 Choose Text Only from the Save As Type text box.

4 Select Save In and find the Proof folder, where your main dictionary is stored.

5 Save the file as MSSP2_EN.EXC.

Your best protection against spelling and grammatical errors is to proofread your documents carefully, with a dictionary by your elbow. Ultimately, a typo is one mistake you can't blame on the computer.

True, Word's spell checker alerts you to these errors. But there's a better and more satisfying way to cover your tracks: AutoCorrect.

AutoCorrect automatically fixes a misspelling or typo on the spot. If you type "relevent," for example, AutoCorrect immediately replaces it with "relevant."

How to add words to AutoCorrect

AutoCorrect is a list of text strings and their replacements. Word starts you with more than 400 entries. To add to the list, choose <u>A</u>utoCorrect from the <u>T</u>ools menu. Enter the text you want fixed in the <u>R</u>eplace text box and the correction in the <u>W</u>ith text box, then click <u>A</u>dd (see fig. 6.4).

Fig. 6.4
AutoCorrect lets you automatically fix common typos and misspellings.

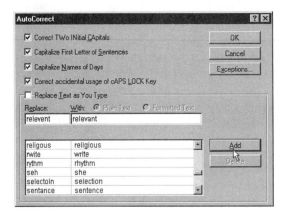

Thereafter, when you type the text that you put in the R<u>e</u>place box, Word immediately replaces it with the correction you entered in the <u>W</u>ith box.

To start automatic correction, make sure the Replace <u>T</u>ext As You Type check box in the AutoCorrect dialog box contains an x.

TIP   **You can add to your AutoCorrect list from the Spelling dialog box**. Enter the word you want to fix in the Not In Dictionar<u>y</u> text box and the correction in the Change <u>T</u>o text box, then click the AutoCorrect button.

Teach AutoCorrect some tricks

The uses for AutoCorrect go beyond correcting spelling errors and typos. You can use it to create shortcuts for long text strings and hard-to-type symbols.

Let's say you write about the Society for the Preservation and Encouragement of Barber Shop Quartet Singing in America (known far and wide as SPEBSQSA). You can use AutoCorrect so that whenever you type **speb**, the full name of the organization is inserted in your text.

The following table lists a few examples of how you can use AutoCorrect creatively.

Replace this	With this
–>	→
NH	New Hampshire
Xerox	photocopy
tel#	1-800-555-1234
Tadz	Tadzhikistan

How to change text into symbols and special characters

Putting "—>" in the Replace text box is simple enough. But how do you get → in the With box?

From your document, choose Insert, Symbol from the menu bar. In the Symbol dialog box, click the Symbols tab and choose Wingdings in the Font drop-down box. Click twice on → to insert the → symbol in your text, then close the Symbol dialog box.

In your document, select the symbol using your Shift and left arrow keys (don't double-click the symbol or you'll return to the Symbol dialog box). Go to the AutoCorrect dialog box. The → symbol appears in the With text box. Type a —> in the Replace text box, then click Add.

Plain English, please!

For our purposes, **symbols** are characters that don't appear on your keyboard, including specially formatted letters and numbers, dingbats such as astrological signs, and funky bullets.

Special characters are a category of symbols that function more as typographic elements; for example, the em dash (—), copyright symbol (©), and single open quote ('). These special characters have their own dialog box to make them easier to find and use. (We discuss symbols and characters in more detail in Chapter 8.)

 TIP **Your AutoCorrect replacement text can include treatments such as italics and underline. For example, you can replace "Moby" with the italicized *"Moby Dick."* See Chapter 8 for more about formatting text.**

Other AutoCorrections

Most of us type like rhinos wearing mittens. The results often include double capitals, sentences that aren't capitalized, and inadvertent Caps Locks. Auto-Correct has ways to help you handle all of these problems.

Got a lazy Shift-key finger?

If you're a speedy typist, chances are one hand sometimes gets a little ahead of the other and you end up with two capital letters at the beginning of a sentence. AutoCorrect to the rescue! When you select the Correct TWo INitial CApitals check box, Word automatically changes the second capital letter to lowercase (for example, "TWo" becomes "Two"). This option does not affect two-letter acronyms.

You can force Word to accept two initial capitals by undoing the Auto-Correct (press Ctrl+Z or click the Undo button). AutoCorrect adds the double capital to an exceptions list, which you can view or change by choosing Exceptions from the AutoCorrect dialog box and clicking the INitial CAps tab.

Starting sentences with capitals

Either you accidentally use two caps to start a sentence, or you don't use any. Fortunately, AutoCorrect can fix that, too. Word automatically capitalizes the first letter of a sentence when you select the Capitalize First Letter Of Sentences check box. It assumes that you're starting a new sentence if the previous word ends with a terminal punctuation, such as a period or question mark.

The time may come when you'll actually want a sentence to start with a lowercase letter (for example, "e.e. cummings was a poet..."). Rather than go through the bother of turning off Capitalize First Letter Of Sentences, use Undo. Press Ctrl+Z or click the Undo button immediately after the letter changes to uppercase. Word undoes the AutoCorrect and forces the letter to stay in lowercase.

To prevent Word from incorrectly capitalizing a word that follows an abbreviation, AutoCorrect includes an Exceptions list. For example, Word won't capitalize a word that follows the abbreviation "Assoc." To see or add to the Exceptions list, click the Exceptions button in the AutoCorrect dialog box, then click the First Letter tab.

Caps Lock confusion solved!

For many computer users, the most aggravating keyboard screw-up comes when they forget to release Caps Lock. hOW OFTEN DOES IT HAPPEN THAT YOU HAVE TO GO BACK AND CORRECT SENTENCES LIKE THIS AFTER USING CAPS LOCK TO CAPITALIZE A HEADING OR ACRONYM?

Word finally has a solution to the problem. In the AutoCorrect dialog box, select the Correct Accidental Usage Of cAPS LOCK Key check box. When you press Caps Lock to make text uppercase, and then type a word that consists of a small letter followed by capitals, Word automatically reverses the cases. As a bonus, it then releases Caps Lock and puts you back in lowercase.

Let's say you have Correct Accidental Usage Of cAPS LOCK Key turned off. You use Caps Lock to add emphasis to the words DO NOT FORGET in the following sentence. You forget to release Caps Lock after "FORGET," and the next sentence comes out like this:

DO NOT FORGET! rETURN ALL BOOKS BEFORE FRIDAY!

But with Correct Accidental Usage Of cAPS LOCK Key on, Word changes "rETURN" to "Return" as soon as you type the space that follows the word. Word then releases Caps Lock, and you type the rest of the sentence in normal upper- and lowercase.

Grammar Moses: Word's handy grammar checker

The grammar checker actually checks grammar and style, but the distinction between the two is unimportant for your purposes. Together, they include all those subjects that so engrossed you in your high school English classes—punctuation, passive voice, subject-verb agreement, contractions, prepositions, and so on. In all, the checker can look for 48 different types of problems.

Formal or informal?

Before you run the grammar checker, decide if you want it to alert you to all rules, only the rules that apply to business writing, or only those rules that govern informal writing.

Choose Tools, Options from the main menu and click the Grammar tab. Under the Grammar tab, choose an option from the Use Grammar And Style Rules list box (see fig. 6.5).

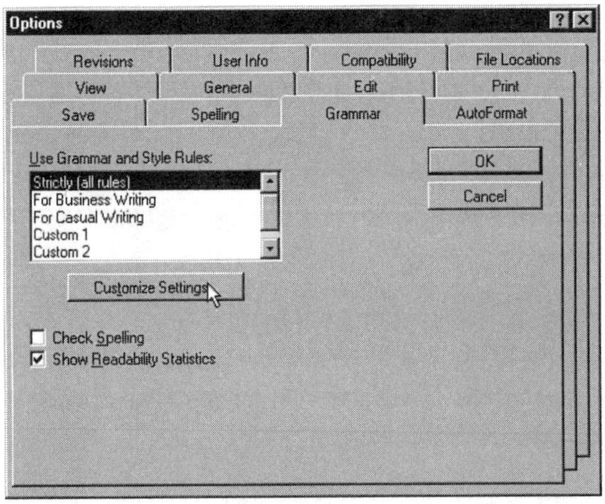

Fig. 6.5
The grammar checker lets you choose from three styles of writing or create your own style.

What are the differences between the three writing styles? We could spend the next 200 pages talking about the nuances of grammar and barely scratch the surface, but here are a few general recommendations:

- Choose the Strictly (All Rules) option if you want to cover every rule of grammar and style. But be warned: the grammar checker will probably query you half a dozen times per sentence (at least, it'll seem that way).

- Choose the For Business Writing option to enforce all grammar rules but ignore a few style rules, such as those governing clichés and homonyms.

- Choose the For Casual Writing option if you want to keep most of the grammar rules but turn off most of the style rules.

We suggest you start with a strict check for all your writing. This will give you an idea of what each rule covers.

It's not likely that you'll want to use a strict check all the time. Your checks will seem to take forever, and Word will drive you crazy querying you on nonexistent problems. ("Yes, I *know* it's a contraction. I *want* contractions!") Decide which rules you don't want to apply and turn them off. We'll take a look at how to deselect rules and create custom checks in a moment.

 **TIP**   **If you run the spell checker, turn off Check <u>S</u>pelling in the** Grammar dialog box.

How to use the grammar checker

To run the grammar checker, choose <u>T</u>ools, <u>G</u>rammar from the menu bar. The grammar checker works a lot like the spell checker. When the grammar checker runs into a possible error, it displays the Grammar dialog box, as shown in figure 6.6.

Fig. 6.6

The Grammar dialog box shows you the offending sentence and explains what it thinks the problem is. The grammar checker is not always right.

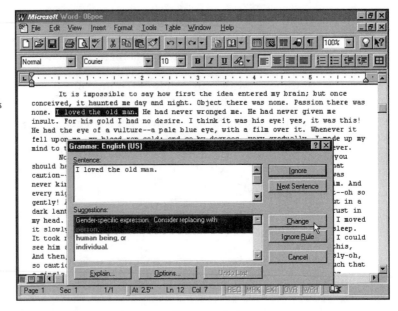

Figure 6.6 is from Edgar Allan Poe's grammar check of his short story "The Tell-Tale Heart." In this case, the grammar checker questions whether Ed is being politically correct with his use of the gender-specific word "man." It shows the entire sentence highlighted in the upper text box, and suggests in the lower text box that a non-gender-specific term might be more appropriate.

When the grammar checker shows you a potential problem, you can take one of the following actions:

- Get more detail on the potential problem by clicking the Explain button. The grammar checker displays a Grammar Explanation text box.

- Ignore the grammar checker's suggestion by clicking Ignore. The checker will go on to the next potential problem.

- Skip the sentence by clicking Next Sentence.

- Make the grammar checker's suggested change by clicking Change. In figure 6.6, the checker will replace "man" with "person." If you prefer one of the checker's other options, click it and choose Change.

- Tell the grammar checker to throw out the rule by clicking Ignore Rule. The checker will skip all further instances of the potential problem for the rest of the document. In figure 6.6, for example, the checker will no longer query Poe on gender-specific expressions.

- Make another change to the sentence. Choose the Sentence text box. An insertion point appears. Delete, insert, and add text using your standard editing tools. For instance, Ed could change "man" to "guy" (he didn't).

Grammar checker overkill

The grammar checker doesn't always hit the mark. It picks more nits than most English teachers know exist—and sometimes, it's flat-out wrong.

For example, the grammar checker will tell you that contractions are unacceptable in formal or technical writing. Many technical writers and editors disagree. Contractions are useful in technical writing because they help make difficult material easier to read.

When you want the checker to stop nagging you about a nonexistent infraction, just tell it to stop. Modifying the grammar checker is easy.

How to modify the grammar checker

Choose Customize Settings from the Options dialog box. The Customize Grammar Settings dialog box appears (see fig. 6.7).

Fig. 6.7
You can tell the grammar checker to stop enforcing grammar and style rules that you're sick of being nagged about. Click the Explain button to get descriptions of each rule.

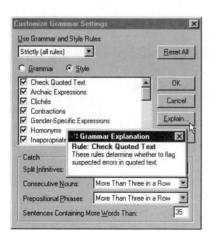

You can modify the existing set of rules, but it's better to keep them as they are and create a new set. In the Use Grammar And Style Rules selection box, choose Custom 1, Custom 2, or Custom 3. Then scroll through the list of grammar rules and remove the checks from the boxes next to the rules you don't want. Click the Style button and do the same.

Unless reading grammar books is your idea of fun, you'll probably need details on some options. You can get a description of any rule by clicking the Explain button.

 TIP **At the end of every grammar check, Word displays an information** box called Readability Statistics. Though buried and poorly documented, the statistics below the Averages and Readability headings can help you refine your writing skills.

Roget is turning over in his sepulcher: using the thesaurus

Last among Word's writing aids is its electronic thesaurus.

The thesaurus lets you find synonyms for any word. Using it is easy. Place your insertion point on the word and choose Tools, Thesaurus (or press Ctrl+F7). The Thesaurus dialog box pops up, as shown in figure 6.8.

The word in the document that we want to look up appears here.

The word that has been selected in the Meanings text box also appears here.

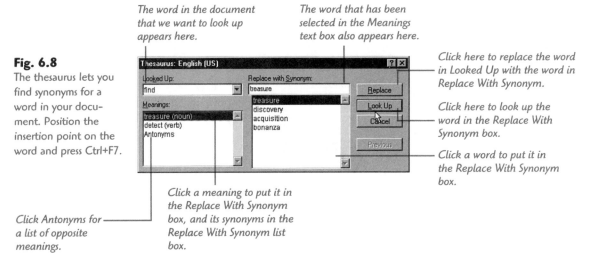

Fig. 6.8
The thesaurus lets you find synonyms for a word in your document. Position the insertion point on the word and press Ctrl+F7.

Click here to replace the word in Looked Up with the word in Replace With Synonym.

Click here to look up the word in the Replace With Synonym box.

Click a word to put it in the Replace With Synonym box.

Click a meaning to put it in the Replace With Synonym box, and its synonyms in the Replace With Synonym list box.

Click Antonyms for a list of opposite meanings.

Inside the Thesaurus dialog box

The word for which you want a synonym is automatically inserted in the Looked Up text box. Below it, in the Meanings text box, are the different uses of that word. The meaning that is highlighted in the Meanings text box is inserted in the Replace With Synonym text box. Underneath is a list of synonyms for that particular meaning.

For example, in figure 6.8, the word being looked up is "find." In this case, the thesaurus provides synonyms for the noun that means "treasure." Other words for the noun "find" are "discovery," "acquisition," and "bonanza."

Choosing an option

To automatically replace the word in your document with the one in the Replace with Synonym box, select Replace. You can also choose from these options:

- To look up synonyms for a word in the Replace With Synonym list box, click once on the word, then click Look Up.

- To look up synonyms for another word in the Meanings list box ("detect" in figure 6.8, for example), click the word.

- To look up a new word, type the word in the Replace With Synonym text box and click Look Up.

- To retrace your steps, click Previous.

How to use a thesaurus

Many inexperienced writers view a thesaurus as a quick route to building a bigger vocabulary without a lot of work. But bigger is not always better. The trade-off is that you risk using words inappropriately and altering your natural voice. You should use a thesaurus only for the following reasons:

- To avoid the repetitive use of a word. For example, if you've used the noun "speech" three times in a paragraph, the thesaurus will suggest "address" or "lecture" as an alternative.

- To jog your memory for a word that's temporarily slipped your mind.

- To find a shorter, simpler word for one that's too long.

When you find a word that you think is appropriate, use it only if you can answer "yes" to the following questions:

- Do you know what it means? All synonyms are not alike; they often have subtle but different definitions. For example, the list of synonyms for "sexy" includes "desirable" and "lewd," but they have somewhat different connotations when used to describe your significant other's lips.

- Is it a word you would use in normal conversation? At one time or another, we all feel as if our vocabulary is too limited. But most of us know more than enough words to express ourselves. The solution is to work harder with the tools you have, not depend on your word processor for a quick electronic fix.

7

Prepare to Print!

● In this chapter:

- It won't print! How to avoid and solve common printer problems

- What will my document look like? Print Preview reveals all

- Can I print just selected pages or text?

- I need to adjust my page margins

- Special jobs: Easy envelopes and lively labels

Word's vast array of printing tools lets you print documents quickly and easily . . . . ➤

We may have thrown out our typewriters, but most of us still need to put our documents on paper. The good news is that today's printers give you good quality at good prices. The bad news is that they're still a pain in the port to set up and operate.

Windows and Word have gone about as far as possible to make printing foolproof. In theory, you should be able to install Word, open a document, choose File, Print, and let 'er rip.

But a printer is like a leash-trained dog. It will behave itself most of the time, but you can't anticipate the cat that unexpectedly leads your baying mutt through the briar patch.

Given the nearly infinite combinations of hardware and software (not to mention cranky networks with shared printers), we can't possibly trouble-shoot every malfunction and hold this book to less than 100,000 pages. If you do everything right and your printer still doesn't work, you probably need the help of a highly trained professional, such as your 12-year-old nephew.

Or you can turn to the extensive on-line Help that Word and Windows 95 provide. We'll tell you where to look a little bit later, once you've taken a crack at printing a few documents.

That said, we'll try to give you some universal advice on common problems as we go along. And if you're new at walking the print dog, read on for some information that might help you avoid a few hardcopy headaches.

Sneak previews: using Print Preview

You can usually tell what a document is going to look like on paper. But when your documents include tables, footnotes, graphics, nonstandard margins, columns, and other formatting, you risk printing documents that don't come out the way you want them to. To save yourself time and paper, use Word's Print Preview command to get a glimpse of the final product.

 Open Print Preview by choosing it from the File menu, or by clicking the Print Preview button on the Standard toolbar. Once in the window, you can see an entire document page as it will appear when printed. You can also see how pages of a book will look side by side.

To see how Print Preview works, look at the flyer shown in figure 7.1. It includes a variety of type treatments that won't fit into the document window. But when the flyer is in a preview window, as shown in figure 7.2, its type, spacing, and borders are easy to assess. If you don't like how an element looks, close the preview window, edit the document, and then preview it again.

A printer and a prayer

When you install Word, it should detect your printer and make it available to you. But problems inevitably arise. Here are a few questions to ask yourself as you prepare to use your printer for the first time:

Is the printer plugged in and turned on?

Check this first; it's the culprit more often than you think!

Is the printer cable connected snugly to both the printer and the computer?

Printer cables are notorious for loosening at night after the lights are out.

Is the printer on line?

Usually, there's an on-line button and corresponding light on your printer's control panel. Make sure the light's on. Some printers have a small display that says Ready.

Does the printer have paper? If the paper is in a tray, is the tray pushed all the way in?

Loose trays are common on laser printers. Also, if your printer has selectable options such as single-sheet or tractor feeding, make sure the right one's selected.

Does the printer that's hooked up to your computer correspond to the printer Word is set up to use?

If, for example, Word expects a Canon Bubble Jet and finds a daisywheel printer, your document won't print as it appears on the screen. Mismatches shouldn't be a concern unless you've got more than one printer available (through a network, for example) or you have reason to believe that someone has changed your setup.

To find out what printer Word expects, Choose File, Print. Word shows you the name of the printer in the Print dialog box. If it doesn't match what's connected to your machine, click the Name text box and see if the right printer is listed.

A mismatched printer doesn't necessarily mean you won't be able to print. You might have a printer that's compatible with the one you've got listed in your Print dialog box. The only way to find out is by printing some documents.

Fig. 7.1

Only part of this yard sale flyer is visible in the document window. Use Print Preview to see how the document will look when printed.

Fig. 7.2

Here's the same flyer as seen in Print Preview.

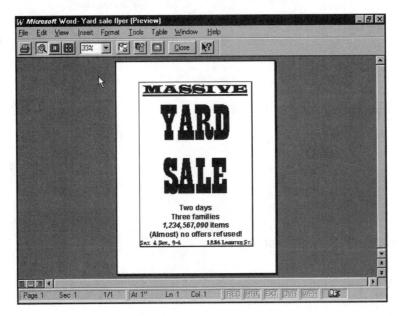

Q&A *Do I have to keep switching between Print Preview and Normal view if I want to make editing and formatting changes?*

No. Your editing and formatting commands are still available to you in Print Preview. You can even add the Standard and Formatting toolbars to your Print Preview screen. Choose View, Toolbars from the main menu and click the Standard and Formatting buttons.

To make your Print Preview page large enough to work in, click the Magnifier button on the Print Preview toolbar. Your insertion point turns into a magnifying glass when you place it in the document. Click the mouse button to enlarge the document to 100 percent. After you've made your changes to the document, click the mouse button again to reduce the page to its previous size. Click the Magnifier button again to turn off magnification.

Previewing multiple pages

Print Preview lets you display several pages of a document on one screen. Click the Multiple Pages button on the Print Preview toolbar and sweep the mouse across the pages in the drop-down box. In figure 7.3, for example, the display is about to change from three pages to four pages.

You can use the Page Up and Page Down keys to page through your document.

When you display more than a handful of pages, they start looking like postage stamps. Don't dismiss these miniature pages just because you can't read them. They can help you identify dense copy, unwanted patches of white space, and poorly placed graphical elements.

The page entitled "Exploring the Print Preview toolbar" later in this chapter describes the buttons on the Print Preview toolbar.

Fig. 7.3
The Multiple Pages button lets you preview several pages at once.

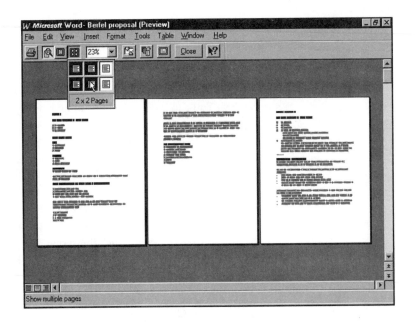

Can I print now?

Enough preparation—let's get down to printing some text. We'll assume for the moment that you've opened a plain document with regular margins and no oddball formatting.

 TIP **It's a good idea to save your document before printing, in case** your computer chokes on the document and you have to reboot.

Quick-printing a document

 If you want to print a document without going through the Print dialog box, click the Print button on the Standard toolbar. Word sends the entire document posthaste to the printer. (If you want to print only part of the document, you need to use the Print dialog box; see the page entitled "Inside the Print dialog box" later in this chapter.)

Exploring the Print Preview toolbar

Print
Displays the Print dialog box

View Ruler
Displays horizontal and vertical rules

Magnifier
Magnifies or shrinks the document page

Shrink to Fit
Tries to shrink document to one page

One Page
Displays the whole page in Page Layout view

Full Screen
Hides all screen elements except pages and Print Preview toolbar

Multiple Pages
Displays multiple pages

Close
Closes Preview

Zoom Control
Enlarges or reduces pages

Help
Provides on-line Help

If background printing is turned on, a message telling you what's happening appears on the left-hand side of the status bar, and a blinking printer appears on the right-hand side. After a few moments, Word prints the open document. (Actually, Word passes the document to Windows 95, which in turn dishes it out to the printer.) If background printing is turned off, a message box appears in the middle of your screen and Word prints the document without pause.

❝ *Plain English, please!*

Background printing lets you continue working while Word prints the document. When background printing is turned off, you have to wait until Word finishes the print job before you can get back to your document. Background printing is slower, so turn it off if you need a long document immediately. ❞

TIP **To turn background printing on or off, choose T̲ools, O̲ptions from** the main menu and click the Print tab. A check in the B̲ackground Printing check box means that background printing is turned on.

To cancel the print job before it's done, double-click the blinking printer.

When to push the panic button

After you send the document to the printer, you will likely hear a series of grunts and groans that sound like a weight lifter preparing to bench press a motorcycle. Don't worry—these noises are normal. On many systems, Word sends the document to a temporary file on the hard drive and the printer must prepare itself to receive the file.

You might also experience a moment (or several moments) of silence some time after you send your file. Again, stay calm. If Word hasn't displayed an error message and you don't see any smoke, chances are Word is just chewing its cud and all is well.

If minutes pass and the printer still hasn't coughed up your document, do *not* try to reprint it. You might end up printing multiple copies. Review the earlier sidebar, "A printer and a prayer," to make sure your printer is ready. Check your Print dialog box settings to make sure you haven't accidentally sent the document to the wrong place (to a file or another printer, for instance).

If you're still not getting any satisfaction, it's time to jump to Windows' printing and diagnostic tools. Read the next section, "Troubleshooting printer problems with on-line Help."

CAUTION **Networks are notorious cud-chewers. When several people print** at the same time, the documents line up for processing like cows waiting to be milked. If your document does not print, do not resend it; go to your network administrator for help. Your administrator can also tell you what kinds of delays you can expect under normal circumstances.

Inside the Print dialog box

For anything other than a quick print of the whole document, go to the printing command center, the Print dialog box. Press Ctrl+P or select File, Print from the menu bar.

The Print dialog box lets you choose a printer, what you want to print, and how many copies. Make your choices, then click OK.

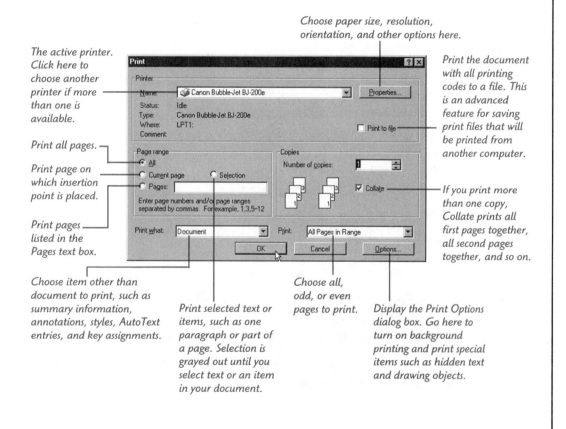

Choose paper size, resolution, orientation, and other options here.

The active printer. Click here to choose another printer if more than one is available.

Print the document with all printing codes to a file. This is an advanced feature for saving print files that will be printed from another computer.

Print all pages.

Print page on which insertion point is placed.

Print pages listed in the Pages text box.

If you print more than one copy, Collate prints all first pages together, all second pages together, and so on.

Choose item other than document to print, such as summary information, annotations, styles, AutoText entries, and key assignments.

Print selected text or items, such as one paragraph or part of a page. Selection is grayed out until you select text or an item in your document.

Choose all, odd, or even pages to print.

Display the Print Options dialog box. Go here to turn on background printing and print special items such as hidden text and drawing objects.

Troubleshooting printer problems with on-line Help

Printer problems can be tricky to figure out because the fault might lie with either Word or Windows 95. Fortunately, both offer informative and thorough Help files that will help you diagnose and solve most common printer problems.

Start with Word's Answer Wizard. Choose Help, Answer Wizard from the main menu, type **My printer won't work!** in the Type Your Request text box, then click the Search button. The Answer Wizard gives you a number of topics that relate to printer problems.

The logical place to start is with the first topic, Troubleshoot Printing. Here you'll find a list of specific printing problems to choose from, including:

- Nonprinting documents and envelopes
- Text running off the edge of the page
- Nonprinting graphics
- A dimmed Print command on the File menu
- A Too many fonts error message

If you can't find what you're looking for here, go back to the Answer Wizard and try another topic on the list.

Several of Word's Help screens refer you to Windows 95's Help files. One of these Windows Help files can actually check out your printer for you and suggest what the problem might be.

Click Help on the Windows 95 Start menu. Choose the Index tab and start to type **print troubleshooting** in the Type The First Few Letters text box. Click the Print Troubleshooting index entry and follow the instructions.

I just want to print a few pages

Often, you don't want to print the entire document. You just need to print the table on page 14, replace page 6, or print the appendix on pages 67 to 75. Word gives you complete control over what you print, using the options under Page Range in the Print dialog box (refer to the previous page). Table 7.1 shows you how to use these options.

Table 7.1   How to print parts of a document

To print this...	Do this
Selected text	Select the text or item and choose Selection.
The page you're working on	Choose Current Page or choose Pages, and enter the page number in the text box.
Adjacent pages	Choose Pages and enter the range in the text box (for example, **14–18**).
Several single pages	Choose Pages and enter the pages in the text box (for example, **1,4,6**).

Q&A *How do I print two-sided documents?*

This is a two-step print job. Choose File, Print. In the Print dialog box, choose Print, then choose Odd Pages from the drop-down box. Word prints only the odd pages of your document. Reinsert the paper in your printer so that it will print on the back of page 1 first, the back of page 2 second, and so on. Choose File, Print again. This time, choose Even Pages from the Print drop-down box. Word prints the even pages on the back sides of the odd pages.

One caveat: Some printers don't like paper that's already been printed on. Make sure the paper is flat and that no sheets are clinging together.

Printing files from a disk

You can print a file or several files from the Open dialog box without opening them first.

Select the file to print. If you want to print several files, choose each one by holding down the Ctrl key while you click the left mouse button.

Click the right mouse button and choose Print from the shortcut menu. Word displays the Print dialog box. Select your options and click OK.

Preparing your document for printing

Not all documents print alike. For example, you might need to print a legal document on 8.5 x 14-inch paper, print a wide table sideways, or use wider margins to fit long headings. You can set up your printer to accommodate these different types of print jobs. Here are some common printing problems and how to solve them.

How do I get a different paper size?

If you're printing a document to paper that's other than 8.5 x 11 inches, choose File, Page Setup from the main menu and click the Paper Size tab in the Page Setup dialog box. Pick the paper you want from the Paper Size drop-down box (see fig. 7.4). The last choice in the box, called Custom Size, lets you define irregular dimensions. Click OK when you're done.

Fig. 7.4

Choose the paper size from the Page Setup dialog box.

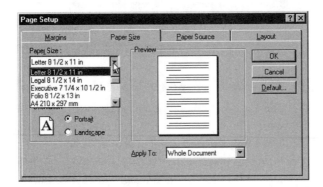

I need to print this document sideways

You can print a document in either **portrait** or **landscape** orientation. Which is which? Take a piece of paper and hold it normally, from top to bottom. That's portrait orientation. Now turn it sideways so that what was the left edge is now the bottom edge. That's landscape orientation.

For documents that are wider than they are long, printing in landscape orientation is the best choice. Choose File, Page Setup from the main menu and click the Paper Size tab in the Page Setup dialog box. Under Orientation, choose Landscape.

You don't need to adjust your printer to use landscape; your computer does the work of printing the document sideways instead of across.

TIP The landscape option works with laser, inkjet, and dot-matrix printers, but not with impact printers.

Adjusting the margins

By default, your text boundaries are 1.25 inches from the left and right page borders and 1 inch from the top and bottom page borders. (We'll look at how to use the ruler to change indents in your document in Chapter 9.) You change your margins from Page Setup; for example, if you need more space for a document or want to shift the document image to widen a margin.

Let's say that your document spills onto a second page by two lines. Here's how to shrink the margins so the document fits on a single page:

1 Choose File, Page Setup from the main menu.

2 Click the Margins tab in the Page Setup dialog box (see fig. 7.5).

3 Decrease the top and bottom margins enough to fit the extra lines. For example, you might change the top margin from 1 inch to 1/2 inch, or both margins from 1 inch to 3/4 inch.

Fig. 7.5

The Page Setup dialog box lets you change your margins to accommodate documents of different sizes.

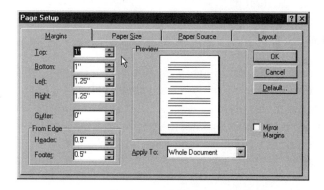

If your new margins will apply only to new pages in the document, choose This Point Forward in the Apply To list box.

Special print jobs: envelopes

Printing envelopes has always been a chore. You've got to set up your printer, configure your word processor, align the envelope, try to print the envelope, unjam the envelope, realign the envelope, print the envelope, throw the envelope away when the address comes out upside down, and repeat the whole process until you get it right.

In the same time, you could hand-address envelopes for the entire Cleveland Symphony Orchestra, and listen to a couple of fugues to boot.

You might be shocked, then, to learn that printing envelopes with Word is almost fun. Maybe not slam-dancing, blues-shouting, bar-walking, let's-have-a-karaoke-party-and-print-envelopes-until-dawn fun, but at least more fun than defrosting your refrigerator.

Here are some of the features that make printing envelopes palatable:

- You can pick the envelope size from a convenient list.

- You can choose how you feed the envelope from a group of graphical buttons.

- You can print the address and return address in any typeface and type size, as well as with such attributes as italics, small caps, and underlining.

May I have the envelope, please?

Choose Tools, Envelopes and Labels from the main menu. Click the Envelopes tab in the Envelopes and Labels dialog box (see fig. 7.6). In the dialog box, fill in the Delivery Address and Return Address text boxes. You also have the option of making the return address permanent, if it isn't already. If you want to exclude the return address for a particular envelope, choose Omit.

Fig. 7.6

Start your envelope by typing the delivery and return addresses under the Envelopes tab in the Envelopes and Labels dialog box.

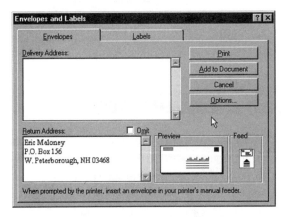

Next, you need to tell Word what size envelope you're using. Click Preview, or click the Options button and click the Envelope Options tab. If the Envelope Size text box doesn't show the proper size, click the box and choose the right one from the drop-down list.

Finally, align the envelope in your paper tray the same way it appears in the little graphic under Feed in the lower right-hand corner.

That's it! Just click <u>P</u>rint and behold the fruits of your labor.

 TIP **Like shoes, envelopes come in standard sizes. For example, a** standard business envelope (4 1/8 x 9 1/2 inches) is a number 10 envelope. Most envelopes you buy at the stationery store have both the dimensions and the number printed on the box.

How to fix alignment problems

If your printer chews up your envelope or doesn't print it the way it's supposed to, try putting it in a different way.

Click Feed in the lower right-hand corner under the <u>E</u>nvelopes tab, or click the <u>O</u>ptions button, and click the <u>P</u>rinting Options tab.

Choose the new alignment from the box under Feed Method. Click OK, insert an envelope, and print it.

Fun with fonts

If you've got a printer that can handle different fonts, you can use them to give your addresses some variety, as shown in figure 7.7. In the envelope shown on top, the return address is done in a font called Shelley Allegro, and the delivery address is in Frutiger Ultra Black. The bottom envelope assumes a more corporate look by using a font called Trajan Bold.

The fonts on your computer might be different, but the steps you take to use them are the same.

Choose <u>T</u>ools, <u>E</u>nvelopes and Labels, then choose <u>O</u>ptions under the <u>E</u>nvelopes tab. In the Envelope Options dialog box, choose <u>F</u>ont for the delivery address or Font for the return address (keyboarders should note the difference between underlined letters). Under the Fo<u>n</u>t tab, choose the typeface, style (bold, italic, or bold italic), and size (see fig. 7.8). You can also pick from among several types of underlines in the <u>U</u>nderline drop-down box. (We'll talk more about fonts, styles, and effects in Chapter 8.)

Fig. 7.7
Two examples of
envelopes printed
with fancy fonts.

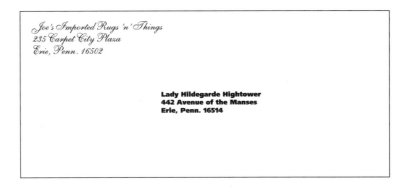

Fig. 7.8
In the Envelope Return
Address dialog box,
choose the Font tab to
choose a new font,
style, or size for your
delivery or return
address.

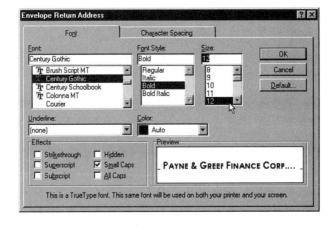

If you want your final selections to be permanent, click Default. Click OK when you're done, then click OK from the Envelope Options dialog box.

Q&A *Can I change the position of the addresses on the envelopes?*

You can raise or lower the delivery and return addresses. From the Envelopes and Labels dialog box, choose Options, then Font or Font for the delivery or return address, respectively. Choose the Character Spacing tab. Choose Position, and then choose Raised or Lowered from the drop-down box. Word automatically adjusts the address by three points—about 1/24 of an inch. You can increase or decrease the adjustment by choosing the By text box and typing a new number (you don't need to type "pt") or clicking the up and down arrows until you get the points you want. Each 18 points adjusts the address by a quarter of an inch. Click the OK button when you're done.

Special print jobs: labels

When you think of labels, you probably think of the kind that go on envelopes. But Word lets you print nearly 60 different kinds, including labels for audio and video tape, name tags, and file folders. You can also use the label-printing option to print business cards, rotary cards, and index cards.

Word gives you the dimensions of the label so you know which one to buy.

Word lets you print a single label, a sheet of the same label, or a sheet of different labels. You can also create and save a file of labels for later use.

Let's work from the ground up and start with the single label.

How to print a single label

Choose Tools, Envelopes and Labels and click the Labels tab (see fig. 7.9). Type the label in the Address box. Under Print, choose Single Label. Word assumes the label is the first one on the sheet in your printer.

If you've already used some of the labels on your sheet, adjust Row and Column accordingly. For example, if the first available label is in the third column of the second row, change the Row spin box to 2 and the Column spin box to 3. Either choose the box and type a new number, or click the arrow keys until the number you want spins into view.

Fig. 7.9

Choose the Labels tab in the Envelopes and Labels dialog box to print single or multiple labels. You can also save labels to use later.

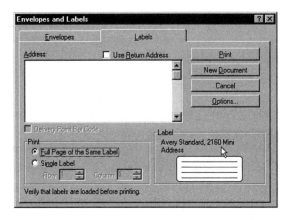

Make sure the label you're set up for is the same as the label in your printer. Word shows you a sample label in the lower right-hand corner.

If you want a different label, click the sample label. In the Label Options dialog box, click Options, or click the sample label in the lower right-hand corner. Scroll the Product Number text box until you find the right one. The dimensions of the label and the label sheet are given in the Label Information box.

The Product Number box gives you stock numbers for Avery labels. If you're using something other than Avery labels and you can't find measurements that match, select Label Products and choose Other. The Product Number box gives you the names of other label-makers' products.

You can see a picture of a label, along with its dimensions and margins, by selecting Details.

 TIP **To print return address labels, check Use Return Address under** the Labels tab in the Envelopes and Labels dialog box. Word uses the return address you entered for envelopes. If you haven't entered a return address yet, choose Tools, Options, User Info and enter it in the Mailing Address text box.

How to print multiple labels

To get the most out of multiple labels, you need to know a little about tables, which we discuss in Chapter 11. We'll give you the basics now, and you can return later to polish your label-making skills.

First, make sure you've selected the right label under the Labels tab in the Envelopes and Labels dialog box. Then choose Full Page Of The Same Label and click the New Document button.

Word opens what looks like a normal document, but it's really a special document that uses Word's Table feature to format the page for the labels. Also, the document's margins are set for the label sheets you'll be feeding the printer.

To see where the labels are, choose Table, Gridlines. In figure 7.10, for example, Word has set up a table to handle Avery Standard 2180 Mini File Folder labels.

Fig. 7.10

When you click New Document, Word opens a special document that's formatted for the labels you want to print.

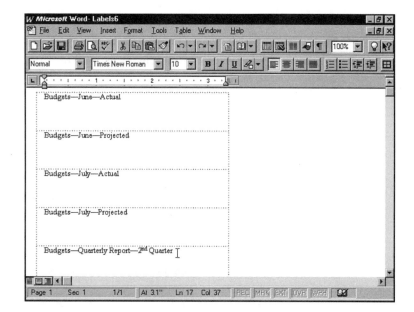

Entering label information

Position your insertion point in the first label and type the information. Press the Enter key after each line. Don't worry about entering too much information; the table keeps you from typing more than the label can hold.

When you're done with the label, press the Tab key to move the insertion point to the next label.

You learn how to edit tables and move around in them in Chapter 11. For now, here's what you need to know:

- Tab moves you to the next label.

- Shift+Tab moves you to the previous label.

- You can move to a label by clicking it with the mouse.

TIP **Would you like to use fonts and styles for your labels like you can** for envelope addresses? You can play with your type just as you would any other document. Chapter 8 tells you how.

Adding pages

To add a page to your label document, press the Tab key when you're done with the last label. Word automatically starts a new page and creates its first label.

Printing and saving your labels

Your multiple labels are a document that you can print and save like any other document. Just make sure you've got your labels in the printer tray before choosing File, Print.

Save your file with the standard Save command, and you can print the same sheet of labels whenever you need it.

TIP **You can save label pages by printing your labels on a blank sheet** of paper first. Hold the sheet against the label page to make sure the labels align properly.

Part III: Live Fast, Die Young, and Leave a Good-Looking Document

Character Sketches: Formatting Your Type

● In this chapter:

- **Fonts a-plenty: choosing from Word's abundance of types**

- **How do I get bold, italics, and underlines?**

- **A few points about type sizes**

- **Subscripts, drop caps, and other typographical trickery**

- **Do it this instant! Reformatting text with Format Painter**

- **Can I insert symbols and special characters in my text?**

Word's smorgasbord of types will make your documents easier to read and nicer to look at. . . . . ▶

You wouldn't serve dinner guests plain spaghetti. Sure, it's palatable, but your guests would be a lot more impressed if you added a tasty sauce, a few spices, and maybe even a garnish.

An unadorned Word document often needs the same kind of attention. It may be functional, but is it inviting? Does it hold your reader's interest from beginning to end? Wouldn't a different font here or a bold heading there make your document a bit more flavorful?

At first glance, using different fonts and type treatments might seem like a sizable undertaking. After all, this is the sort of matter we see in publications prepared by experienced designers. But you don't need to be an artist or desktop-publishing maven to create attractive documents. Formatting is easy to learn and even easier to do. A few minutes is all you need to turn a drab report into one that grabs people's attention and demands to be read.

Word gives you a variety of ways to change the look of your text. You can change a font, underline (or **boldface** or *italicize)* a few words for emphasis, or resize your type. You can apply most of these formats from the keyboard, simply by selecting text and clicking buttons on the Formatting toolbar.

Let's start by looking at the most important ingredient in Word's design kitchen: the font.

The types, they are a-changin'

At first glance, you might think the polished document shown in figure 8.1 was done by a highly trained layout specialist. Actually, it was done by one of the authors, who knows about as much about design as he does about theoretical chemistry.

Creating this document involved no desktop publishing or tricky text formatting. It was done entirely from the Formatting toolbar and Font dialog box, and involved only four actions:

- Changing typefaces
- Changing font styles (bold and italic)
- Changing sizes
- Adding underlining and small capitals

Fig. 8.1

A few simple changes to the text turn a plain document into one that's attractive and more readable.

JOURNALISM 200
INTRODUCTION TO MASS MEDIA

Instructor: Eric Maloney (Elliot 253)
Class Hours: Monday through Thursday, 9:30-11:10
Office Hours: Before or after any class by appointment

COURSE DESCRIPTION
J200 studies the techniques and effects of mass media, with an emphasis on understanding the relationship between people and their sources of information. We will analyze the subject from historical, technical, political, and social perspectives.

OBJECTIVES
- To survey the function of each medium.
- To review the history of mass media.
- To investigate the relationship of the media to economic and political systems.
- To review mass media literature to find out what media professionals think.
- To develop a critical point of view about mass media based on personal research.
- To attribute and document ideas to authoritative sources in research.
- To differentiate between fact and opinion.

METHODOLOGY
This course will be lecture-discussion with class participation an important component. You will be responsible for material presented in lectures, including material not in the text.

TEXTS
Agee, Warren K., Phillip H. Ault and Edwin Emery, *Introduction to Mass Communications*, 11th edition.

ASSIGNMENTS
You are required to complete all assignments for written and oral presentation.

We'll take a look at how we can change the body type in figure 8.1. This will introduce you to the relevant part of the Formatting toolbar, where much of the work is done.

Then we'll step back and take a broader look at the decisions that you must make to format your type. Along the way, we'll talk about some general principles of text formatting and how you can use them to make your documents more attractive and readable.

Selecting and changing the body type

In its original incarnation, the document was written in 10-point Times New Roman, the standard format for all new Word documents created with the Normal template. That's the template Word uses when you click the New button on the Formatting toolbar or press Ctrl+N. Figure 8.2 shows a portion of the original text.

Here's how to change body type, using the part of the Formatting toolbar shown in figure 8.2:

1 Select the entire document by pressing Ctrl+A.

2 Choose the Font Size text box in the Formatting toolbar by either clicking the down arrow or pressing Ctrl+Shift+P. Choose a new size from the drop-down text box or type it in the box. Sizes are given in points (more on that later).

3 Choose the Font text box by either clicking the down arrow or pressing Ctrl+Shift+F, then choose a new font.

 Plain English, please!

A **font**, or **typeface**, is a set of letters, numbers, symbols, and punctuation marks that have the same general look. Some examples of fonts include Times New Roman, Arial, and Courier.

 Q&A *How can I see what characters are available for a particular font?*

Choose Insert, Symbol from the main menu and click the Symbols tab. Most of the dialog box is occupied by a chart that shows the characters available for the font in the Font drop-down box. To look at the characters for a different font, choose the Font drop-down box and select a new font.

Click here to change the font.   *Click here to change the type size.*   *Click here for* ***boldface***.

Fig. 8.2

This is the way the document in figure 8.1 began. Use the Formatting toolbar to change the way your type looks.

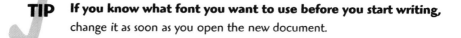

Click here for *underline*.

Click here for italics.

Changing selected elements

The steps for changing the blocks of text, headings, and other elements are the same: just select the text and change it. For example, if you want to make your text bold, like the main heading in figure 8.1, do the following:

1 Select the paragraphs you want to change.

2 Choose bold by clicking the Bold button on the Formatting toolbar or by pressing Ctrl+B.

TIP **If you know what font you want to use before you start writing,** change it as soon as you open the new document.

Q&A *Do I have to start each document with 10-point Times New Roman?*

No, you can start new documents with any font and size you want. Choose Format, Font from the main menu. Select the font and size you want and click the Default button. Choose Yes when Word asks you if you want to change the default. The next time you quit Word, you'll be asked if you want to change the template. Choose Yes. If Word does not ask, choose Tools, Options from the main menu, click the Save tab, choose Prompt To Save Normal Template, and click OK.

The Font dialog box

We took care of the body text in figure 8.2 using the Formatting toolbar exclusively. While the toolbar is better for quick changes, especially when you know what you want, the Font dialog box does much more. For example, the Font dialog box is where you find small caps like the ones used for the headings in figure 8.1.

Choose Format, Font to display the Font dialog box (see fig. 8.3).

Change the font here.　　*Change the font style here.*

Fig. 8.3
The Font dialog box includes all of the essential text-formatting tools.

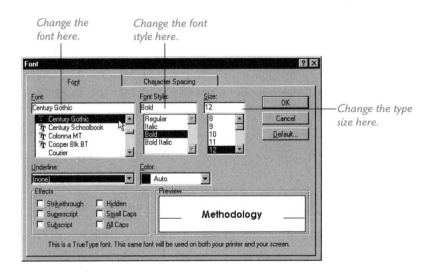

Change the type size here.

The Font dialog box has one big advantage over setting preferences using the toolbar—the Preview box in the lower right-hand corner. The Preview box lets you see what your choices look like before you use them.

Preview is terrific if you can't decide what font or style to use. For example, if you don't know what font you want for a heading, just select the text, click the Font list box, and scroll through the list of fonts. As you move down the list, Preview gives you a sample of each font.

The Font dialog box gives you several type treatments that aren't available on the Formatting toolbar. These include four types of underlines, subscripts and superscripts, small caps, and strikethrough. We'll look more closely at these functions a little later.

 Q&A *Some of my fonts just give me a lot of garbage characters. Is there something wrong with them?*

No need to adjust your set. These are special fonts that consist mostly of symbols. These fonts include Monotype Sorts, MT Extra, Symbol, and Wingdings. You usually insert these symbols using the <u>I</u>nsert, <u>S</u>ymbol command, which we'll discuss toward the end of this chapter.

Choosing the best font for the job

Your first step when you format a document is to decide if Times New Roman is the font that's appropriate for the work you're doing. It's fine for columnar material or short reports, both of which need to pack a lot of information in a small space. But for books, manuals, reports, and letters, in which more space between letters and words helps make the material more readable, consider something more stylish.

To look at the fonts you have available, choose F<u>o</u>rmat, <u>F</u>ont from the main menu to display the Font dialog box. Choose the Fo<u>n</u>t tab. The names of the fonts appear in the <u>F</u>ont list box, and as you scroll through the list box, you can see what each font looks like in the Preview box.

The chances are good that your fonts will be different from the ones shown in figure 8.3. Your selection partly depends on what software you have installed. Also, some printers can't print certain fonts; other printers come with packages of their own fonts.

 TIP **You can save time experimenting with fonts if you create and** print a document with examples of all your typefaces. Post a copy next to your computer for quick reference.

Basic rules for body type

Don't be confused by all the fancy fonts and funny names. The rules for picking a nice body type are simple:

- Use a serif type. **Serif** types have letters that are finished with little "flags" (like the letters you're reading now). **Sans serif** types have letters that are smooth and rounded, like this. Sans serif types are more appropriate for display types. (Some designers will argue against this rule. Common practice still argues for it.)

- Avoid screwy fonts such as Braggadaccio, Wide Latin, Britannic Bold, or Matura MT Script Capitals. They're designed as display types and are unreadable as body types.

- Century, Bookman, and Garamond are good fonts for reports, manuals, documentation, instruction sheets, books, and brochures. They're readable, and you can fit a lot of copy in little space. Also, these fonts are attractive in bold and italics.

- Courier is appropriate when you want a less formal look for letters and reports. It's the type you get on most typewriters. Don't use Courier if you want to **justify** your type (make both margins even). Also, Courier is not a good choice if you want to use bold and italics or if you want to use sans serif elements (for headings, for example).

- Avoid using more than one body type in any single document. Use a different font in headings for contrast. In figure 8.1, for example, the main heading and subheadings are in Century Gothic, the sans serif version of Century Schoolbook.

  You can also use a different font for tables and charts. For example, in figure 8.4, which is the second page of the syllabus that appears in figure 8.1, the Reading assignment schedule is in Century Gothic.

- Above all, remember that whatever you do to your type must make your document more readable. Otherwise, what's the point?

 Plain English, please!

Body type is type that you use mostly for plain text. **Display type** is type that is suited for large characters that are meant to grab a reader's attention, such as what you see in a newspaper ad.

TIP **If you haven't selected any text and change your font in the** middle of a document, the new font applies to whatever text you type from the current insertion point position.

When to use sans serif type

Earlier, we suggested that sans serif type is better for headings than for body type. There are exceptions.

Sans serif can be effective for short documents. It gives press releases, letters, and resumes a more contemporary feel. Also, you can use sans serif to set off short bursts of text such as quotes, sidebars, and footnotes.

The rules for picking a sans serif type are much the same as they are for serif: stick with the simple, easy-to-read fonts. Arial, Century Gothic, and MS Sans Serif are good choices.

 TIP **Check out Word's templates for ideas on how to use fonts and** styles. For example, the Contemporary press release mixes serif and sans serif types, while the Elegant press release uses only serif type.

 Q&A *Some of my fonts change all of my lowercase text to* *uppercase. How can I fix this?*

You can't. The font supplies only uppercase letters. Such fonts—for example, Desdemona—are designed as display types, not for body text.

A word about TrueType and other font mysteries

Windows and Word come with a variety of Microsoft fonts called **TrueType fonts**. They're the ones preceded by a double TT in the Font text box. TrueType fonts have two important characteristics that other fonts sometimes lack:

- You can enlarge or shrink them to most any size and get good results.

- What you see on the screen is what you get from the printer.

But your font list might include many fonts that do not come from Microsoft. They don't always behave. For example, a font might not display properly, or the font you get on the screen might not match the one you get on paper.

Fig. 8.4

Page 2 of the document that started in figure 8.1 includes an example of how you can use a sans serif type to help set off a table.

All assignments completed outside of class must be typed in MLA style. An MLA handbook is available at the library reference desk, or you can buy one at the bookstore.

All papers that include summaries of library materials will include a photocopy of the original.

All papers must be typed and double-spaced.

Any paper found to be plagiarized will receive an F, and the student's status in the class will be jeopardized.

Grammar, spelling, and punctuation will be important. If writing problems render your assignments unacceptable, you will be asked to rewrite and resubmit.

I will not accept late work unless you have an excused absence or have made prior arrangements.

ATTENDANCE

Attendance is required. You are permitted three excused absences. An excused absence must be as a result of extenuating circumstances (for example, illness or a family emergency).

Being late for class will count against your grade for participation.

READING ASSIGNMENTS

You are responsible for all reading assignments, even when they're not discussed in class. Expect periodic quizzes on the book. Supplementary readings will be assigned as appropriate.

Reading assignment schedule

Week	Section	Pages
May 23	Part One	1-82
May 30	Part Two	83-206
June 6	Part Three	207-264
June 13	Part Four	265-400
June 20	Part Five	401-474
June 27	Part Six	475-end

Grading

Assignments count for 40 percent of your grade, the midterm for 20 percent, the final for 20 percent, quizzes for 10 percent, and class participation for 10 percent. You will lose points for unexcused absences.

This is not the place to describe all of the hobgoblins that lurk in the gloomy hollows of Windows' font forest. But you'll have a better idea of how to use fonts if you know something about TrueType fonts and their kin.

CAUTION   **Hundreds, perhaps thousands, of fonts are available for the taking** from bulletin boards and user groups. Resist the temptation to become a font collector. Most of them not only are useless or duplicates, but they take a surprising amount of disk space. A mere 200 fonts might occupy as much as six megabytes. Choose a few good serif and sans serif body types and a few complementary display types, and forego the rest.

Display types, plain and simple

Most of Word's fonts are display types. They're designed to be big and bad, with the goal of attracting attention rather than enhancing readability. You can use display types to put together effective flyers and notices, such as the yard sale flyer in figure 8.5, which started out looking like this:

MASSIVE

YARD

SALE

Two days

Three families

1,234,567,090 items

(Almost) no offers refused!

SAT. & SUN. 9-4 1234 LASSITER ST.

As you can see, this flyer is nothing more than a glorified document. Putting it together involves no desktop publishing or tricky text formatting—just the tools you use to spruce up body type.

Formatting display type, such as the word "MASSIVE" in the flyer, takes only a few steps:

1 Select the text that you want to format.

2 Choose the Font text box and change the font (for example, "MASSIVE" in figure 8.5 is in Wide Latin).

3 Choose the Font Size text box and change the size ("MASSIVE" in figure 8.5 is 44 points).

4 Choose your font styles by clicking the Bold, Italics, or Underline button on the Formatting toolbar ("MASSIVE" in figure 8.5 is in bold and underlined).

Making a point about size

When you choose a size for your body type, you need to think about two factors: readability and space. The smaller the type, the harder it is to read but the more you get on a page. There are three important rules governing type size:

Fig. 8.5
From rags to riches—converting a puny document into a muscular yard sale flyer.

Font: Wide Latin
Style: Bold
Size: 44 points
Other: Underlined

Font: Playbill
Style: Bold
Size: 198 points

Font: Arial
Style: Bold, Italic
Size: 28 points

MASSIVE

YARD

SALE

Two days
Three families
1,234,567,090 items
(Almost) no offers refused!

SAT. & SUN., 9-4   1234 LASSITER ST.

Underline is part of word "MASSIVE."

Font: Arial
Style: Bold
Size: 28 points

Font: Algerian
Style: Regular
Size: 22 points
Effects: Small capitals

- The longer the line of type, the larger the type size should be. If you're using letter-size paper, for example, anything less than 12 points is hard to read.

- Go to a larger type size only if you have a special reason for doing so, such as for overhead transparencies or documents that will be posted.

- Use a smaller type for columns, particularly if they're justified. Otherwise, Word might have trouble inserting spaces between letters and characters, and you'll end up with type that looks squeezed or too spread out. Newspapers generally use an 8- or 9-point type.

Plain English, please!

A **point** is the unit printers use to measure the size of the type. There are 72 points in an inch, so a 12-point type is about 1/6 of an inch. However, some 12-point types appear to be smaller than other 12-point types because the characters themselves take less space.

Figure 8.6 shows you how different type sizes look when used with columns. (See Chapter 13 for more information on how to use column type effectively, including how to fix spacing problems with kerning and hyphenation.)

Fig. 8.6
As these examples show, the width of your column determines how large your type can be.

> A line that runs across a full page is hard to read when you use a small type such as this 9 point Times New Roman.
>
> Use 12 point type such as is in this sentence, or 11 point type if space is tight.
>
> On the other hand, when you use narrow columns, 9 points will give you much better spacing. This is particularly true if you justify the column (that is, make the type fill the line).
>
> If you use 12 points, you often will end up with awkward-looking spaces, particularly if you use a veritable cornucopia of polysyllabic words.

The changing face of type

We've looked at how to change fonts and font sizes. Next on the agenda are font styles—bold, italic, and bold italic. We'll also take up underlining here. The Underline button is on the Formatting toolbar, and underline serves the same purpose as a style, although Microsoft doesn't consider it to be a style.

You can add bold, italic, or underlining to any text. You can also use them in any combination. Just select the text and click the appropriate button on the Formatting toolbar. If you prefer the keyboard, press Ctrl+B for bold, Ctrl+I for italic, and Ctrl+U for underlining.

How to use styles effectively

Boldface, italics, and underlining have specific purposes. Use them conservatively, following these guidelines:

- Use bold to draw the reader's eye to a particular spot on the page, such as for headings or special messages. If you use too much bold, the elements compete for the reader's attention, and the bold defeats its own purpose.

- Use italics to emphasize words in text or for composition titles.

- Use underlining to literally underscore a point. Underlining headings or column heads can also be effective.

- Don't use bold, italics, or underlining for large blocks of body text. You can, however, use bold and italics effectively for small blocks of text that you want to highlight, such as quotes, tables, or charts.

- Don't combine too many styles, such as underlined bold italics. Your text will start to look messy and harder to read.

TIP **Word has four types of underlines to choose from:**
single underline, words only, double underline, and dotted underline. The Underline button on the Formatting toolbar gives you a single underline. To use one of the other types, highlight the text, choose F̲ormat, F̲ont from the main menu, and choose the U̲nderline text box.

Special effects

Last, and in many ways least, we come to special effects such as strikethrough and superscripts.

These options are not on the Formatting toolbar. To use them, select your text and choose F<u>o</u>rmat, <u>F</u>ont. Check the effect under the Effects heading in the lower left-hand corner of the Font dialog box (refer to fig. 8.3).

You'll probably never need most of these effects, but they're good to know about, just in case:

- **Stri<u>k</u>ethrough** runs a line through a portion of text, ~~like this~~.

- **Su<u>p</u>erscript** gives you a raised character often used in mathematical formulas, such as $A^2+B^2=C^2$.

- **Su<u>b</u>script** gives you the lowered character used in text to reference a footnote, such as Footnote$_1$.

- **H<u>i</u>dden** hides selected text from being displayed or printed. You use hidden text for notes and comments that you don't want in the printed document.

    You can display hidden text by choosing <u>T</u>ools, <u>O</u>ptions, clicking the View tab, and checking H<u>i</u>dden Text under Nonprinting Characters. Word displays hidden text with a dotted underline.

- **S<u>m</u>all caps** turns lowercase letters into SMALL CAPITAL LETTERS that are about the size of the letters they replace. Uppercase letters stay uppercase, as in the subheadings in figure 8.1.

- **<u>A</u>ll caps** look the same as ALL UPPERCASE. The differences are technical and don't matter enough to get into here. The Shift key is the easier alternative to get uppercase letters.

Drop caps

Occasionally, a document will be broken into sections, but each section won't have its own heading. To distinguish one section from another, try beginning each one with a **drop cap**—a large capital letter (or an entire word of large capital letters) that starts a paragraph. Figure 8.7 features several examples of drop caps.

To insert a drop cap, place your insertion point anywhere in the sentence. You don't need to select the text unless you want to drop more than one character. Choose Format, Drop Cap from the main menu to display the Drop Cap dialog box. Choose Dropped, which sets the cap inside the text, or In Margin, which positions the cap to the left of the text.

You can change the font of the drop cap in the Drop Cap dialog box; just choose the Font drop-down box and pick your new font. You can also change the font, as well as the style and size, right in the document. Click the letter twice or the space inside the drop cap box three times and make your changes as you would to any other selected text.

A sneaky way to get raised caps

The cap in the last example in figure 8.7 rises above the text rather than drops into it. That's called a **raised cap**. The Drop Cap dialog box has no raised cap option, but you can create a raised cap with a little sleight of hand.

Create a regular drop cap. Place your insertion point to the right of the drop cap and press the Enter key one less time than then number of lines the cap is dropped. For example, in figure 8.7, the drop cap was dropped three lines, so the Enter key was pressed twice.

Reapplying text treatments—a clever shortcut

If you change formats often in a document, selecting and reformatting each new block can get tedious. Word takes away some of the pain with the Format Painter button on the Standard toolbar. Essentially, the Format Painter borrows the format from one part of your document and applies it to another part of your document.

For example, figure 8.8 shows a document with 12-point Book Antiqua body text. The name of the first entry, "Northern White Cedar," has been changed to 14-point Arial bold, and the Latin name, *Thuja occidentalis*, has been reduced to 10 points and italicized. The task is to change the second and third entries—four one-line paragraphs in all—to match.

Fig. 8.7

A sampling of drop cap formats. Choose Format, Drop Cap from the main menu.

This is an example of drop caps. You can embed drop caps into the text or place them in the margin. You cannot see how drop caps will look on paper unless you use page layout mode (View, Page Layout) or Print Preview.

This is an example of drop caps. You can embed drop caps into the text or place them in the margin. You cannot see how drop caps will look on paper unless you use page layout mode (View, Page Layout) or Print Preview.

This is an example of drop caps. You can embed drop caps into the text or place them in the margin. You cannot see how drop caps will look on paper unless you use page layout mode (View, Page Layout) or Print Preview.

This is an example of drop caps. You can embed drop caps into the text or place them in the margin. You cannot see how drop caps will look on paper unless you use page layout mode (View, Page Layout) or Print Preview.

This is an example of drop caps. You can embed drop caps into the text or place them in the margin. You cannot see how drop caps will look on paper unless you use page layout mode (View, Page Layout) or Print Preview.

Fig. 8.8

Format Painter makes it easy to take a style from one part of your document and apply it to another.

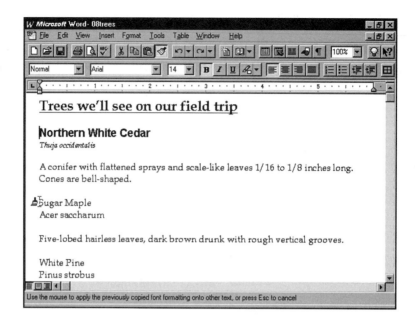

Formatting the Sugar Maple and White Pine entries individually involves at least twenty steps. But Format Painter can cut the number of actions in half. Here's the procedure:

1 Place the insertion point anywhere in the paragraph whose format you want to borrow; for example, "Northern White Cedar" in figure 8.8.

2 Click the Format Painter button on the Standard toolbar.

3 Move your mouse pointer to the left of the paragraph you want to reformat. If the pointer turns into a little paintbrush, keep moving it to the left until it's a standard arrow. (The paintbrush has a specific function that we'll talk about in a minute.)

4 Click the mouse button. Word selects the paragraph and then reformats it.

Brushing up: how to reformat selected text

The above steps reformat one paragraph with the format of another paragraph. You can also borrow a format from selected text and apply it to another block of selected text.

Select the text that contains the format you want to borrow. Click the Format Painter button on the Standard toolbar. Move the mouse pointer to the text you want to reformat. The pointer turns into a paintbrush. Holding down the mouse button, run the brush over the text you're reformatting. Word selects the text as you move the brush. Then release the mouse button.

How to reverse formats

You can remove formatting from text—that is, change the text to the formats you started the document with. Select the text whose formats you want to reverse and press Ctrl+spacebar. If you're removing formats for a single word, put the insertion point anywhere in the word.

Ctrl+spacebar removes all formats that you've applied, including fonts, styles, sizes, and effects.

The key word here is "applied"—you must have taken an action from the Formatting toolbar or the Font dialog box. Formats that are part of a paragraph style, which is not the same as a font style, will not be affected. If this sounds confusing, Chapter 12 should help to clarify matters.

Symbolic victories

You can use symbols in a number of ways to embellish your documents. For example, you might use a pair of scissors along the border of a clip-n-save coupon, check boxes for checklists, mathematical symbols for your latest theorem explaining the origin of the universe, or your astrology sign for responses to personal ads.

Open dialog box, insert symbol

To insert a symbol, choose Insert, Symbol from the main menu and click the Symbols tab in the Symbol dialog box (see fig. 8.9). Select a font from the Font drop-down box. The symbols for each font appear in the grid below the Font drop-down box.

Click a symbol to magnify it (as the thumbs-up symbol in figure 8.9 is shown). You can scan the symbols with your arrow keys. When you find the symbol you want to insert, press the Enter key, double-click the symbol, or choose Insert.

Fig. 8.9

The Symbol dialog box lets you insert a variety of symbols ranging from the practical to the frivolous.

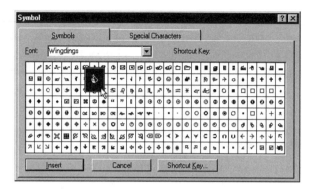

 TIP You can move between the Symbol dialog box and your text by clicking the inactive window with your mouse or by pressing Alt+F6.

How to create a keyboard shortcut

If you've got a symbol that you want to use repeatedly, you'll probably tire of opening the Symbol dialog box for each insertion. The more efficient method is to create a shortcut key. For example, if you assign Ctrl+Alt+X to the check box, you can use that key combination to insert a check box whenever you want.

You create a shortcut by clicking Shortcut Key in the Symbol dialog box. In the Customize dialog box that appears, choose Press New Shortcut Key. In the text box, press Ctrl or Alt, followed by a letter or number (for example, Alt, then M). The string Alt+M appears in the text box.

Word displays a message under the text box that warns you if the key already has a shortcut. If so, press the Backspace key to delete the shortcut and choose another one.

 TIP To delete, copy, move, or size a symbol, you first need to select it. Click the symbol or put your insertion point before the symbol, then press Shift+right arrow.

Inserting special characters

You might have noticed in the Symbol dialog box that there's also a tab titled Special Characters. These characters are similar to symbols, only they're more like text: different types of dashes, hyphens, and spaces; copyright, register, and trademark symbols; ellipses; and a variety of quotation marks. You insert special characters the same way you do symbols.

9

Formatting Paragraphs and Blocks

● **In this chapter:**

- **How do I center text?**

- **Indenting paragraphs the easy way**

- **Just put it on my tab stop!**

- **I want to double-space my paragraphs**

- **Right on target with bulleted lists**

- **Highlighting text with boxes and shading**

Tired of documents that are unbroken blocks of gray type? Add some pizzazz with different alignments, indents, and bulleted lists. . . . . ▶

Remember the days when TV dads never took off their suits? At dinner, on weekends, or at Beaver's ball game, Ward Cleaver always looked like he was on his way to a business meeting. Ward probably even wore his tie in the shower.

Word is set up to produce documents that Ward would have appreciated: plain type, single-spaced, aligned unobtrusively against the left-hand margin. But we don't live in a cautious world anymore. While conservative dress still has its place, there's also room for style and even decoration.

Most documents have lists, quoted material, and other blocks of text that deserve (or even demand) to be highlighted. A bulleted list here, a centered head there, and an indented paragraph over there can transform even the blandest document into a more interesting reading experience.

Word has commands and buttons to take care of most paragraph formatting. We'll start with the formatting commands available to you on the Formatting toolbar, shown in figure 9.1.

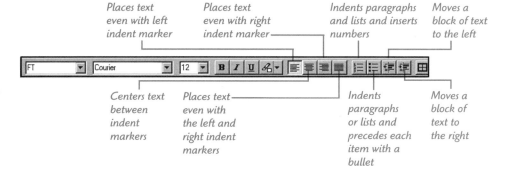

Places text even with left indent marker   *Places text even with right indent marker*   *Indents paragraphs and lists and inserts numbers*   *Moves a block of text to the left*

Centers text between indent markers   *Places text even with the left and right indent markers*   *Indents paragraphs or lists and precedes each item with a bullet*   *Moves a block of text to the right*

Fig. 9.1
Use these buttons on the Formatting toolbar to handle simple text alignments.

Center, right, and justified alignment

You can use alignments to format part or all of a document. In most cases, however, centering and right alignment are used to give variety to headings and small blocks of text. Figure 9.2 shows a head that is centered and a date that is flush right. Justified type aligns the left and right sides of text with their respective indent markers. Use justified type to give body text a neater, more formal look.

Fig. 9.2
Different text align–
ments separate
elements of type and
give a document more
visual appeal.

Centering automatically
aligns text so that it's the
same distance from each
indent marker.

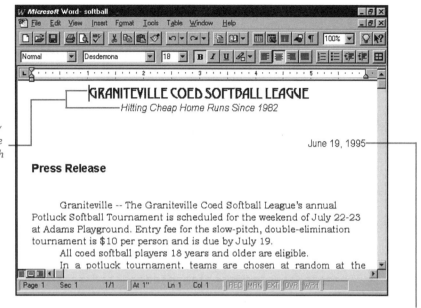

Right alignment brings type
against the right indent marker.

Here's the easy way to align paragraphs:

- To center the heads, select them and click the Center button on the Formatting toolbar.

- To align the date flush right, place the insertion point anywhere in the line of text and click the Align Right button on the Formatting toolbar.

- To justify the body type, select the entire page (Ctrl+A) and click the Justify button on the Formatting toolbar.

Alignment tricks you should know

Here are a few extra pointers to make text alignment easier:

- You don't need to select a paragraph or line when you realign it; just put the insertion point anywhere in the text you want to realign, then click the appropriate button.

- To align text that you are about to type, choose the alignment you want and start typing.

- The shortcut keys for aligning text are Ctrl+L for flush left, Ctrl+E for align center, Ctrl+R for align right, and Ctrl+J for justification. While the buttons usually are better for fixing alignment in a finished document, the shortcut keys are quicker when you're aligning text as you type it.

Indenting paragraphs made easy

Pages of gray, monolithic text are boring to look at and hard to digest. How does your reader know, for instance, that your three points about why the company needs new fax machines are more important than your grumbles about the flickering fluorescent lights?

One solution is to set off the text by indenting it. Figure 9.3 shows examples of the most common types of indents: the **paragraph indent**, the **hanging indent**, and the **negative indent**.

Fig. 9.3

Paragraph indents and their corresponding ruler settings. You can move the ruler markers by dragging them with the mouse.

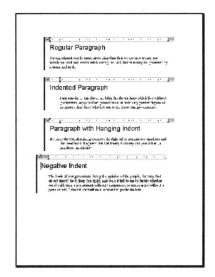

You can get any indent easily by dragging the indent markers on the ruler. Figure 9.4 identifies the markers and other elements of the ruler.

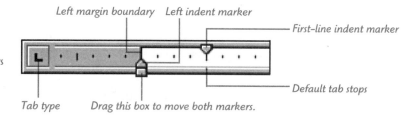

Fig. 9.4
Use the indent markers to create different kinds of paragraph indents.

Note that Word gives you two different left indents. The first is for the first line of a paragraph; it's controlled by the first-line indent marker on the top of the ruler. The second is for the rest of the paragraph. You set it with the left indent marker on the bottom of the ruler.

You can drag either marker separately, or you can slide them together with the box attached to the indent marker.

When you drag a marker, a dotted line extends the length of the page to help you align your text.

The paragraph indent

You indent a paragraph by placing the insertion point anywhere in the text and dragging both indent markers to the new location.

 More conveniently, you can click the Increase Indent button on the Formatting toolbar. Word moves the indent markers to the first tab and indents the selected paragraph accordingly. Word increases the indent by one tab for each subsequent button click.

 The easiest way to reverse an indent is to click the Decrease Indent button on the Formatting toolbar, or you can drag the indent markers on the ruler back to the margin boundary.

 TIP **To indent more than one paragraph, select the text before you** drag the indent markers. To indent an entire document, select the document first by pressing Ctrl+A.

The hanging indent

Bored with paragraph indents? Try a hanging indent. The difference is that the left indent marker (that's the one on the bottom) is to the right of the first-line indent marker. To create a hanging indent, place the insertion point in the paragraph you want to indent and do either of the following:

- Click the Increase Indent button on the Formatting toolbar, then drag the first-line indent marker back to where you want the first line of the paragraph to begin. The body of the paragraph hangs down from the first tab.

- Drag the left indent marker to the spot where you want the body of the paragraph to hang.

The negative indent

With most paragraph indents, the indented text is pushed into the page. The negative indent does the opposite—it pushes the selected text into the left margin, to the left of the margin boundary.

Be cautious when you use a negative indent with body text; it can make your document look ragged and disorganized. The negative indent is most effective as a way to emphasize headings or the first lines of your paragraphs.

To give text a negative indent, place your insertion point anywhere in the paragraph and drag the box below the first-line indent marker to the left. As you move the two indent markers past the margin, the ruler above the left margin becomes visible.

If you want to apply a negative indent to just the first line of a paragraph, drag only the first-line indent marker.

CAUTION **The size of the page limits how far you can push text into the** margin. Text that extends beyond the page boundary won't print. Use File, Preview to make sure your negative indents are printable.

Meanwhile, on the other end of the ruler...

A paragraph indent is a great way to set off a block of text, but why not go one step further and indent it from the right margin too? A little bit of space on both sides of a block quote, a list, or important instructional material attracts the reader's eye and balances the design of your page.

To indent text from the right margin, drag the right margin marker as you do the other markers.

Figure 9.5 shows an example of how to use a right margin indent. The paragraph is indented 3/4 inch from both the left and right margin boundaries.

Fig. 9.5

Indent a paragraph on both sides to give it more emphasis. Here, each side is indented 3/4 inch.

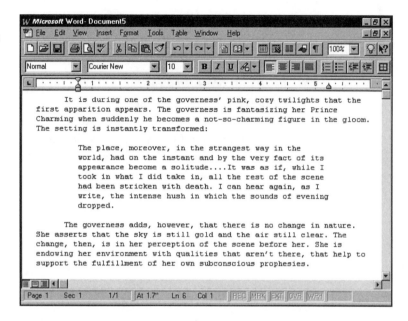

A little tab will do you

Tabs were once important for preparing tables and columnar material. But most of these functions have been stolen by Word's Table and Columns commands, which are easier to use and have far more design and editing power.

Still, tabs have their place if all you need is a simple two- or three-column listing—a price or inventory list, for example, or a schedule of events.

Word places default tab stops at 1/2-inch intervals (they're little gray marks just underneath the ruler). These usually aren't practical for aligning tabular material because they're so close together; you often have to press the Tab key half a dozen times to align your text properly. The more efficient way is to set your own tab stops.

Setting new tab stops

Figure 9.6 shows a simple to-do list. It consists of two columns, the second starting at 3 inches. The start of the second column is marked on the ruler by a tab stop, which looks like a squat, boldfaced L. The default tab stops before the set tab stop are gone.

> ### *Plain English, please!*
>
> A **tab stop** is where your insertion point stops when you press the tab key and is marked on the ruler. A **tab**, on the other hand, is what you get when you press the Tab key—the space between your tab stop and where your insertion point was. Tabs are usually hidden, but you can see them by clicking the Show/Hide Paragraph Marks button on the Standard toolbar; they're the bold arrows in figure 9.6.

Fig. 9.6

A simple two-column table created with a single tab stop at 3 inches on the ruler.

The Tab Alignment button shows what kind of tab you'll create by clicking the ruler.

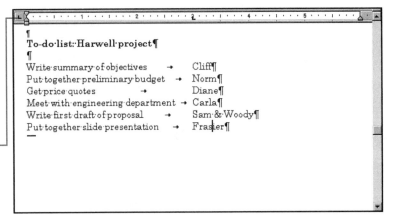

Here's what you do to create tabular material:

1 Click the ruler where you want the tab stop. Word inserts the new tab stop and deletes the default tab stops to its left.

2 Start typing your text. When you reach the end of an entry in the first column (`Write summary of objectives` in figure 9.6, for example), press the Tab key. Your insertion point slides to the tab stop. Type the entry for the second column and press the Enter key.

If you decide you want the tab stop somewhere else on the ruler, click it with the mouse and drag it to its new location. To help you align your column, Word drops a dotted line from the tab through your text.

You can insert as many tab stops as will fit on the ruler. However, if you find yourself with a table that has more than two or three simple columns, check out Word's table feature (see Chapter 11). It's easier to use and gives you more editing options.

When you reach the end of your table, you can reinstate Word's default tab stops by clicking the tab stop you set and dragging it off the ruler.

Q&A *How do I set tab stops for a list or table I've already typed?*

Start by highlighting the text. Click the ruler where you want the tab stop. Of course, you must have tabs at the appropriate places between columns to align the text.

Q&A *OK, I created a two-column list following your instructions. So how come the text in the second column doesn't align with the tab stop?*

If you used Word's default tab stops to align your second column of text *before* you set your new tab stop, there's a good chance you have extra tabs. Also, to make your text line up properly, you probably used more tabs in some lines than you did in others. Delete the extra tabs, and you should be set.

Different tabs for different tables

Figure 9.6 uses a left-aligned tab; that is, the text of the second column starts at the tab stop. You can also set tabs for right and center alignment, and for decimals. Figure 9.7 shows examples of right and decimal alignment. Notice that right alignment in the table labeled "Schedule" neatly lines up the times. In the second table, "Costs," decimal alignment lines up the figures, even the ones that don't have a decimal.

Center alignment balances a column so that each entry has equal amounts of text on either side of the tab. You can center-align the middle column of a three-column table to give the table more balance. Center alignment is also effective for columns that consist of single words.

Fig. 9.7

The first table shows an example of how you can use a right-aligned tab to line up lists such as times. The second uses decimal alignment to line up dollar amounts.

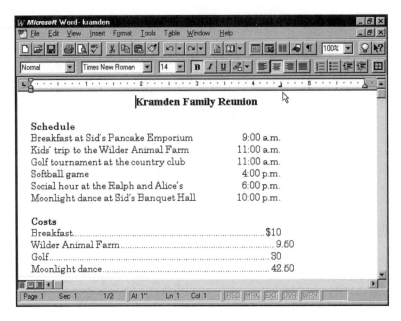

You choose the type of tab stop you want with the Tab Type button at the far left of the ruler. Click the ruler until the tab you want appears, then click the ruler where you want to put the tab stop. The following table shows what the different tab stop markers look like.

Click this...	To get this
L	Text flush left to tab stop
⅃	Text flush right to tab stop
⊥	Text centered on tab stop
⊥·	Decimals in numbers aligned

Q&A *I finished my table, then tried to change a tab stop by dragging it on the ruler. The tab stop changed for only one line! How do I change the tab stops for all of the lines in the table?*

Select the entire table first, then drag the tab stop. When no text has been selected, dragging a tab stop affects only the line on which your insertion point is positioned.

Take me to your dot leaders

Most phone books have little dots that connect each name with its phone number. The dots, collectively called a **leader**, make the listings easier to read.

While you might not be creating a phone book any time soon, you should consider leaders for long lists in which the columns are spread apart; for example, phone lists, indexes, tables of contents, and schedules. The second table in figure 9.7 shows dot leaders; Word also lets you replace tabs with dashed leaders or a solid underline leader.

If you're creating a new table, set up your leaders after you set your tab stop and before you start typing. If you've already created a table and you want to add leaders, select the table text first. In either case, then follow these steps:

1 Click a tab stop twice; the Tabs dialog box appears (see fig. 9.8).

2 Under the Leader heading, choose the type of leader you want.

3 Click OK, and Word replaces the tab before the tab stop with the leader.

Fig. 9.8
Set and clear tabs from the Tabs dialog box. You can also use this dialog box to insert leaders.

Word inserts a leader only for the tab stop you've clicked. If you want to use a leader with another tab stop in the same selected text, click <u>S</u>et instead of OK. Select the tab stop from the <u>T</u>ab Stop Position list box, choose another leader, and click <u>S</u>et. When you've got as many leaders as you want, click OK.

Q&A *I tried creating leaders in my document, but I don't get any. What am I doing wrong?*

Have you set tab stops to align your tabular material? Leaders don't work with Word's default tab stops.

Clearing tabs

The easiest way to clear a tab stop is to drag it up or down off the ruler. If you want to clear all tab stops, click the Clear <u>A</u>ll button in the Tabs dialog box (refer to fig. 9.8). Word resets all tabs to the default shown in the De<u>f</u>ault Tab Stops text box.

Vertical leaps—line and paragraph spacing

Long reports are easier to read if you add space between lines and paragraphs, and Word gives you the commands to do both.

In figure 9.9, for example, the body text is double-spaced and the space between the indented quotes has been reduced to 6 points.

Fig. 9.9

Use line and paragraph spacing to make text more readable and emphasize indented text.

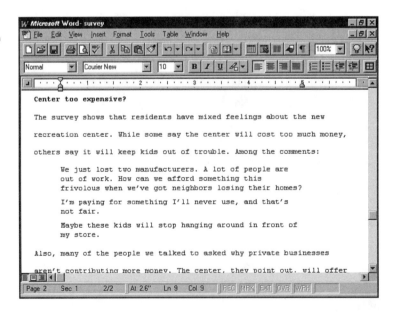

How to adjust line spacing

To double-space paragraphs, press Ctrl+2 before you start typing. Double-space a single paragraph by placing the insertion point anywhere in the text and pressing Ctrl+2. You can also use Ctrl+2 to double-space selected paragraphs.

Press Ctrl+1 for single space; press Ctrl+5 for one and a half spaces.

If you want to adjust your spacing to something else—triple space, for instance—use the Paragraph dialog box (see fig. 9.10). Choose F̲ormat, P̲aragraph from the main menu and click the I̲ndents and Spacing tab. Choose the Li̲ne Spacing drop-down box and choose Multiple. Type the new spacing in the A̲t text box (for example, type **3** for triple spacing).

Plain English, please!

Points are used by printers to measure type sizes and the distance between lines and paragraphs. One inch contains 72 points, so adding 3 points between two paragraphs adds 1/24 of an inch.

Fig. 9.10
Use the Paragraph dialog box to adjust the space between lines or paragraphs.

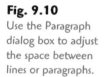
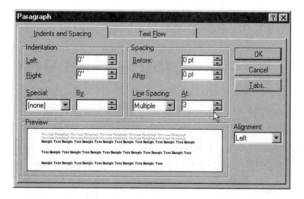

Fine points

You can adjust line and paragraph spacing by the point. This lets you control your spacing with much greater precision. Figure 9.11 shows examples of 10-point Bookman, with line spacing ranging from 6 to 14 points.

Fig. 9.11
You can adjust line
spacing by the point to
put more text on a
page or give the text
more space.

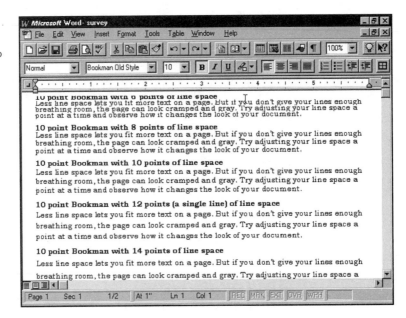

To expand or tighten line spacing by the point, choose Exactly from the Line Spacing drop-down box, and enter the new spacing followed by pt in the At text box (refer to fig. 9.10). For example, to change spacing to 10 points, type **10 pt**.

How to adjust paragraph spacing

Adjust the spacing between paragraphs in the Paragraph dialog box, in the Before and After text boxes under Spacing (refer to fig. 9.10). For example, to get the 6 points shown in figure 9.9, select the indented paragraphs *except for the last one* and enter **6 pts** in the After text box. You don't select the last indented paragraph to avoid adding space between the indented text and the body text.

Q&A *I selected a double-spaced paragraph, pressed Ctrl+1, and nothing happened. What did I do wrong?*

There's a good chance the person who wrote the document pressed the Enter key after each line (this is a common mistake among inexperienced users). Click the Show/Hide Paragraph Marks button on the Standard toolbar and look for telltale paragraph markers. Delete all but the one that ends the paragraph.

Bulleted and numbered lists

Bulleted and numbered lists are excellent ways to emphasize points or organize instructional material. Figure 9.12 shows a few simple examples.

Fig. 9.12

Three types of lists with numbers and bullets. In the numbered list, I boldfaced the numbers and increased the text indent.

These are the standard bullets and indents you get when you click the Bullets button.

Here the bullets are replaced with check boxes.

Click the Numbering button to get this list.

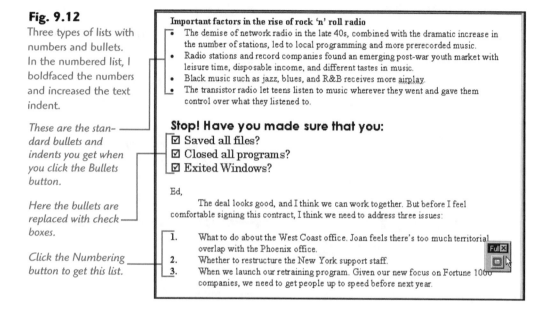

Creating a bulleted or numbered list is as easy as aligning text. You can also change the appearance of such lists in several ways, for example:

- You can change the bullet into a special character, such as the check box in the second example in figure 9.12.

- You can change the font, style, and size of numbers.

- You can change the spacing between the bullets or numbers and the text.

Lists made easy

If you're creating a list from scratch, put the insertion point where you want to start the list. Click the Numbering button if the list is numbered, and the Bullets button if the list has bullets.

Word inserts the number or bullet and moves the insertion point to where your text begins. Type the first item on your list. If your text is longer than one line, Word automatically indents your text so that subsequent lines are indented evenly.

Press the Enter key at the end of each item. Word inserts the next number or bullet. When you're done, double-click the Enter key to switch back to your regular format.

To add numbers or bullets to a list that you've already written, select the text and click the Numbering button or the Bullets button.

 Q&A *How do I get rid of my bullets? I tried the Delete key, but it doesn't work!*

Highlight the list items and click the Numbering or Bullets button. If you want to delete a single bullet or number, the easiest way is to put your insertion point between the bullet or number and the following text and press the Backspace key.

Not by the numbers—clever tricks for numbered lists

It's not unusual to create a numbered list and then find you need to change it. Here are a few tricks that will make editing lists easier:

- To insert an item in the middle of a numbered list, put your insertion point at the end of the previous item and press the Enter key. Word starts the next line with the correct number and automatically renumbers the items that follow.

- Word also renumbers a list if you delete an item.

- You can move an item in a list by using keyboard shortcuts. To move an item above the previous item, put the insertion point anywhere in the item and press Alt+Shift+up arrow. To move an item below the next item, press Alt+Shift+down arrow. Word renumbers the list for you.

- To skip numbering a paragraph in the middle of a list, put your insertion point anywhere in the text of the item you don't want numbered and click the Numbering button. From the keyboard, put the insertion point at the beginning of the item and press the Backspace key. Word renumbers the items that follow so they stay in sequence.

- If you want to break a list into two lists, press the Enter key after the item that will end your first list. This inserts a blank line. Put your insertion point on the blank line, click the right mouse button, and choose Stop Numbering (see fig. 9.13). Word creates a new list, starting with No. 1, below the blank line. Use the blank line to insert your heading for the second list (see fig. 9.14).

Fig. 9.13

To break a list into two separate lists, insert a blank line after the last item of the first list, click the right mouse button, and choose Stop Numbering from the shortcut menu.

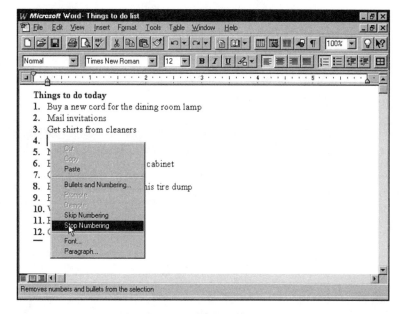

Fig. 9.14

To finish breaking your list in half, enter your heading for the second list in the blank line.

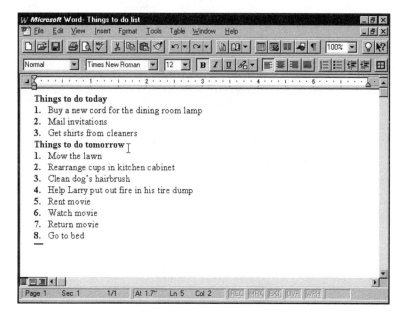

Formatting fandangos

If you get tired of plain old numbers, Word gives you a nearly endless variety of formatting options.

Figure 9.15 gives you an example. The numbers have been replaced with letters preceded by the word "Item," the typeface has been changed to Century Gothic bold, and the space between the letters and the text has been widened.

All of the work was done from the Bullets and Numbering dialog box. Let's walk through the procedure.

Fig. 9.15

Spice up plain old numbers in a numbered list by adding descriptive text.

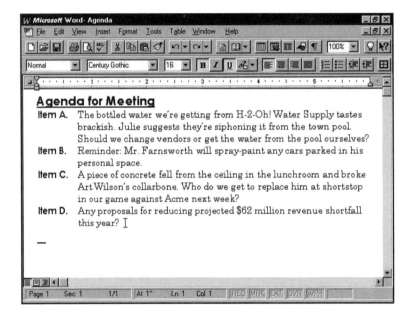

Changing the numbers

We'll assume that you're changing an existing list, although you can just as easily choose your options before you start.

Select the numbered text you want to work with and choose F<u>o</u>rmat, Bullets and <u>N</u>umbering from the main menu. On the Bullets and Numbering dialog box that appears, click the <u>N</u>umbered tab (see fig. 9.16). Click one of the six ready-to-go formats (for our example, the first one in the second row).

Fig. 9.16

Click the Numbered
tab in the Bullets and
Numbering dialog box
to change the format
of a numbered list.

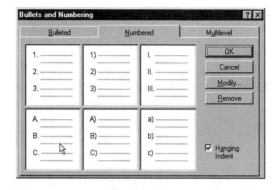

Next, click the Modify button to display the Modify Numbered List dialog
box (see fig. 9.17). The list in figure 9.15 requires only two changes: typing
the word "Item" in the Text Before edit box and changing the Distance From
Indent To Text to 0.6".

Fig. 9.17

The Modify Numbered
List dialog box lets you
add text before or after
the numbers in a list.

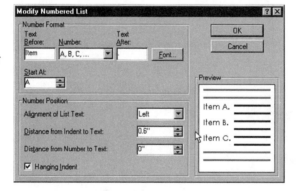

Figure 9.17 also displays your other options. Putting together a numbered
list often takes some experimenting, so try different combinations and see
how they look in the Preview box.

 TIP **If you apply a format that you don't like, you can click**
the Undo button on the Standard toolbar to bail out.

Changing fonts and styles

To change the character of the type, click the Font button in the Modify
Numbered List dialog box (refer to fig. 9.17). Word displays the Font dialog
box. It's the same dialog box you get when you're changing body or display

text, except that the changes you make affect only the numbers (or letters) that precede your list items. (Chapter 8 gives you more information on how to use the Font dialog box.)

Hit the bullseye with fancy bullets

You don't have quite as many options for playing with bullets, but you can replace them with any character and change their size. Figure 9.18 shows you a few possibilities.

Fig. 9.18

For special effects, replace your plain bullets with symbols.

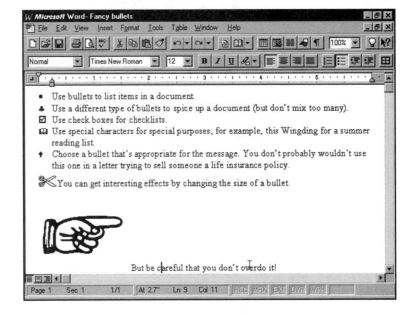

Choose Fo̲rmat, Bullets and N̲umbering from the main menu. The B̲ulleted tab looks like the N̲umbered tab, with six types of bullets you can choose from.

The real action is in the Modify Bulleted List dialog box (see fig. 9.19). Here's where you change the size of a bullet or pick a new one.

Click the M̲odify button from the B̲ulleted tab of the Bullets and Numbering dialog box. To change the size of a bullet, select it from the buttons below Bu̲llet Character and enter a new number in the P̲oint Size text box.

Fig. 9.19

The Modify Bulleted List dialog box lets you change a bullet's size or pick new bullets.

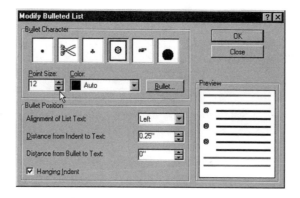

Picking new bullets

If you want a new bullet, click the Bullet button. Word opens the Symbol dialog box. Click the Symbols From drop-down box and choose a font. Click the symbol you want, then click Insert.

For more information on symbols and special characters, see Chapter 8.

Borderline decisions: how to box paragraphs

Fonts, bullets, indents—these are all devices you can use to emphasize parts of your document. But if you *really* want to set off a block of text, check out Word's borders and shading.

A well-placed border can do for text what a frame does for a painting. It contains the text and separates the document into segments that make the page easier to read. Shading a block does much the same thing with more subtlety.

You can box or shade text using either the Paragraph Borders and Shading dialog box or the Borders toolbar. For heavyweight boxers, the toolbar is the fastest way to go, but let's do a little sparring first with the Paragraph Borders and Shading dialog box, where your options are easier to select.

Boxing lessons

You can border or shade any paragraph. Start by placing your insertion point anywhere in the paragraph you want to format. You can format several paragraphs by selecting them first. In figure 9.20, for example, the three lines of the letterhead are selected.

Fig. 9.20

An example of a letterhead with a shadowed box and shading.

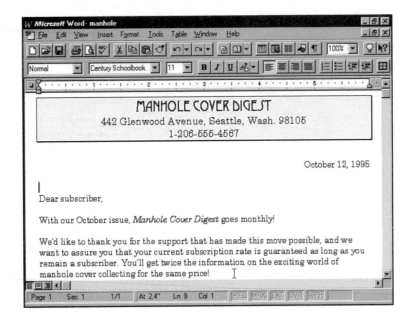

Choose Format, Borders and Shading from the main menu and click the Borders tab (see fig. 9.21). Choose Box or Shadow under the Presets heading. A box is, well, a box—lines of equal weight on all four sides. If you choose Shadow, Word gives your box a three-dimensional effect.

Fig. 9.21

The Paragraph Borders and Shading dialog box lets you choose the type of border you want.

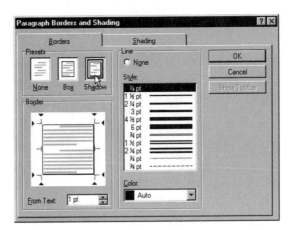

Next, choose the type of border you want under Style. You can get an idea of what the border will look like in the Border preview box.

You can also choose how much space you want between the borders and your text in the From Text text box. For most uses, 1 point is about right.

Opening the border

If your text is feeling claustrophobic and starts clamoring for air, you can open your box by deleting one or more of its sides. Click the border you want to get rid of in the Border preview box. For example, to give the letterhead in figure 9.20 top and bottom lines but no sides, click the left and right borders.

Made in the shade

To add a shaded background to your selected text, choose Format, Borders and Shading and click the Shading tab. (You can shade paragraphs without borders, but shades usually look neater when they're boxed.)

Select the degree of shading you want from the Shading selection box. Word gives you a range of choices, from 5 percent to 90 percent. The higher the percent, the heavier the shade.

The shading in figure 9.20 is set at 10 percent. You usually don't want to go much above 30 percent; anything heavier begins to overwhelm your text. You might need to experiment to find out what shades are most attractive on your printer.

While you're puttering around with shading, take a peek at the special shades at the bottom of the Shading selection box. Word provides a variety of diagonal, horizontal, and vertical lines that you can use for those times when, for example, you want your reader to feel as if he's reading your document through Venetian blinds.

Boxer shorts

After you've gone a few rounds in the Paragraph Borders and Shading dialog box, try using the Borders toolbar to box or shade text. Click the Borders button at the far end of the Formatting toolbar. That pops up the Borders toolbar.

Using the Borders toolbar has two advantages:

- You can select top, bottom, left, and right borders with the first four buttons.

- You can work in your document and click the toolbar when you need it. This lets you change borders and shading without going through the menu bar.

10

Formatting Your Page

● In this chapter:

- I'd like to start a new page, please

- How do I create and format sections?

- I want page numbers on my document

- Can I keep blocks of text together?

- This document needs headers (or footers)

- The dating game: adding the date and time

Give me a break! And while you're at it, how about some footers, page numbers, and dates?. . . . . ▶

As you develop more elaborate documents, you may have specific needs that Word's basic formatting tools can't fulfill. How do you create a separate page in the middle of your document? Prevent Word from splitting a block of text or table between two pages? Put a title and page number on each page? We'll take up these topics and more in this chapter.

Divide and conquer: inserting page and section breaks

As documents become larger, they're easier to read if you break them into smaller units. For example, you might want a table on its own page or a report broken into chapters. Sound complicated? It's not. Word's Break command lets you do these things in just a few simple steps. Breaks have another important function—they make formatting and editing easier. For example, if you break your document into sections, you can use a different sequence of page numbers for each section.

 Plain English, please!

A **page break** is the spot where Word ends one page and begins the next one. An **automatic page break** is one that Word inserts when it reaches the end of the page. The break moves as you add or delete text above it. A **manual page break** is one that you insert; it's permanent, regardless of how you change previous text. A **section break** creates a new section, somewhat like the chapter of a book, that you can format separately from other sections.

How to start a new page

When you insert a page break, Word ends the page at that point and starts a new page. Word marks a manual page break in Normal view with a dotted line and the words Page Break, as shown in figure 10.1.

The easiest way to insert a page break is with the keyboard shortcut Ctrl+Enter. You can also choose <u>I</u>nsert, <u>B</u>reak from the main menu and then <u>P</u>age Break in the Break dialog box.

Delete a page break by putting the insertion point on it and pressing the Delete key.

Fig. 10.1

Insert a page break to force Word to start a new page.

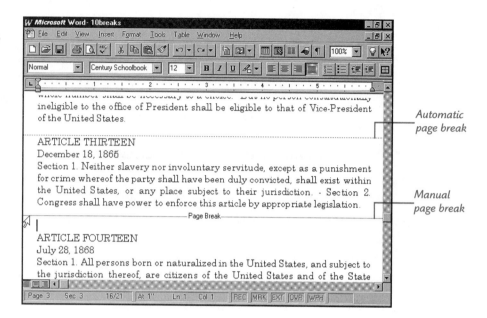

Automatic page break

Manual page break

 To see how a page break affects your document, Choose <u>V</u>iew, <u>P</u>age Layout from the main menu, or click the Page Layout View button to the left of the vertical scroll bar. Choose <u>F</u>ile, Print Pre<u>v</u>iew, or click the Print Preview button to see how the break will look in the printed document.

CAUTION **If you insert, delete, or move a lot of text after you insert a manual page break, be careful of double page breaks—an automatic page break followed by a manual page break with no text between them. You'll get a blank page in the middle of your document.**

Breaking a document into sections

At first glance, a section break looks a lot like a page break. Both segment a document, but a section break has several important differences:

- You can do some types of formatting by the section. For example, if you have an extra-long table, you can put it in a section and tell Word to print just that section lengthwise, using landscape orientation.

- You can give each section separate page numbers.

- You can put a new title on each page of a new section in a header or footer.

 ### Plain English, please!

A **header** is information, such as a title or page number, that Word automatically inserts at the top of each page. A **footer** is the same as a header, except that it appears at the bottom of the page.

How do I start a new section?

To insert a section break, place the insertion point where you want the section to start and choose Insert, Break from the main menu. Under Section Breaks in the Break dialog box, Word gives you the following options:

- *Next Page* starts the new section on the next page.

- *Continuous* inserts a section break that you can format separately, but it does not start a new page.

- *Odd Page* starts the new section on the next odd-numbered page. For example, if you insert a section break on page 41, the new section will start on page 43 and leave page 42 blank. Use this break when you print on both sides of your paper and want your sections to always start on right-hand pages, like the chapters in this book.

- *Even Page* is the same as Odd Page, only the new section starts on the next even-numbered page.

Word marks a section break in Normal view with a double dotted line and the words End of Section. Use Page Layout view or Page Preview to see how a break will look in the printed document.

The status bar tells you what section you're working in.

Delete a section break by putting your insertion point on it and pressing the Delete key.

TIP **Use the Go To command to move quickly to the beginning of a** section. Press the F5 function key, choose Section in the Go To What text box, type the section number in the Enter Section Number text box, and click the Go To button. Use the Next and Previous buttons to move from one section to another.

Formatting sections

The Columns and Page Setup dialog boxes have an Apply To text box in which you can tell Word what part of the document you want to format. If you don't have section breaks, your choices are Whole Document or This Point Forward. (If you've selected text, then This Point Forward is replaced by the Selected Text option.) If you have inserted section breaks, Apply To adds This Section as an option.

Section formatting is most useful when you want to print part of your document with different margin settings. In the document in figure 10.2, for example, the margins for the second section beginning on the right-hand page have been reset to 2 inches.

Fig. 10.2
Use section breaks if you want to reset the margins for a particular part of a document.

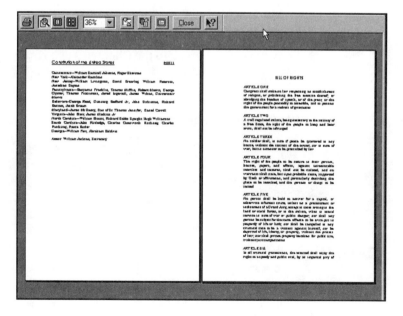

We'll look more closely at another example—using a new header for a separate section—when we discuss headers and footers later in this chapter.

Can I copy a section break?

You can copy a section break to another part of your document. This is a useful shortcut if, for example, you want to use the same margins in another section.

However, copying section breaks does not work quite the way you might expect. You have to mark and cut the break *after* the section whose format you want to copy. Likewise, you have to paste the break *after* the section whose format you want to change.

Let's say you're working in a document with regular margins set up for portrait printing. In the middle of the document, you create a wide table that you need to print sideways, in landscape orientation. You insert a section break above the table and format section 2 for landscape printing. When you're done, you want to resume typing your document with regular margins. Here's how you do it:

1 Insert a section break after the table. This ends section 2, which contains the table, and starts section 3, in which you'll continue typing your document.

2 Select the section break that separates section 1 and section 2.

3 Copy the section break to the Clipboard by pressing Ctrl+C or clicking the right mouse button and choosing Copy from the shortcut menu.

4 Put your insertion point after the section break that ends section 2 (the section with the table).

5 Paste the first section break by pressing Ctrl+V or clicking the right mouse button and choosing Paste from the shortcut menu.

6 Continue typing your document in the section above your new section break.

CAUTION **When you create and format a section, Word stores the** formatting information in the section break at the end of the section. If you delete the break, the section *above* the break assumes the format of the section *below* the break. For example, if the second section is set up for landscape printing, deleting the page break changes the first for landscape printing.

Q&A *I put my section break in the wrong place. How do I move it?*

Select the section break. Click the selected break and hold down the mouse button. A small checkered box appears at the tail of your mouse pointer, and Word displays the message Move to Where? in the status bar. Drag the section break to where you want it, and release the mouse button.

Saving and reusing a section format with AutoText

If you have a section format that you use often, save it as an AutoText entry. The section will be available whenever you open a new document.

Select the section break and choose Edit, AutoText. Give the section a name and click Add. To insert the break, type the name and press F3. (For more about AutoText, see Chapter 5.)

How to prevent breaks

You can prevent Word from breaking a paragraph that you want to keep in one piece. Put your insertion point in the paragraph. Choose Format, Paragraph from the main menu and click the Text Flow tab. Select the Keep Lines Together check box. Word will not place an automatic page break within the paragraph.

Word treats the paragraph as an unbreakable block even if you move it to another part of the document, unless you insert a manual page break, a paragraph return, or a section break within the block.

I want these paragraphs to stay on the same page

If you have two paragraphs that you want on the same page, put the insertion point in the first paragraph and choose Format, Paragraph from the main menu. Click the Text Flow tab and select the Keep With Next check box.

You can use the same method for keeping more than two paragraphs together. Select all but the last paragraph and follow the steps above.

Headers and footers

Rare is the book, magazine, or long report that doesn't include such text as the title, page number, date, or author on each page. This information—called a header when it's at the top and a footer when it's at the bottom—serves as an important reference for the reader, who never has to guess where she is in the document or what she's reading. A header or footer also ties the pages of a document together visually, giving each page at least one element in common with all other pages.

Word has a command that lets you insert headers or footers automatically on designated pages. The command is easy to use and comes with a variety of formatting options.

You usually use a header or footer to put a page number, title, or chapter heading on each page. Your header can also include text, the date, the time, or anything else you want.

You format the contents of a header or footer the same way you format body text. You can choose a different font, styles such as bold and italics, alignments such as centering and flush right, and tabs with leaders. You can even give your header or footer a border or shading (see Chapter 9 for information on the Borders and Shading command).

 Plain English, please!

A **leader** is a line of dots or dashes that appears between two pieces of text separated by a tab. See Chapter 9 for information on how to create leaders.

For convenience, we'll focus on headers; the steps for creating footers are identical.

Starting your header

To start your header, choose <u>V</u>iew, <u>H</u>eader and Footer from the main menu. Word displays the Header box and the Header and Footer toolbar shown in figure 10.3.

Type the text you want in the header. You can format the header with Word's Formatting toolbar and main menu. In figure 10.3, for example, the text has been changed to 14-point Century Gothic and underlined. The page number is moved to the right margin with a tab, and "Page" is formatted for small caps.

Fig. 10.3
You can format the text in your header the same way you do the text in your document.

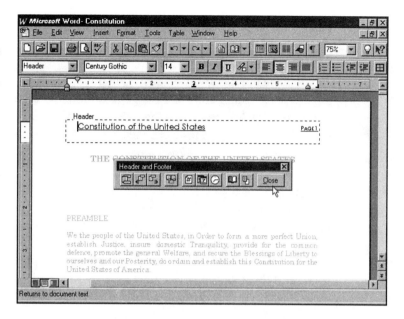

 TIP **You can include just about anything in a header or footer that** you can include in your document, including graphics and symbols. See Chapter 16 for information on pictures and objects; see Chapter 8 for more on symbols and special characters.

How do I see my new header?

  When you're done, click Close on the Headers and Footers toolbar. Don't be alarmed if the headers don't appear in your document; they won't if you're in Normal view. Choose Page Layout from View on the menu bar, or click the Page Layout View button at the beginning of the vertical scroll bar. The header appears in light gray. Click the Print Preview button or choose File, Print Preview to see what the header will look like when you print the document.

 TIP **To change a header into a footer, select the header text, cut it** with Ctrl+X or the Cut button, press the Down arrow, and paste the text with Ctrl+V or the Paste button.

Adding page numbers, dates, and times to a header or footer

To add page numbers, put the insertion point where you want the number in the header or footer and click the Page Numbers button on the Header and Footer toolbar (see the following page entitled "Close-Up: the Header and Footer toolbar"). Word inserts a page field. The page number changes automatically for each following page.

 Plain English, please!

> A **field** is a code that automatically inserts information into a document, header, or footer. For example, the date field inserts the date while the time field inserts the time.

You insert the date or time field by clicking the Date and Time buttons, respectively.

You can instruct Word to update your date and time automatically when you open the document. Choose Tools, Options from the main menu and click the Print tab in the Options dialog box. Choose Update Fields under Printing Options and click OK.

You can update either one manually by clicking it with the right mouse button and choosing Update Field from the shortcut menu.

 Q&A   *I tried to insert page numbers, but all I get is the word "PAGE" between two squiggly brackets! Why isn't this feature working?*

> What you see, {PAGE}, is the name of the field. You can change it to the actual page number in one of two ways. If you're in a header or footer, right-click the field and choose Toggle Field Codes from the shortcut menu. If you're not in the header or footer, choose Tools, Options from the main menu and click the View tab. Under the Show heading, choose Field Codes to remove the check in the checkbox.

I don't want a header on the first page

Title page and first pages often don't need a header or footer. To force Word to start your header on page 2, click the Page Setup button and choose Different First Page under Headers and Footers. Word presents you with a blank header; ignore it and click Close.

Close-Up: the Header and Footer toolbar

 Switch between Header and Footer
Click here to switch between the header and footer.

 Show Previous
Click here to show the previous header or footer.

 Show Next
Click here to show the next header or footer.

 Same as Previous
Click here to insert the contents of the previous header or footer.

 Page Numbers
Click here to insert a page number field.

 Date
Click here to insert a date field.

 Time
Click here to insert a time field.

 Page Setup
Click here to change the page setup of the selected sections.

 Show/Hide Document Text
Click here to show or hide the text in the document.

 Close
Click here to close Header/ Footer view and return to your document.

TIP **To remove a header or footer, choose Edit, Headers and Footers.** Delete the text in the header or footer box, then click Close.

Inserting a new header or footer

When you want a different header or footer for a new section, go to that section and choose View, Header and Footer. Click the Same as Previous button. This deselects the button and gives you a blank header or footer. Enter your new text, then click Close.

CAUTION **It's important to turn off Same as Previous *before* you start your** new header or footer. Otherwise, your previous headers or footers will change to match your new one.

What about page numbers?

If you want only page numbers, choose <u>I</u>nsert, Page N<u>u</u>mbers from the main menu to display the Page Numbers dialog box (see fig. 10.4).

Fig. 10.4

Use the Page Numbers dialog box to position and align your page numbers.

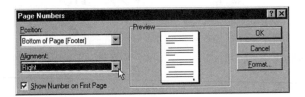

In the <u>P</u>osition drop-down box, choose whether you want the page number to appear at the top or bottom of the page. Then choose the alignment—left, center, right, inside, or outside—from the <u>A</u>lignment drop-down box.

If you're printing a two-sided document with facing pages, Outside alternates your page numbers so that they're always close to the outside margin. That is, the number is on the left side of even-numbered pages and the right side of odd-numbered pages. Choose Inside to insert them next to the inside margin.

To hide the page number on the first page of a document, click the <u>F</u>ormat button in the Page Numbers dialog box and remove the check mark from the <u>S</u>how Number On First Page check box.

 TIP **To use Roman numerals for prefaces and introductions, click the** <u>F</u>ormat button in the Page Numbers dialog box, then choose the Roman numeral format from the Number <u>F</u>ormat drop-down box.

Dates and times

You can insert the current date or time in one of two ways:

- As plain text

- As a field that updates to reflect the current date or time

In figure 10.5, the top time is plain text that you can edit like any other text. The bottom time, on the other hand, changes when you click it and choose Update Field from the shortcut menu.

Fig. 10.5

The top time is plain text that remains fixed. The bottom time is a field that updates to the new time whenever you reopen the file or choose Update Field from the shortcut menu.

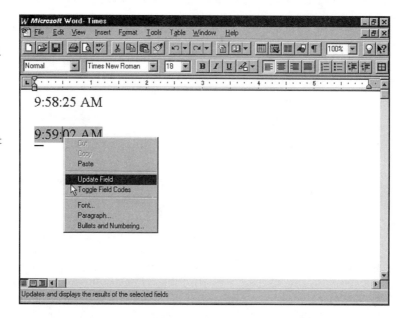

Choose Insert, Date and Time from the main menu. Word displays the Date and Time dialog box shown in figure 10.6. Select the format you want from the Available Formats list box. If you want a time or date that can be updated, select the Update Automatically (Insert As Field) check box.

Fig. 10.6

Now when was it I printed this document? Choose the Update Automatically (Insert As Field) check box to help you keep track.

Inserting file names, your name, and other information

How often have you stared at two printed versions of the same report and wondered which one was the most recent? Wouldn't it be nice if you could include information that identifies a document, such as the author, date the document was created, and the size of the file in which the document was stored? And just to make life a bit easier, how about the document's file name so you could quickly find it on your disk?

Word lets you put this information, and a lot more, in your document. You do it the same way you add the current date and time, by inserting a field. Some of the information, such as the author's name and address, is useful in headers and footers. Other fields, such as the creation date and file name, are appropriate for a cover sheet or at the top of your document.

You can insert any field with the Field command. Put your insertion point where you want the information and choose Insert, Field from the main menu. In the Field dialog box, choose a category from the Categories selection box, then choose a field from the Field Names selection box. Word describes each field at the bottom of the dialog box. When you've found the field you want, click OK, and Word inserts the field in your header or footer.

Table 10.1 lists some of the more useful fields that are available.

Table 10.1 Inserting information in headers and footers

Choose this field	To get this information	For example
Author	Author from File, Properties	Dashiell Hammett
CreateDate	Date document was created	06/26/95 4:15 PM
Date	Current date	08/08/95
EditTime	Time document has been open	832
FileName	File name of document	Report
FileSize	Size of document, in bytes	43520
NumChars	Number of characters in document	23196
NumPages	Number of pages in document	19
NumWords	Number of words in document	4883
Page	Number of current page	13
PrintDate	When document was last printed	08/08/95
RevNum	Number of times document has been saved	62
SaveDate	Last time document was saved	08/01/95 11:03 AM
Section	Number of current section	1
SectionPages	Number of pages in current section	20
Time	Current time	10:31 AM
UserAddress	Address from Tools, Options, User Info	General Delivery San Francisco, CA 94114
UserInitials	Initials from Tools, Options, User Info	DH
UserName	Name from Tools, Options, User Info	Dashiell Hammett

11

Turning the Tables

In this chapter:

- **Creating a table: one click is all you need**

- **How to insert, delete, and move rows and columns**

- **Table out of order? Try sorting it**

- **How do I add borders and shading?**

- **AutoFormat—Word's instant table formatter**

Wait a minute! That's about all it takes for Word's Table command to organize anything from a plain list to a boring ledger page into an attractive visual . . . . ⊗

Using tables to create eye-catching effects

Tables are good for more than just lining up columns of data. You can also use them to mix text and graphics or different sizes of text.

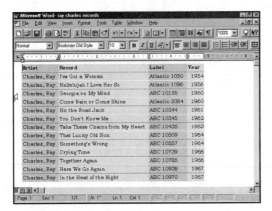

Borders and shading give this table a 3D effect.

Use a table to put text of different sizes next to one another.

This three-column table includes a graphic in the middle column.

A two-column table formats a list suitable for posting.

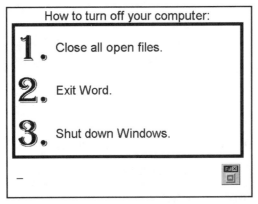

n the world of consumer products, "fast" too often means "mediocre." Whether you're talking about instant food, snap-together furniture, or five-minute-a-day exercise machines, you usually lose as much in quality as you gain in speed and convenience.

Word's Table functions buck the trend. Fast? Very. But mediocre? Hardly. Word's Table command is the quintessential combination of speed and power. The first table shown in the graphics page, for example, took less time to set up than it takes to make instant oatmeal.

And don't think a table is just a glorified way to punch the Tab key. You can't use the Tab key to create the tables shown in the graphics page. Nor can you so deftly move, delete, insert, size, box, shade, format, and otherwise bend columns and rows to your will.

Word gives you two basic ways to create a table. The first assumes you haven't typed the text yet; that is, you're going to create the table and then fill it in. The second assumes you already have the text typed; in other words, you want to create the table from existing material.

How to create a table from scratch

First, let's look at how you create an empty table:

1 Click the Insert Table button on the Standard toolbar. A panel of squares representing the cells of your table drops down.

2 Drag your mouse across and down the grid until it's the right size. The dimensions appear at the bottom of the grid. In figure 11.1, for example, the resulting table will be 14 rows deep and four columns wide. The dimensions of your grid might vary depending on where your Insert Table button is located and how much screen space is available.

3 If you don't see grid lines as shown in the table in figure 11.2, turn them on by choosing Table, Gridlines from the main menu.

Fig. 11.1
Use the Insert Table button to create a table from scratch. This table will be four columns wide and 14 rows deep.

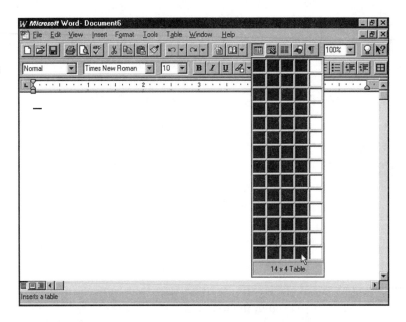

Fig. 11.2
If you don't see the table when you're finished designing it, choose Table, Gridlines to show the grid.

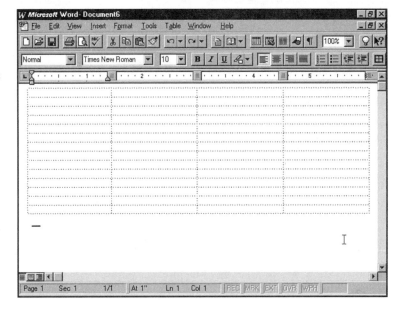

Don't worry about getting the number of rows or columns right. As we'll see later, they're as easy to add as pressing the Tab key, and not much harder to delete.

Plain English, please!

A **cell** is the location in a table where a row and column intersect. You see a cell on the screen as a box. A table is simply a **grid** made up of many cells.

Grid lines are thin, dotted lines on the screen that outline a table's cells. Grid lines don't appear on printouts. A **border**, discussed later in this chapter, is a line that you add to a table. It remains visible on the screen at all times and appears as part of your printout.

Creating tables with the Table command

Many users prefer to create their table, fill it in, and tinker with the formatting details later. But if you're the type who likes to get the job done right the first time, you can specify how your table will look before you create it, using the menu commands Table, Insert Table followed by Table, AutoFormat.

However, these options probably won't do you much good until you learn how to format your tables manually. Otherwise, you'll be stuck with tables you don't know how to edit or reformat. Understand the basics first, then we'll tackle the more advanced tricks at the end of this chapter.

How to fill out the table

Place your insertion point in a cell and type your text. When you reach the right grid line of the cell, notice how Word wraps the text to the next line and extends the cell vertically to fit the text. When you're done typing, you have these options:

- Press the Tab key to move to the next cell to the right. You can also use the right arrow key if you're at the end of the text.

- Press Shift+Tab to move to the next cell to the left. The left arrow key also works if you're at the beginning of the text.

- If you're on the last line in the cell, press the down arrow to move down one cell.

- If you're on the first line in the cell, press the up arrow to move up one cell.

If you run out of table space, you can add a row to the bottom by placing the insertion point in the lower right-hand cell and pressing the Tab key.

 TIP   **Press Ctrl+Tab in a cell to insert a normal tab in your text.**

How to create a table from text

So far, so good. But what if you've already typed your table, using tabs to make your columns? Do you have to retype or copy the text into the new table?

Probably not. If you set your tabs properly, you can select the text and drop the grid lines on top of it.

The key to converting text into a table is to make sure you have only one tab between items in a row. In most cases, this means setting tabs for each column rather than using the default tabs. If you've got four columns, set the tabs for columns 2, 3, and 4. When you convert your text to a table, you'll get the nicely formatted table shown in figure 11.3. Otherwise, you might end up with an unsightly mess such as the table shown in figure 11.4.

Fig. 11.3

If you create columns in text by setting your tabs and convert the text into a table, Word will format the resulting table properly.

Columns set up using four custom tabs:

| Charles, Ray | I've Got a Woman | Atlantic 1050 | 1954 |
| Charles, Ray | Crying Time | ABC 10739 | 1966 |

Above text converts to this table:

Charles, Ray	I've Got a Woman	Atlantic 1050	1954
Charles, Ray	Crying Time	ABC 10739	1966

Fig. 11.4

If you create columns with default tabs, your table columns might not line up.

Columns set up using default tabs:

| Charles, Ray | I've Got a Woman | Atlantic 1050 | 1954 |
| Charles, Ray | Crying Time | ABC 10739 | 1966 |

Above text converts to this table:

Charles, Ray		I've Got a Woman		Atlantic 1050		1954	
Charles, Ray		Crying Time			ABC 10739		1966

Once you've got your tabs right, select the text and click the Insert Table button on the Standard toolbar. Choose T<u>a</u>ble, Grid<u>l</u>ines to see the table lines.

> **TIP** **If you have a table set up with default tabs, choose <u>E</u>dit, R<u>e</u>place** and, in the Replace dialog box, replace all back-to-back tabs with single tabs. (Your columns won't line up anymore, but it doesn't matter; the final table will look the way it's supposed to.) You get the tab character in the Fi<u>n</u>d What and Re<u>p</u>lace With text boxes by clicking Sp<u>e</u>cial and then <u>T</u>ab Character from the selection box.

Modifying your table

A new table is rarely perfect. You'll probably need to add, move, or delete rows or columns. These are uncomplicated tasks but require that you know how to select parts of your table.

Selecting columns, rows, and cells

To select a column, position the pointer at the top grid line of the column until it's an arrow pointing down, then click the mouse button (see fig. 11.5).

Fig. 11.5
To select a column, touch the top grid line until your pointer turns into an arrow, then click once.

Final vote totals—Seat 12

	Lang (D.)	Rutherford (R.)	Clesson (L.)	Stowe (I.)	Other
Ward 1	222	145	14	2	6
Ward 2	198	199	16	4	12
Ward 3	431	542	34	12	36
Ward 4	98	102	2	0	8
Ward 5	167	154	15	8	11

To select several contiguous columns, point to the top of the first column to select it, then click and drag the mouse across the table. You can also select the first column, hold down the Shift key, and click the last column.

To select a row, put the pointer to the left of the row and click once (see fig. 11.6). Drag the pointer down to select several columns.

Fig. 11.6

To select a row, put the pointer in the left margin and click once.

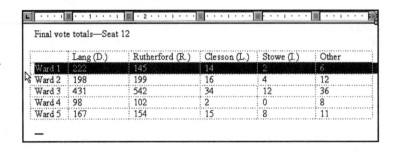

To select a cell, click the space between the left grid lines of the cell and the text. The entire cell becomes highlighted, as shown in figure 11.7. Select several contiguous cells by dragging the pointer across the cells.

Fig. 11.7

To select a cell, point at the space between the left grid line and the text and click once.

	Lang (D.)	Rutherford (R.)	Clesson (L.)	Stowe (L.)	Other
Ward 1	222	145	14	2	6
Ward 2	198	199	16	4	12
Ward 3	431	542	34	12	36
Ward 4	98	102	2	0	8
Ward 5	167	154	15	8	11

Final vote totals—Seat 12

You can also select cells using the keyboard. Put the insertion point at the beginning of the text in the cell and press Shift+down arrow until you reach the last line of text; then press Shift+End. To select several cells to the right, press Shift+End for each cell. Use Shift and the appropriate arrow key to move left, up, or down. Here are a few other useful keyboard shortcuts:

- To select the next cell in the row, press the Tab key.

- To select the previous cell in the row, press Shift+Tab.

- To select the current and previous cells in the row, place the insertion point at the beginning of the cell and press Shift+right arrow.

To select the text in a cell, select it as you would regular text—only the text will be highlighted (see fig. 11.8).

Fig. 11.8
Select the text in a cell by double-clicking the text.

Final vote totals—Seat 12

	Lang (D.)	Rutherford (R.)	Clesson (L.)	Stowe (I.)	Other
Ward 1	222	145	14	2	6
Ward 2	198	199	16	4	12
Ward 3	431	542	34	12	36
Ward 4	98	102	2	0	8
Ward 5	167	154	15	8	11

To select the entire table, hold down the Alt key and double-click anywhere in the table, or choose Table, Select Table from the main menu. You can also press Alt+Num5 (the number 5 on the numeric keypad); make sure that NumLock is off.

TIP **If you're going to perform an action on a single column or row** such as cutting, copying, or pasting, select it with the right mouse button. A shortcut menu with common table commands pops up.

How to change column widths

When you create a table using the Insert Table button, Word automatically sets all columns to the same width and stretches the table from margin to margin. You'll likely want to change the widths of a column or two.

The easiest way to change the width of a single column is to drag the border marker on the ruler with the mouse. But Word gives you three ways to re-size. You have to be careful of how the method you choose will affect your other column widths.

In figure 11.9, the goal is to widen column 3 so that the text fits on one line. But the method used for the third example narrows column 4 too much, and the method used to get the fourth example pushes the table beyond the right margin. Only the second example has properly formatted columns.

Fig. 11.9

Word gives you three ways to widen a column, each affecting subsequent columns differently.

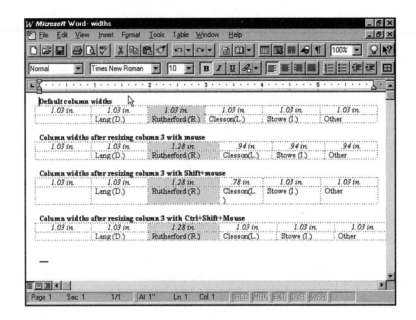

Here are the three options you can choose from:

- If you drag with the mouse only, all columns to the right change proportionately, as in the second example in figure 11.9. The table width stays the same.

- If you drag the mouse while pressing the Shift key, only the next column to the right changes, as in the third example in figure 11.9. The table width stays the same.

- If you drag the mouse while pressing Ctrl+Shift, all columns to the right stay the same, as in the last example in figure 11.9. The table width changes size accordingly.

Q&A *My ruler isn't showing. How do I change column widths?*

You can change a column's width by dragging the grid line in the table. Select the column, then touch the right grid line with the pointer until it changes into two vertical lines between two arrows.

If you'd rather use the ruler, you can make it visible by choosing View, Ruler.

How to change several columns at once

To change several column widths at the same time, select the columns and choose Table, Cell Height and Width from the main menu. In the Cell Height and Width dialog box that appears, enter the column width in the Width Of Column text box, then click OK.

CAUTION　**When you select a column to change its width, make sure the** entire column, not just the top cell, is highlighted. Otherwise, you'll change the width of only the selected cell.

Perfect fit: how to adjust column widths automatically

Wouldn't it be convenient if Word adjusted your column widths automatically? It can, with a command called AutoFit. Word expands or shrinks the columns according to the text they contain. Figure 11.10 shows the table in figure 11.9 with the columns automatically adjusted.

Fig. 11.10

When you use AutoFit, Word decides what the best column widths are.

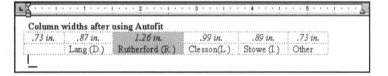

Here's how to use AutoFit on selected columns:

1 Select the column whose width you want to adjust.

2 Touch the right grid line of the last selected column until your pointer changes into two vertical lines between two arrows.

3 Double-click the grid line.

You can also use AutoFit from the keyboard. Select the columns you want to adjust. Choose Table, Column Height and Width from the main menu, click the Column tab in the Cell Height and Width dialog box, and click AutoFit.

Changing the width of a single cell

You can change the width of a single cell by selecting the cell and dragging the border markers or grid lines. In figure 11.11, for example, the selected cell has been widened on either side so that the text will fit without wrapping to a second line.

Fig. 11.11
To change the width of a single cell, select the cell and drag the border markers or grid lines.

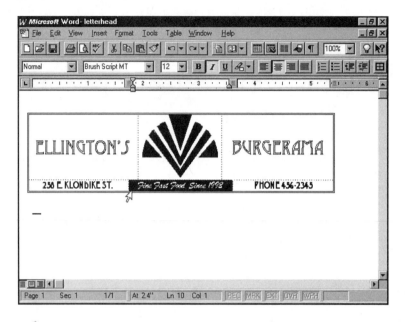

 TIP **If you change the widths of many individual cells in a table, some** cells might *appear* to realign themselves under different columns. In fact, cells remain with their original columns, no matter where they are on the screen. If you need to see which cells make up a column, select the column by clicking its top grid line.

Inserting a row

You can't always know exactly how many rows and columns you need when you create a table. Conveniently, Word gives you more ways to insert rows and columns than you can shake a pointer at. Let's start with how to add rows.

 If your insertion point is in the row that will follow the new row, click the Insert Rows button on the Standard toolbar. (The Insert Rows button is the Insert Table button, only with a new name and function.)

You can also take the following steps:

1 Place the mouse pointer in the left margin next to the row that will follow the new row.

2 Press the right mouse button. The row is highlighted and Word displays a shortcut menu.

3 Choose Insert Rows from the shortcut menu (see fig. 11.12).

Fig. 11.12
Click to the right of a row and choose Insert Rows to insert a row above the one that is selected.

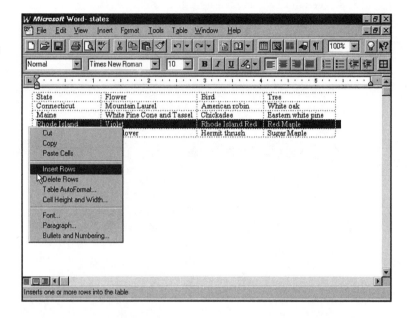

Your new row will include any formats contained in your selected row.

Inserting a column

The steps for inserting a column are a lot like those for inserting a row. Select a column and click the Insert Columns button on the Standard toolbar. (The Insert Columns button is the Insert Table button, only with a new name and function.)

Alternatively, you can select the column, click the right mouse button, and choose Insert Columns from the shortcut menu.

How to insert several rows or columns at once

Once you've inserted a row or column, you can make additional insertions by clicking the Insert Rows or Insert Columns button on the Standard toolbar.

To insert several rows at the same time, select the same number of rows that you want to insert and click the Insert Rows button. For example, to insert six rows, select the six rows below the insertion point and click the Insert Rows button.

From the keyboard, choose Table, Insert Rows from the main menu after you select the cells (see fig. 11.13).

Fig. 11.13

In this table, two rows are being inserted to make room for New Hampshire and Massachusetts.

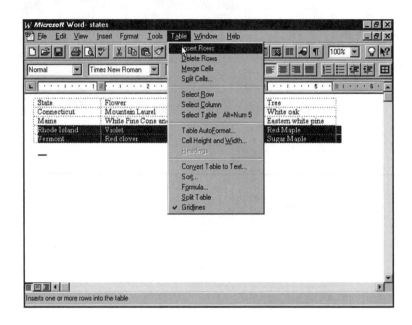

The same technique works for inserting several columns. Select the same number of columns that you plan to insert and either click the Insert Columns button or choose Insert Columns from the shortcut menu.

Going, going, gone: deleting rows and columns

Word provides several ways to delete rows or columns, but the easiest method is to select them and then take either of these steps:

- Click the right mouse button and choose Delete Rows or Delete Columns from the shortcut menu.

- Choose Table from the main menu, then choose Delete Columns or Delete Rows from the Table menu.

When you delete rows and columns, you erase them completely. If you want to insert them somewhere else in your table or document, then cut them instead. We'll cover cutting and pasting in a moment. (See Chapter 5 for details on the differences between deleting and cutting.) Select the rows or columns and use one of the following methods:

- Click the right mouse button and choose Copy from the shortcut menu.

- Click the Copy button on the Standard toolbar.

- Press Ctrl+C.

Q&A *Oops! I accidentally deleted a column. Is it gone forever?*

Not if you deleted it recently. If the deletion was your last action, choose Edit from the main menu and choose Undo Delete Columns. The shortcut for Edit, Undo is Ctrl+Z. If you've taken some actions since the delete, click the down arrow next to the Undo button on the Standard toolbar. Find Delete Columns in the selection box and click it. Note, however, that Word also undoes all actions above Delete Columns.

Anywhere you want it: moving rows and columns

Once you've got a vegetable garden planted, it's pretty tough moving your rows of plants around. If you decide you really wanted the carrots next to the radishes instead of the lettuce, you just have to wait until next year.

Fortunately, a Word table is a bit more flexible. Moving a row or column is not much more complicated than cutting and pasting regular text. You cut the row or column, move your insertion point to the row or column's new location, and paste.

Let's look at the steps to move a column. (The steps to move a row are nearly identical.) In figures 11.14 through 11.16, for example, we'll move the Bird column to between the State and Flower columns. Here's how to do it:

1 Select the column you want to move by clicking its top grid line with the right mouse button. The shortcut menu appears, as shown in figure 11.14.

2 Choose Cut from the shortcut menu.

3 Select the column that follows the point at which you want to insert the column by clicking the right mouse button on its top grid line (for example, the Flower column in figure 11.15). The shortcut menu appears.

Fig. 11.14

To move a column, first select and cut it.

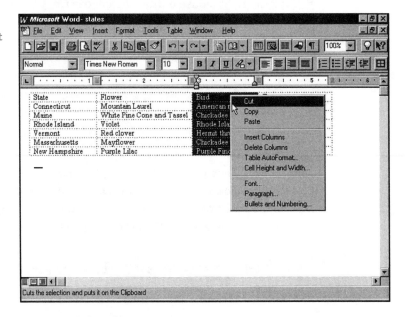

Fig. 11.15

Select the column to the right of where you're going to insert the column and choose Paste Columns.

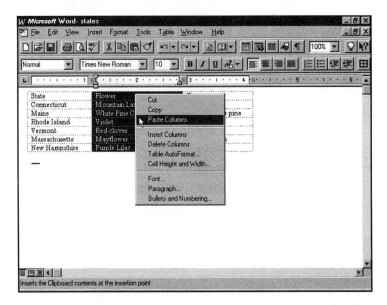

4 Paste the column by choosing Paste Columns from the shortcut menu.

Figure 11.16 shows the results.

Fig. 11.16
Word puts the column
in its new spot.

Moving a row is almost the same:

1 Select the row to move by clicking the right mouse button to the left of the row's left grid line.

2 Choose Cut from the shortcut menu.

3 Using the right mouse button, select the row below which you want to paste.

4 Paste the row by choosing Paste Rows from the shortcut menu.

All together now: moving several rows or columns

You can use the shortcut menu to cut more than one selected column or row, or you can cut them by clicking the Cut button on the Standard toolbar. If you prefer the keyboard, press Ctrl+X. You can also use the shortcut menu to paste the rows or columns (follow step 4 in the previous two examples).

Table out of order? Try sorting it

Sorting is one of the best ways to make a table easier to read. Your personal or office phone list is a perfect example: you'll find "Aadaabandaah, Hubert" a lot quicker if he's at the top of the table and not buried between "Zerph, Meg" and "Kasper, Kenny" somewhere in the middle.

In Word, you can sort a table using the Sort command. Word lets you sort by any column in the table (if, for example, you want your phone list sorted by the numbers), sort by several columns (for example, to sort your phone list first by department and then alphabetically within each department), and sort in ascending (A through Z) or descending (Z through A) order.

To sort a table, put your insertion point anywhere in the table and choose Table, Sort from the main menu. The Sort dialog box appears (see fig. 11.17).

Fig. 11.17
Use Table, Sort to sort your table. In this example, the table is sorted first by the Department column and then by the Name column.

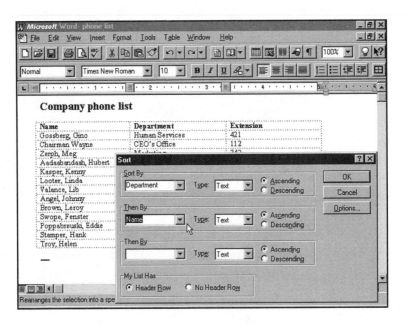

If your table has a row of headings, choose Header Row under My List Has. This prevents Word from including the header in the sort. In the Sort By text box, choose the heading of the column by which you want to sort the table (Department in fig. 11.17). You can also choose additional column headings in the Then By text boxes (Name in fig. 11.17). When you finish making your selections, click OK.

Can I format my table text?

A table is rarely complete without a few extra formatting touches. How about bold headings? Centered text in a column? Or even a bulleted list in a cell? These and most other types of formats you use in regular text are readily available.

To format text in a row, for example, select the row and choose your formatting options. In figure 11.18, the column headings are boldfaced and centered by clicking the Bold and Center buttons on the Formatting toolbar.

Fig. 11.18

Format text in a row by selecting the row and choosing the formatting options you want.

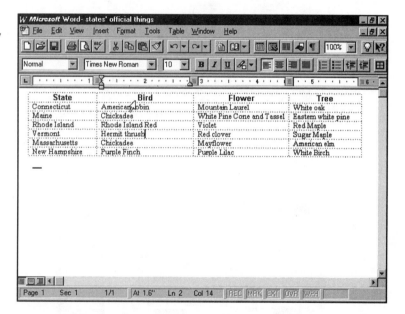

Adding borders and shading

Dressing a table doesn't stop with formatting its text. You can embellish the table itself by adding different types of borders and shading.

As figure 11.19 shows, borders and shading don't have to be just cosmetic. They can make text more readable by subtly blocking off columns and directing the reader's eyes across rows.

Word gives you many options for adding borders and shading to a table. You can use either for the entire table or selected cells, and you can mix different border widths and shading densities.

You add borders and shading from the Table Borders and Shading dialog box (see fig. 11.20).

Fig. 11.19
Borders and shading improve the appearance of a table and make it more readable.

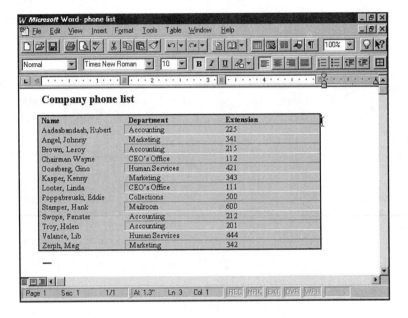

Fig. 11.20
The Table Borders and Shading dialog box lets you spiff up your table with a variety of border lines.

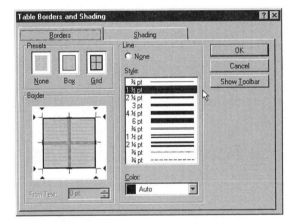

Placing an order for borders

Putting a box around a table or adding border lines is simple. Place the insertion point anywhere in the table. Choose F<u>o</u>rmat, <u>B</u>orders and Shading to display the Table Borders and Shading dialog box, and click the <u>B</u>orders tab. Choose Box or Grid under the Presets heading. Choose the type of line you want in the Style list box, then click OK. Figure 11.21 shows what you get if you choose a grid and a 3/4-point double line.

Fig. 11.21

Use the Format, Borders and Shading command to create quick borders and grids.

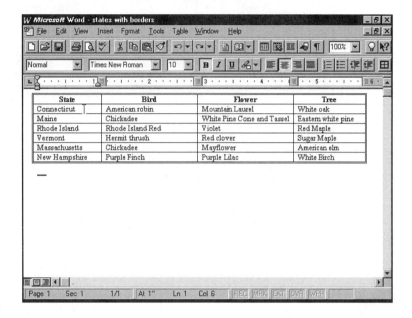

State	Bird	Flower	Tree
Connecticut	American robin	Mountain Laurel	White oak
Maine	Chickadee	White Pine Cone and Tassel	Eastern white pine
Rhode Island	Rhode Island Red	Violet	Red Maple
Vermont	Hermit thrush	Red clover	Sugar Maple
Massachusetts	Chickadee	Mayflower	American elm
New Hampshire	Purple Finch	Purple Lilac	White Birch

Fine-tuning borders

Once you've got your borders in place, you can tinker with them. For example, you might want to highlight certain cells by boxing them with a different border, or you might want to remove some borders entirely.

Notice in figure 11.21 that Word automatically chooses 3/4-point single lines for the borders to go with the 3/4-point double-line box. The easiest way to choose different lines for individual rows, columns, and cells is by using the Borders toolbar. The Borders toolbar also lets you format lines for a table's top or side grid line, outside grid lines, or the entire grid.

For example, to change the table in figure 11.21 so that a double line separates the headings from the text, follow these steps:

1 Select the heading row.

2 Click the Borders button on the Formatting toolbar to display the Borders formatting toolbar shown in figure 11.22.

Fig. 11.22
Use the Borders toolbar to fine-tune your borders. Here, a 3/4-point double line is added to the bottom border of the row that contains the column headings.

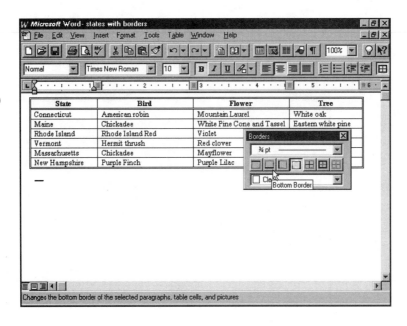

3 Choose a 3/4-point double line from the Line Style drop-down box at the left end of the Borders toolbar.

4 Click the Bottom Border button on the Borders toolbar.

Made in the shade

Borders aren't the only way you can emphasize certain parts of your table. Shading is also effective, particularly for subtly setting off column headings or for highlighting columns or rows.

Select the cells you want to shade and click the Borders button on the Formatting toolbar. (You can also choose Format, Borders and Shading from the main menu and click the Shading tab.) Click the Shading drop-down box and select the shading you want. Word shades the selected text. In figure 11.23, for example, the row that contains the headings has been given a 20 percent shade. (For more details about shading, check out Chapter 9.)

TIP **To shade an entire table, put the insertion point anywhere in the** table without selecting anything, choose Format, Borders and Shading, click the Shading tab, and choose the shading you want from the Shading list box. Click OK when you're done.

Fig. 11.23
The Borders toolbar is the fastest and easiest way to shade selected text. Here, the heading row is given a 20 percent shade.

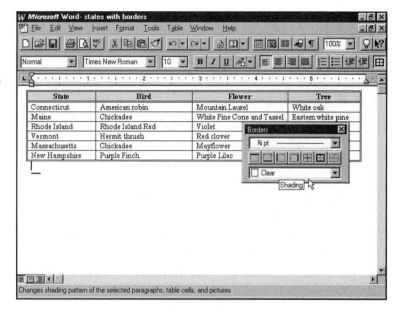

AutoFormat—table formatting for the masses

Formatting a table is easy. But the variety of formats, borders, and shades can be bewildering. What are the most attractive borders? How much shading is too much? What's the best way to make a table more attractive while maintaining its readability?

Enter AutoFormat, Word's automatic table formatter. AutoFormat lets you choose from among 37 formats that you can apply to your table. Some of the formats aren't much more than unadorned grids, while others include fancy shading and 3D effects. Using AutoFormat is like trying to find the best frame for a picture. You can quickly apply a series of formats to your table and then pick the one you like best. The Table AutoFormat dialog box also lets you choose which parts of the format you want to apply. For example, if you like the format except for the shading, you can remove the shading.

Using AutoFormat

To use AutoFormat, choose T**a**ble, Table Auto**F**ormat from the main menu. Word displays the Table AutoFormat dialog box shown in figure 11.24.

Fig. 11.24

AutoFormat lets you choose from among 37 prefab formats that you can use to create a table.

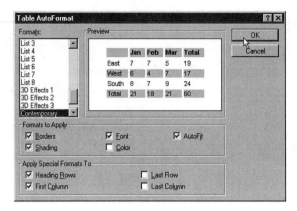

To select a format, scroll the Formats list box. You can see a sample of each in the Preview box. Select or deselect whatever items you wish under Formats To Apply or Apply Special Formats To. The Preview box changes to reflect your choices.

When you find and adapt the format you want, click OK, and Word automatically formats your table.

Once you've formatted a table with AutoFormat, you can reformat parts of the table manually using the formatting tools we've discussed in this chapter.

Table Wizard, for fast and easy tables

If you work a lot with numbers, Table Wizard is designed to set up tables made for displaying numerical data. For example, if you wanted a table that showed monthly revenue figures for a 10-person sales staff, Table Wizard can create a table with a column for each month and a row for each staff person. It'll automatically insert column headers for quarters and months, as well as format how the numbers will align in the table cells.

Table Wizard creates a table by asking you a series of questions on what elements and formats you want to include. When done, it passes you along to AutoFormat, with which you determine the table's overall appearance.

Table Wizard works only if you're starting a table from scratch. Choose Table, Insert Table from the main menu and click the Wizard button. Word displays the Table Wizard dialog box, which gives you six basic table formats to select from. Pick one, then click Next.

Subsequent dialog boxes let you choose your column and row headings. Included among your options are months, quarters, days, or years. Word then asks you if you want your table to print landscape or portrait. Finally, the wizard opens the Table AutoFormat dialog box and lets you choose a format.

12

Word Documents are Never Out of Style

Some people do anything in the name of style. Swallow goldfish, buy fancy cars—you name it. But for a stylish Word document, all it takes is a couple of mouse clicks . . . . ⊘

Styles change. Two hundred years ago, no stylish man would have been seen in public without snappy silk hose under his breeches. When English dandy Beau Brummell started wearing trousers in the early 1800s, men stopped worrying about runs in their leg wear. Trousers were a great innovation, though they didn't do much for Brummell. He wound up in debtor's prison, his fortune wasted on clothes (gambling played a part too).

Literary styles are just as changeable. But good ones, like sensible fashions, endure. Jonathan Swift's *Gulliver's Travels* reads as clearly to us as it did to his contemporaries, nearly three centuries years ago. Swift had this to say about literary style: "Proper words, in proper places, make the true definition of a style."

That still holds, though if Swift had used Word instead of a quill pen, he might have modified his definition. Word **styles** are formatting elements that you apply to text. You can assemble, name, and save your own styles, or you can use Word's built-in styles. "Proper words, in proper places, with proper formatting" is how Swift might have defined style today.

What do I need to know about styles?

Whenever you write something the old-fashioned way, with pen and paper, you're formatting a document in a particular style: your handwriting (mine is called the "illegible style").

Word does the same thing when you start typing. Any new text is formatted in the Normal style, which is why you see the word Normal in the Style box on the Formatting toolbar. The Normal style is just one of the styles that makes up the Normal template (see Chapter 2 for more on templates). Shift+click the Style box drop-down arrow to see all the other styles available in the Normal template, as shown in figure 12.1.

 Q&A *How come the list in the Styles box keeps changing?*

When you open a new document, you get a handful of common styles in the Style box list. As you add features to your document, headers and footers for example, or tables of contents, special styles for those features appear automatically in the Style box. That's why the styles you see listed in the figures in this chapter might not be displayed in the Style box in your own document window.

Additional styles appear on the list as you use the various Word features. Or Shift+click the Style box arrow to see them all.

Fig. 12.1

The styles for a template are displayed in the Style box; just click a style to apply it to the current paragraph.

Character styles are shown with the a.

Paragraph styles are indicated by paragraph marks.

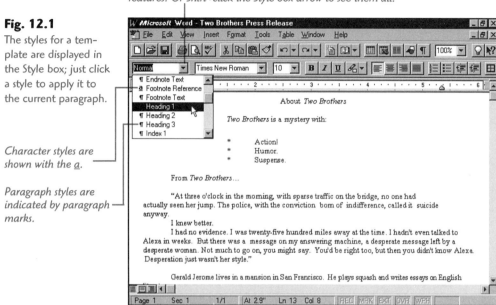

There are two basic kinds of styles (refer to fig. 12.1):

- **Paragraph styles** are applied to entire paragraphs. Position the insertion point in a paragraph, click the style, and the paragraph gets that style.

- **Character styles** are applied to selected characters. Select the characters, then click the character style to apply it. If you select characters and click a paragraph style, the whole paragraph is formatted in that style.

Why use styles in the first place?

- Styles are fast. One click applies formatting that would otherwise involve working your way through several commands and dialog boxes. And if you have several paragraphs formatted in the same style, just change the formatting in the style. That changes the formatting of all the paragraphs in that style too.

- Styles give your documents consistent formatting. If you format all your headings with the Heading 1 style shown in figure 12.1, for example, you avoid the jumbled appearance of documents with too many different formats.

- Styles are versatile. You can create your own mix of fonts and other formatting, name it, and save it as a custom style.

Plain English, please!

Formatting is everything to do with the appearance of text in a document—bold, italicized, indented, and so on. **Styles** are one or more formatting elements that are named and saved, and can then be applied to text. **Templates** are collections of styles and other formatting that you apply to an entire document.

One click, for effortless style

To use any of the paragraph styles listed in the Style box, just position the insertion point anywhere in the paragraph you want to format and click a style. Or select a style and start typing a new paragraph. The entire paragraph, from the first character at the left margin, to the hard return (automatically inserted whenever you press Enter) at the end of the last sentence in the paragraph, is instantly formatted with the font, font size, alignment, and any other formatting commands in that style.

Applying character styles is a little different. You select the words or parts of the word you want to format, then click a character style to apply it.

To apply a different style to the next paragraph, click the style and press Enter.

TIP **Fed up with mousing around in the Style box? Apply a style to a** paragraph, then select the next paragraph you want formatted in the same style. Press Ctrl+Y to apply the style to the selected paragraph. Select additional paragraphs, and every time you press Ctrl+Y, you'll apply the same style again.

Once you've applied a style to a paragraph, you can see exactly what formatting elements make up that style. Click the Help button on the Standard toolbar, and your pointer is joined by the Help question mark (see fig. 12.2). Now click the paragraph you've just styled. A box pops up with details about the character and paragraph formatting you've just applied, as shown in figure 12.2.

Click the Help button to get the question mark.

Fig. 12.2
When you want to see what a style is all about, click the Help button, then click the styled text.

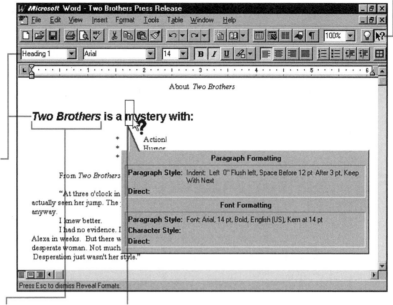

Selecting the Heading 1 style in the Style box formatted this one-line paragraph; the current paragraph's style is displayed in the Style box.

These italics were applied before the style. They were preserved, but applying styles can also remove any previous formatting.

Click any character in the styled paragraph for details on the formatting that makes up that style.

We could have used the F<u>o</u>rmat, <u>F</u>ont command to select the font face, size, and attributes of the Normal template's Heading 1 style, but using the style instead saved us a few clicks.

TIP　**If you use the Heading styles to format your section headings, you** can generate a fast table of contents based on your headings. Click <u>I</u>nsert, Inde<u>x</u> and Tables, Table of <u>C</u>ontents for the Table of Contents tab of the Index and Tables dialog box shown in figure 12.3.

Select a format for your table of contents from the Forma<u>t</u>s list, then click OK. An instant table of contents appears at the insertion point, complete with the styled headings and their page numbers.

Fig. 12.3

Heading styles let you produce an instant table of contents, formatted any way you like.

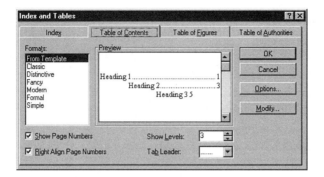

AutoFormat, for instant style

Applying a style to a paragraph is like putting up wallpaper on a wall; click the style, and the current paragraph is "papered over" with the style's formatting.

AutoFormat is more like turning an interior decorator loose on the entire room. This is an unusual interior decorator, though—if you want it to, AutoFormat will format your document as you type! That's like a decorator who follows you around the room, improving your decorating touches as you make them.

To turn on AutoFormat as you type, click Tools, Options. Click the Auto-Format tab in the Options dialog box, for the options shown in figure 12.4.

Fig. 12.4

You even get a choice of what options to display in the Options dialog box.

Click the Show Options For AutoFormat As You Type option button. Then select or deselect any feature you want, or don't want, turned on in your documents.

The Replace As You Type group of options simply replaces your typed text with AutoFormat formatting and symbols. Table 12.1 shows the changes AutoFormat As You Type makes to your typed text.

Table 12.1 AutoFormat As You Type, for on-the-fly formatting!

Type this...	Press the spacebar, and get this
1st or 2nd	1st or 2nd
1/2	$^1/_2$
(c), or (tm), or (r)	©, or ^{TM}, or ®
Quotation marks (" ")	Curly SmartQuotes (" ")

The AutoFormat As You Type feature, for automatic style

Clicking a style in the Style box on the Formatting toolbar to apply heading styles isn't much of a strain, as we've seen. Click the heading, click the style, and you're done.

With AutoFormat As You Type, you can spare yourself even that minimal effort. If you want it to, AutoFormat will supply headings, bulleted and numbered lists, and even solid borders, automatically! Click Tools, Options and click the AutoFormat tab. If all the options in the Apply As You Type group are checked (refer to fig. 12.4), here's what happens:

- For an automatic heading, type a line of text at the left margin. Don't use any punctuation, and capitalize the first letter of the line. Press Enter twice in rapid succession at the end of the line, and the Heading 1 style is automatically applied.

- To get an automatic subheading, press the Tab key or click the Increase Indent button on the Formatting toolbar. Type a line of text with an initial capital and no punctuation. Then press Enter twice in rapid succession at the end of the line. The Heading 2 style is applied automatically. For Heading 3 through Heading 9 styles, just press Tab (or click the Increase Indent button) an additional time for each heading level. For example, for Heading 3, press Tab *twice*, then type your line of text and press Enter twice at the end of the line.

Q&A   *I can't seem to get these automatic headings to work!*

Automatic headings are handy, but fussy. Your text has to begin with a capital letter, it can't have any punctuation, and automatic headings won't work on consecutive lines; you have to have a line of text in between them. If automatic headings are still giving you trouble, you might find it easier to click the heading style you want in the Style box.

- If you want automatic numbered lists, type **1.** and press the spacebar before the first list item. When you press Enter at the end of the first item, AutoFormat automatically numbers the subsequent lines 2., 3., and so on. Press Enter twice after the last item in the list to turn off automatic numbering.

- Need a solid line border? Type three hyphens (---) and press Enter. Instant border, courtesy of AutoFormat As You <u>T</u>ype.

- For automatic bulleted lists, type an asterisk (*) and press the spacebar before the first bulleted item. AutoFormat As You <u>T</u>ype converts the asterisk to a bullet when you press Enter at the end of the line, and automatically bullets the next line. Press Enter twice after the last bulleted item to turn off automatic bullets.

Figure 12.5 shows you the formatting magic AutoFormat As You <u>T</u>ype can work on a document.

Click the TipWizard button to get rid of the wiz's message.

Fig. 12.5

If your documents are peppered with headings, lists, and borders, AutoFormat As You Type will save you a few nanoseconds.

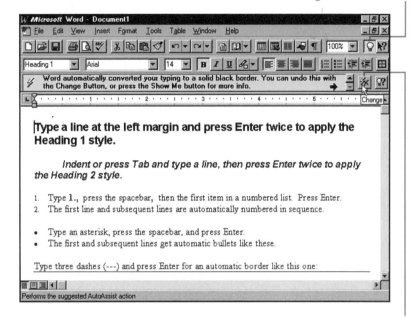

Click the Change button to undo AutoFormat's formatting.

How do I AutoFormat existing text?

AutoFormat As You Type is an amazing feature. Most users will find it pretty handy. Others (I'm neutral on this) may find it a distracting pain. If you fall into the latter category, just deselect the AutoFormat As You Type options on the AutoFormat tab of the Options dialog box.

Even those who like AutoFormat As You Type may have existing documents that haven't benefited from AutoFormat's formatting tricks. Others can take advantage of AutoFormat's convenience by applying it manually and selectively.

To AutoFormat an existing document, open the document and click the AutoFormat button on the Standard toolbar. Word analyzes every paragraph in your document. AutoFormat then automatically applies what it decides are the appropriate styles to each paragraph. Headings get the Headings styles, titles are styled as Titles, body text as Body Text, and so on.

AutoFormat performs a few other tricks, too:

- Copyright, trademark, and registration mark symbols that you've indicated with a (c), (tm), or (r) are replaced with ©, ™, and ®.

- Extra spaces and paragraph and tab marks are cleared. They can creep into documents when you inadvertently hit the spacebar, Enter or Tab keys when you don't mean to. As you continue to type, they get buried in the text, which can result in odd-looking spacing in the final draft. AutoFormat decides which of these marks are unnecessary and wipes them out. Click the Show/Hide Paragraph Marks button on the Standard toolbar to display the paragraph marks in your document.

- Numbered list numbers and homemade bullets are replaced with Word's automatic varieties. Since you've probably created those lists with the Bullets and Numbering buttons on the Formatting toolbar anyway (which produce automatic numbers and bullets), this Auto-Format feature may not be too helpful.

- AutoFormat also replaces straight quotation marks, the kind you produce from the keyboard (") with the curly opening and closing SmartQuotes (" and ").

Do I AutoFormat with the toolbar button or the menu command?

There are two ways of getting at AutoFormat for existing text. Either click the AutoFormat button on the Standard toolbar, or select Format, AutoFormat from the menu bar. What's the difference?

Click the AutoFormat button on the Standard toolbar, and you get instant AutoFormatting. No fuss, no questions asked. If you don't like the job AutoFormat does on your document, just click the Undo button.

When you're working with existing, non-AutoFormatted text, here's the handiest use for the AutoFormat button: select text like 1/2, 2nd, or (c). Click the AutoFormat button on the toolbar, and you get the more professional-looking $\frac{1}{2}$, 2nd, or ©.

Control AutoFormat changes with the menu bar command

Use the Format, AutoFormat menu command if you want to AutoFormat selectively. You get to review each change AutoFormat makes. Accept or reject the changes individually, or accept or reject them all, it's your choice.

To AutoFormat a document and exercise some control over what AutoFormat does:

1 Position the insertion point anywhere in the document and click Format, AutoFormat. That pops up the AutoFormat dialog box shown in figure 12.6.

 TIP **If you don't want to AutoFormat the whole document, select the** text you do want formatted first. AutoFormat will work its magic on only the selected text.

Fig. 12.6

The menu command for AutoFormat involves more steps than the toolbar button, but you get to be selective about your document changes.

The "Before" look: here's our heading in the Heading 1 style, but otherwise the document looks pretty plain.

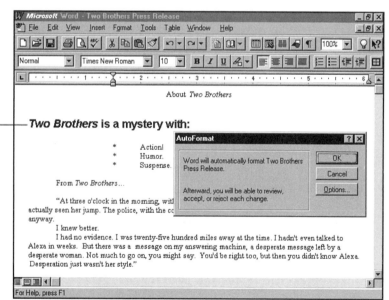

2 Click OK, and AutoFormat gives your document a makeover. When the makeover is completed, the AutoFormat dialog box pops up again, as shown in figure 12.7.

Fig. 12.7
This dialog box floats over the document; you can edit text, and the dialog box stays on the screen.

The title got the Title style. Note that this style wiped out the italics that used to be in the paragraph.

This heading kept its previous style; by default, Auto-Format leaves the document's existing styles alone.

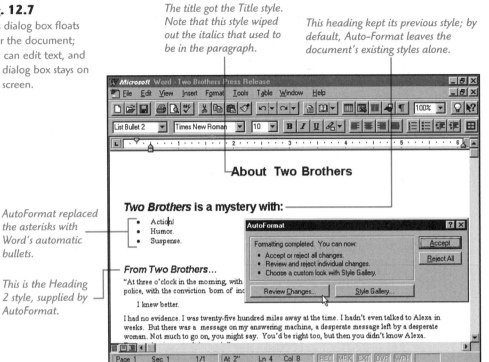

AutoFormat replaced the asterisks with Word's automatic bullets.

This is the Heading 2 style, supplied by AutoFormat.

3 If you like the look of what AutoFormat's done, click Accept in the AutoFormat dialog box. If you don't like it, click Reject All to return your document to its former appearance. Otherwise, click Review Changes for the Review AutoFormat Changes dialog box.

4 Click Find to review the first AutoFormat change. Click Reject if you don't like it, or Find again to leave it and go to the next formatting alteration. Work your way through the entire document if you want to, rejecting or finding each change. Most AutoFormat changes will be of interest only to the most punctilious (see fig. 12.8).

TIP **Using the Find button in the Review AutoFormat Changes dialog** box to search for every single AutoFormat alteration can get old fast. To speed things up, click the document to activate it. Then use the keyboard or the scroll bars to scroll through the document. Eyeball the AutoFormat changes. If you see one you don't like, select it, then click Reject in the AutoFormat dialog box.

Fig. 12.8

Some might mourn the absence of leading white space; most won't care. Just click Find to skip to the next format change.

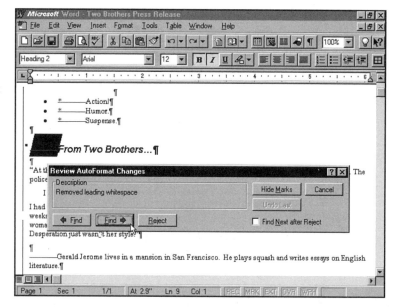

5 When you're done, click the X button in the upper-right corner of the Review AutoFormat Changes dialog box. That returns you to the Auto-Format dialog box. If you're satisfied, click Accept.

6 If you still don't like the document's appearance, click Style Gallery for some major alterations. You get the Style Gallery dialog box, with a preview of the document and a list of document templates. Click any of the templates in the Template list and view the results in the Preview window. Figure 12.9 shows the preview of a document formatted with styles from the Professional Press Release template.

7 When you preview the different template styles in the Style Gallery dialog box, the document's actual formatting doesn't change; it's more like viewing an object through different colored lenses. Sample as many as you like.

8 If find a template you want, click OK. The styles from that template are copied to the current document (the template itself doesn't change). If none of them appeal to you, just click Cancel.

9 When you're happy with the way things look, save your document to preserve the formatting changes, and you're done.

Fig. 12.9
Click any of the templates for an instant preview of a major makeover.

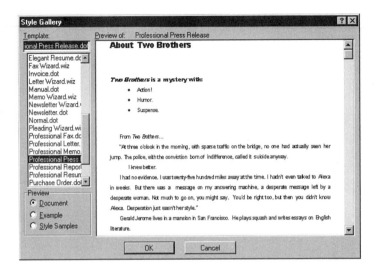

I want my own style

Each of Word's templates, including the Normal template you start out with when you first run the program, comes with its own styles. They can be modified with different fonts and font styles (like bold or italics), and with different spacing and alignments—indents, for example, or centering. Or create your own style, name it, and save it.

Modified or newly created styles are saved in the active document. If you want to use your own styles in other documents as well, just copy them to a template.

How do I change this style?

Want a Heading 2 style subheading, but hate the default font? Just modify the style with a different font. To change a style in the active document:

1 Select the paragraph formatted in the style you want to change. Make sure the style name is displayed in the Style box when you do this; if it's not, click the paragraph, then select it.

2 Make your formatting changes; use the Formatting toolbar to apply boldface or italics, center or right-align the text, or change the font.

3 Click the style name in the Style box on the Formatting toolbar and press Enter. That pops up the Reapply Style dialog box shown in figure 12.10.

I selected a different font, Book Antiqua, for the paragraph in the Heading 2 style.

Fig. 12.10

If you change your mind, select the Reapply The Formatting Of The Style To The Selection? option to restore the style's original formatting.

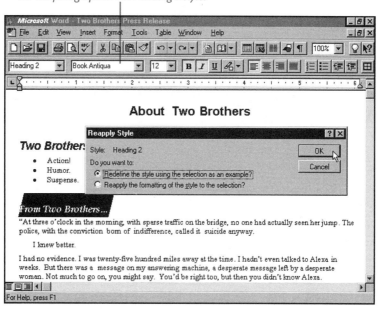

4 Select the option called Redefine The Style Using The Selection As An Example?, and click OK. That modifies the style with the changes you've made. The next time you apply that style, you'll apply the redefined version with your alterations included.

Changing the font of the Heading 2 style (refer to fig. 12.10) changed the font for all the paragraphs formatted in that style throughout the document. Figure 12.11 shows a split-screen view of the document, with another heading in the Heading 2 style. That heading got the same font change when we redefined the Heading 2 style.

Fig. 12.11
Modify a style in a document, and all the paragraphs in that style get the same modifications.

This paragraph's Heading 2 style was modified with a different font.

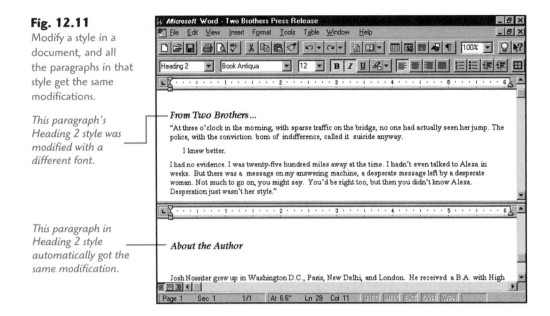

This paragraph in Heading 2 style automatically got the same modification.

You can modify character styles the same way. Just select the characters in a particular character style and make your changes. Click the style name in the Style box, press Enter, then redefine the style as we did above.

Birth of a style: creating a new style

When mere alterations aren't enough, create your own style. You might, for example, want all your document titles in the same custom style. It's easy to do; just create a style called Custom Title.

To create your own style:

1 Select a paragraph and format it. Change fonts, font size, add shading, whatever you like.

Q&A *Why doesn't this new style seem to have all the formatting I added?*

When you create a paragraph style, the formatting you use applies to the whole paragraph. You can't, for example, italicize part of a paragraph and save it as a style. You can always go back to the paragraph later and add more formatting, like italics, to particular words or phrases.

2 Click the style name of the selected paragraph in the Style box.

3 Type a new name for your style. The new text overwrites the old name. Press Enter, or click anywhere outside the Style box, and your new style is born, as shown in figure 12.12.

Fig. 12.12
You can call your style anything you want. Just don't use a backslash, curly braces, semicolons, or asterisks.

Click here to type in the new style name.

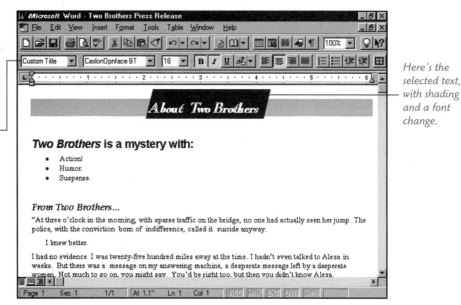

Here's the selected text, with shading and a font change.

The style whose name you eradicated to make room for the new name is unaffected by the change.

I want that new style in my other documents

You'll only want one title in a document. But you might want to reuse that title style in your other documents. Trouble is, when you open a new document, you won't see your new style. It's only saved in the active document.

If you want your style in other documents as well, copy it to the Normal template:

1 Click Format, Style for the Style dialog box, then click Organizer in the Style dialog box to pop up the Organizer dialog box.

2 Select the style you want to copy on the In [document name] list, as shown in figure 12.13.

Fig. 12.13
The list on the left shows the styles in the active document; the To Normal list displays the current template.

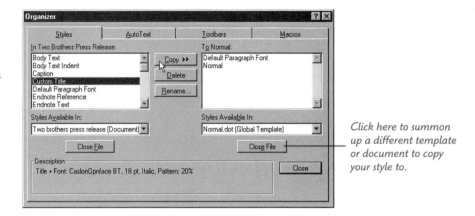

Click here to summon up a different template or document to copy your style to.

3 Click **C**opy to copy the new style to the Normal template.

With your new style copied to the Normal template, it'll be available in all your documents. If you want to copy the style to a different template, or to another document, click the **C**lose File button under the T**o** Normal list (refer to fig. 12.13).

The button turns into an Op**e**n File button. Click it again, and you get the Open dialog box. Double-click the document or template you want to copy to, then click the **C**opy button in the Organizer dialog box.

TIP **To display all the available templates in the Open dialog box, click** the Up One Level button on the Open dialog box toolbar. That displays the parent MSOffice folder in the Look **I**n box. Then click the Files Of **T**ype drop-down arrow and select Document Templates.

Part IV: Be Your Own Publisher

13

Columns, the Pillars of Sturdy Documents

● In this chapter:

- I need columns, fast!

- How do I change column widths?

- These columns are unbalanced

- Can I leave some text out of these columns?

Columns add visual variety and make dense text more readable. Word columns are so easy to work with, anyone can be a successful columnist . . . .

Columns hold things up. One ancient architectural form uses columns, or posts, to support a horizontal beam, called a lintel. Greek temples were built on the post and lintel principal; so was the Lincoln Memorial in Washington.

There's just one problem with the post and lintel design. Lintels, those horizontal beams atop the posts, tend to sag in the middle. The Egyptians pioneered one solution—they just added more posts. The Romans must have thought all those columns were too much of a good thing, so they perfected the arch (thanks to which the Capitol in Washington has a dome instead of a pitched roof).

Documents, like buildings, should be structurally sound. Long lines of text across the page can cause a reader's interest to sag. Columns prevent that by breaking up the page. And just as in architecture, too many columns on a page can be too much of a good thing. Word makes it easy to adjust column sizes and numbers. Propped up with a few columns, Word documents never sag.

Quick columns, for more readable documents

What with news on radio and TV, by computer, and even by fax, the most venerable source of news is sometimes overlooked. But a preference for newspapers doesn't make you old-fashioned. Good newspapers retain plenty of advantages over newer and glitzier media. You can pick and choose what stories to read, for one thing. You can also read as much or as little detail as you want.

By dividing text up into columns, newspapers make it easy for the eye to scan a lot of information quickly. With headlines and subheads as guides, newspaper columns turn a reader's eyes into powerful search tools. Formatting your Word documents with columns confers the same benefits on your own readers.

How do I set this text in newspaper columns?

 Newspaper columns, in which the text automatically flows from the bottom of one column to the top of the next, are easy to work with and easy to read. They're also what you get when you click the Columns button on the Standard toolbar.

Suppose we have a press release about a new mystery on our hands, and we want to format it in columns for quick readability. To set an existing document in columnar format:

 1 With your document open, click the Page Layout View button on the horizontal scroll bar. In Normal view, Word displays all your text in one column, no matter how many columns you've actually inserted. To view multiple columns, use Page Layout view.

TIP **You can also view multiple columns in Print Preview** mode—just click the Print Preview button on the Standard toolbar.

TIP **Because you can't display multiple columns in Normal view, it's** easier to write and edit your document first, and then apply columns to the finished text. You *can* write and edit in Page Layout view, but you might find Word a mite sluggish.

So how come all text isn't laid out in columns?

Just imagine the morning paper with lines of text that stretched all the way from the left margin to the right margin! Those wide pages of newsprint would be unreadable. Smaller-format publications, like tabloids and magazines, use columns to help the eye dart around the page in search of worthwhile information.

Some text doesn't work as well in columns. Henry James wrote sentences that go on for line after line. Broken up in columns, those sentences would be even harder to read. And unlike a newspaper reporter, James expected his readers to read every word in every sentence—no skimming allowed. Long sentences meant to be read from start to finish are better suited to a single, wide-column layout.

2 Click the Columns button on the Standard toolbar. That gets you a palette of four columns. Point at the first column on the left, and drag across to select the number of columns you want to use, as shown in figure 13.1.

Fig. 13.1
As you drag across the Columns button palette, you highlight each selected column.

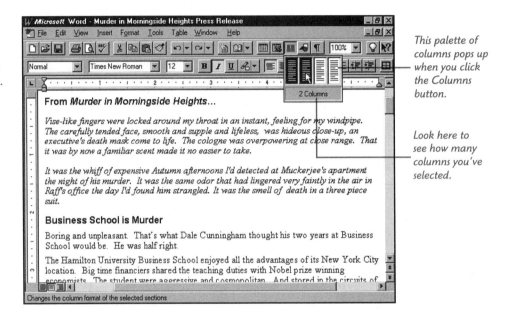

This palette of columns pops up when you click the Columns button.

Look here to see how many columns you've selected.

TIP **If you continue to drag past the fourth column, the columns** palette expands to six columns. Just remember that the more columns you use, the skinnier they get.

3 Release the mouse button, and your document is formatted in as many columns as you selected, as shown in figure 13.2.

How do I adjust these columns?

When you format text in columns, a **column marker** appears on the ruler in between each column (refer to fig. 13.2). You drag the column marker to adjust both the width of the columns and the amount of space in between each column.

Column markers appear on the
ruler in between each column.

Fig. 13.2
Formatting documents
in Word columns is a
simple click-and-drag
operation.

If indented paragraphs
don't look right in
columns, drag the
indent marker to
the left.

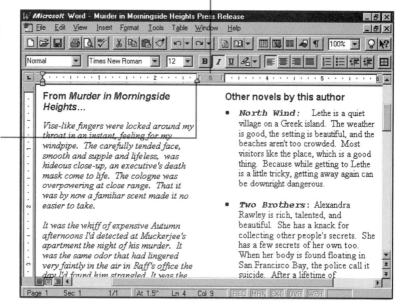

Change the column width...

To adjust column widths, point at the dimpled center of the column marker.
The pointer turns into a two-headed arrow. Now drag left or right to widen
or narrow the columns on either side of the marker, as shown in figure 13.3.

Or adjust the space in between the columns

In printer's jargon, the white space in between columns is called the **gutter**.
A little white space in between columns makes your page more readable,
but don't overdo it. As you increase the space between the columns, the
columns themselves get skinnier.

If you look closely at a column marker, you'll see two indented surfaces
on either side of the dimpled center. To adjust the space in between the
columns, point at either indented surface on the column marker. The
pointer changes into a double-headed arrow. Now drag to the left or right
to increase or decrease the space in between the columns, as shown in
figure 13.4.

Fig. 13.3

As you widen the column on one side of the marker, the column on the other side narrows.

The pointer turns into a double-headed arrow; drag to adjust column widths.

The dimpled center of the column marker

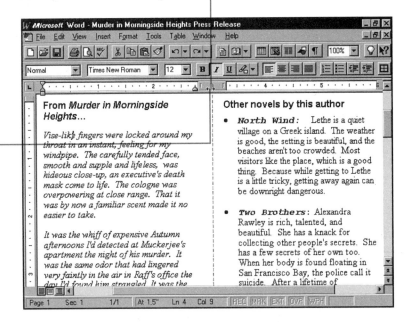

Fig. 13.4

As you drag either side of the column marker, it shrinks or grows to indicate the amount of space in between the columns.

Drag the indented sides of the column marker to increase or decrease the gutter.

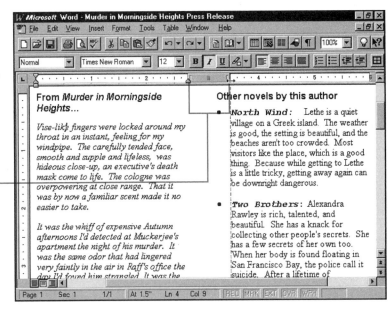

If you drag those indented sides of the column marker far enough, the marker shrinks to a gray sliver. Just drag it out again if you decide you want a wider gutter.

Precision columns are a two-button drag

Dragging column markers makes for fast column and gutter width adjustments. But what if you need exact measurements? Precision page-layout artists can set up columns and gutters to within a hundredth of an inch.

Just press both the left and right mouse buttons at the same time as you drag the column markers. The ruler displays the exact column and gutter widths, as shown in figure 13.5.

Fig. 13.5
For a tightly formatted page, where every fraction of an inch counts, two-button dragging is the way to go.

Drag the column marker's dimpled center with both mouse buttons, and note the width measurement between the columns.

Drag either indented end of the column marker with both mouse buttons, and read the gutter width here.

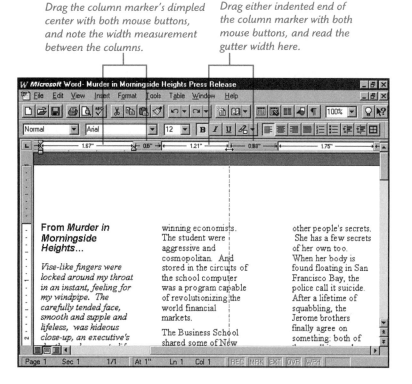

TIP **Find it awkward to drag with both mouse buttons? Press Alt as you** drag a column marker with the left mouse button. The Alt+drag combination gives you the same display as two-button dragging.

These columns are out of balance!

Here's a minor bother you're likely to run into with columns: even though your text fills an entire page, when it's formatted in columns, one column is shorter than the others. To see if your columns came out with uneven lengths, click the Print Preview button.

Figure 13.6 illustrates the problem.

Fig. 13.6

Print preview mode shows you if your columns are unbalanced.

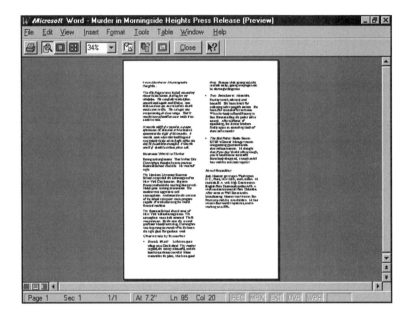

There's a fast fix. To balance your columns:

1 If you're not already in it, switch to Page Layout view so you can see what you're doing. Position the insertion point after the last of the columns you want to balance—if you have two columns, click after the period of the last sentence in the second column.

2 Click Insert, Break for the Break dialog box shown in figure 13.7.

3 Click the Continuous option button, then click OK. Your columns get adjusted to equal lengths, as shown in figure 13.8.

In figure 13.8, the second column is just about one line shorter than the first, which is pretty close, if not perfectly balanced. Unless your columns happen to have exactly the same number of lines, this minor discrepancy is unavoidable. If you want to start a new page after your balanced columns, put the insertion point at the end of the last column and click Insert, Break, Page Break, OK.

Fig. 13.7

Section breaks are used to divide the page into sections with different formatting.

Fig. 13.8

Print Preview mode shows that the columns are now balanced.

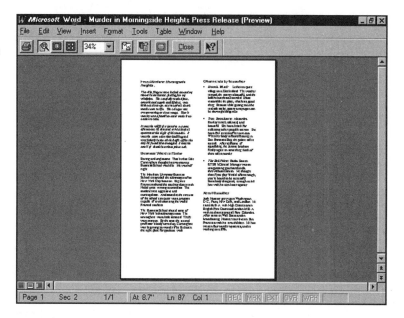

 Q&A   *Why won't my columns balance?*

You've gone through the steps to balance your columns, and they won't balance! Frustrating, but fixable. There are three possible causes:

- Paragraph formatting can prevent columns from balancing. To fix it, click Format, Paragraph, and click the Text Flow tab. Clear all the check boxes in the Pagination group of options and click OK.

- You might find that the top of the last column begins one line below the top of the column to the left of it. That means you've got a paragraph mark at the bottom of the next-to-last column. Click the

Show/Hide Paragraph Marks button on the Standard toolbar and delete the offending paragraph mark.

- If you've converted the document from another word processor or an earlier version of Word, choose Tools, Options. That gets you the Options dialog box. Click the Compatibility tab in the Options dialog box, then clear the Don't Balance Columns For Continuous Section Starts check box. Click OK when you're done.

What else can I do with columns?

Setting up your page in columns is a snap, as we've seen. But what if you want only some of the page in columnar format? Maybe you'd like to add a headline all the way across the top of the page. And while dragging the column markers can give you columns of unequal width, getting the widths just right can be a bit of a drag. There's a shortcut for doing that, and those other items are easily taken care of too.

I don't want the whole page in columns

Some text works better in lines that go from the left to the right margin than in columns. And a page that has both columns and regular text draws attention to each kind. To format only part of the page in columns, just select the text you *do* want in columnar format, click the Columns button on the toolbar, and select the number of columns you want.

If you've already set up the page in columns, then you decide to offset some of the page by formatting it as ordinary left-to-right margin text, here's how to do it:

1 Select the text you want outside the columns.

2 Click the Columns button and select one column, as shown in figure 13.9.

3 When you release the mouse button, the selected text is formatted from the left to the right page margins, as shown in figure 13.10.

If you want columns above and below right-to-left page margin text in the middle of the page, select the text and format it in one column, as we did in figure 13.10. You'll probably have some tweaking to do. Heads and subheads may not come out exactly right, or you might have to prune or add a paragraph mark or two.

Fig. 13.9

You might not have thought of it this way, but ordinary text is formatted in one wide column.

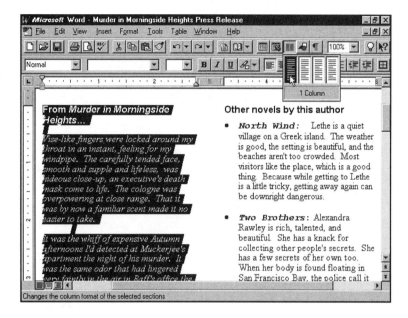

Fig. 13.10

This works best for text at the beginning of the first column or the end of the last column.

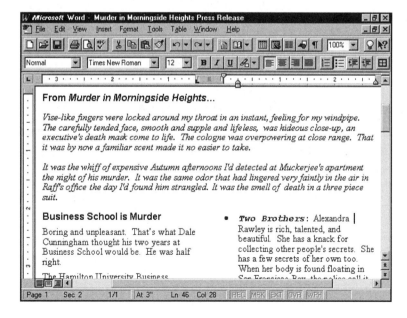

Changed your mind about pulling that text out of columnar format? Here's the fast way to snap it back into your columns: click the Show/Hide Paragraph Marks button on the Standard toolbar. You'll see the End of Section double line after the text you pulled out, as shown in figure 13.11.

Fig. 13.11
Columnar and non-columnar text is treated as different sections of a page by Word.

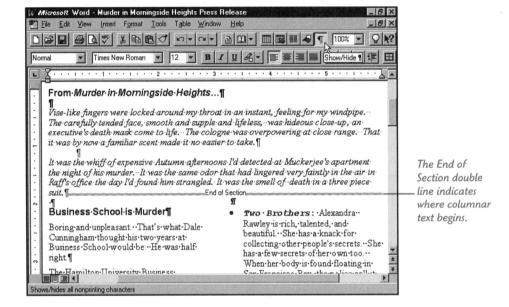

The End of Section double line indicates where columnar text begins.

Position the insertion point next to the End of Section double line and press Delete. Your text snaps back into columnar format.

How about a title for these columns?

Putting a title (also called a **banner headline**) across the top of a columnar page is something you may want to do.

If your page isn't formatted in columns yet, just select the text below the title, click the Columns button, and drag for the number of columns you want.

To add a banner headline to a page already formatted in columns, use the same technique we used to pull text out of columns (refer to figs. 13.9 and 13.10). Type your title at the top of the first column, select it, then click the Columns button and choose a single column. That yanks the selected text out of the column and strings it across the top of the page, just like the title on the front page of a newspaper.

What's the easy way to get columns of unequal width?

Columns of unequal width are a good way of offsetting different subjects in a document. You might also want columns of unequal width just for variety's sake. While dragging the column markers will do the job, getting your widths exactly right might be a chore.

Here's the fast way to get columns of unequal width:

1 With the insertion point anywhere in the document, click Format, Columns for the Columns dialog box shown in figure 13.12.

Fig. 13.12
Use the Columns dialog box to get rid of columns, too—just click One in the Presets group, then click OK.

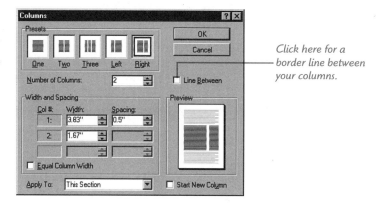

Click here for a border line between your columns.

2 Click Left for a left-hand column half the width of the right column, or click Right for a right-hand column half the width of the left column. Then click OK. Figure 13.13 shows the effect of the Right option.

I need a newsletter, fast!

Somebody has to do it—churn out the company newsletter, that is. If that somebody happens to be you, save yourself a lot of time and aggravation. Summon up the Word Newsletter Wizard and let the wiz guide you through the steps of creating a (nearly) instant newsletter.

To get the Newsletter Wizard, Click File, New for the New dialog box. Click the Publications tab and select Newsletter Wizard for a preview of your newsletter, as shown in figure 13.14.

Fig. 13.13

If your columns of unequal width create too much white space between the columns, just drag the side of the column marker.

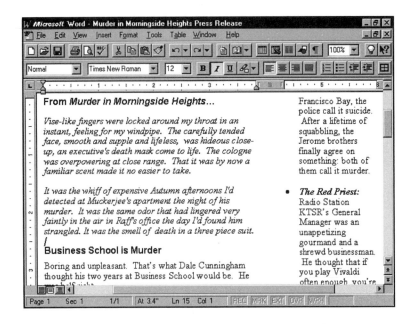

Fig. 13.14

Once you get the hang of columns, you might be tempted to wing your newsletters. Trust me on this: the Wizard is faster.

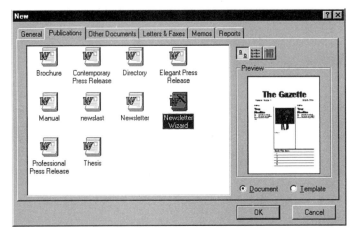

Double-click the Newsletter Wizard icon to pop up the Wizard. Answer the Wizard's questions, give your newsletter a title, and you'll wind up with the formatted shell of a newsletter. Add your own text and graphics, and you'll be done in plenty of time to find somebody else to do the chore before the next issue.

14

Borders, Colors, and Typographical Tweaks

● **In this chapter:**

- **What should I know about borders?**

- **How do I jazz up my document with borders?**

- **Shading and colors, for snazzy effects!**

- **White space isn't flashy, just readable**

- **How come this big title looks odd?**

From the bold and brash to the quiet and refined, Word has formatting tricks to enhance all kinds of documents. . . . . ➤

To a writer, a blank page is an open invitation. The young P.G. Wodehouse, then a clerk at a London bank, was handed a new ledger with a dazzling white first page. The temptation was too great; Wodehouse whipped out his pen and started scribbling. In short order he'd filled the page with a delightful story. Rightly thinking that the bank manager wouldn't feel as he did about his literary effort, Wodehouse cut the page right out of the ledger.

That was the beginning of the end of Wodehouse's banking career. Since he went on to write dozens of novels that sold (and still sell) millions of copies, it was probably the smartest thing he ever did.

For a reader, a page has to have something on it to be inviting. If the writer can catch the reader's eye, odds are the page will be read. One obvious way to grab that first glance is with a page made attractive with borders, colors, and shading. A more subtle approach spaces lines and words so perfectly that the eye can't resist reading them. Word makes it easy to take either approach. Word's special effects won't put you on a best-seller list, but they might draw a little attention to that report you've just written.

All about borders

Borders are lines and boxes that you put around a paragraph. They can be solid lines, double-lines, broken lines—you name it. Borders go above, below, or to the right or left of a paragraph. You can also put a border all the way around a paragraph, or between two paragraphs.

Use borders to:

- Separate columns, or headings and body text.
- Highlight important passages in a document.
- Add a little visual variety to titles and headings.
- Format tables in attractive and readable ways.
- Create interesting frames around graphic objects.

 The Borders toolbar puts a palette of borders at your fingertips. To get the Borders toolbar, click the Borders button on the Formatting toolbar. Figure 14.1 shows the Borders toolbar.

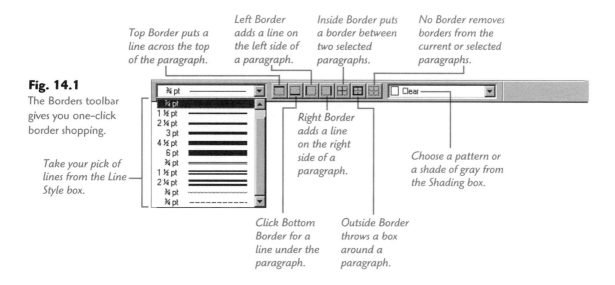

Top Border puts a line across the top of the paragraph.

Left Border adds a line on the left side of a paragraph.

Inside Border puts a border between two selected paragraphs.

No Border removes borders from the current or selected paragraphs.

Fig. 14.1
The Borders toolbar gives you one-click border shopping.

Take your pick of lines from the Line Style box.

Right Border adds a line on the right side of a paragraph.

Choose a pattern or a shade of gray from the Shading box.

Click Bottom Border for a line under the paragraph.

Outside Border throws a box around a paragraph.

To apply any border (except for the Inside Border—see below on how to do that), just click a paragraph, click a button on the Borders toolbar, and you're done.

To get rid of the border again, click the No Border button.

Borders rule!

Printers and page designers also call borders **rules**. Before modern machinery came along to do the job, traditional printing used metal type. The type was arranged by hand in lines to make words and sentences, and held together in a frame (called a form) to make a page. To separate columns of type, or headings and body text, the printer inserted a thin slip of brass into the form. When inked and pressed against a sheet of paper, the metal type left impressions of letters, and the brass slips created straight lines. Those brass slips were called rules, or composing rules; hence rule, as in straight line. Incidentally, printers kept their metal type in cases, one below the other. The upper case held (no prizes here) the capital letters.

How do I add a border?

Adding, formatting, and clearing borders is so easy that you might want to take an experimental approach. Try one, get rid of it, then try another. Keep at it until you achieve exactly the look you want.

For example, here's how to apply an inside border between two paragraphs:

1 Click the Borders button on the Formatting toolbar to pop up the Borders toolbar.

2 Select two adjacent paragraphs and click the Inside Border button on the Borders toolbar. The resulting inside border is shown in figure 14.2.

Then click the Inside Border button to apply an inside border between them.

The Borders button stays "pushed-in" until you click it again to get rid of the Borders toolbar.

Fig. 14.2
Inside borders work well for two-paragraph headings.

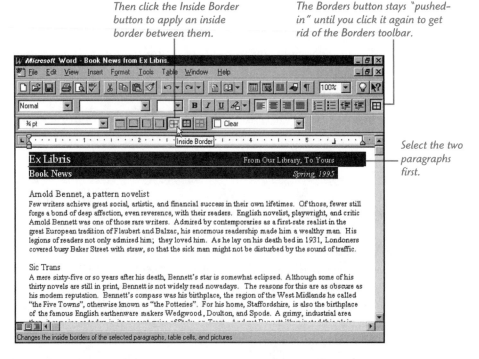

Select the two paragraphs first.

3 The default line style gets you a line 3/4 of a point thick. For a thicker line, click the Line Style drop-down arrow and take your pick. There are double lines, dotted, and dashed lines too, as shown in figure 14.3.

Fig. 14.3

We'll try a 2 1/4-point line for this inside border.

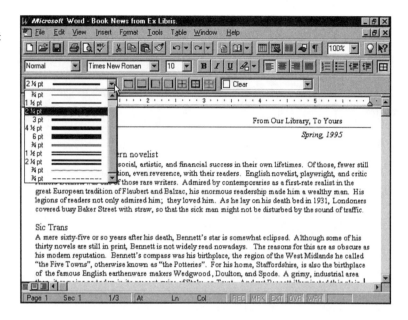

4 To apply a different line style to an existing inside border, select the paragraphs, then select the new line style. Click the Inside Border button again to apply your chosen line style.

Q&A *Why can't I see my inside border?*

If you try to apply an inside border to a single paragraph, you won't see it. But if you then press Enter to split the paragraph in two, or to begin a new paragraph, the inside border appears. Inside borders are only visible in between paragraphs.

What's the difference between a border line and an underline?

One thing about borders you'll notice right away: they're applied to the entire paragraph. Lines and boxes extend all the way from the left paragraph indent to the right indent. If you want to underline only part of a paragraph, select the text and click the Underline button on the Formatting toolbar. Figure 14.4 shows the difference between selected underlined text and a border applied to an entire paragraph.

Fig. 14.4

If you were curious about the difference between borders and underlining, here's the answer: borders are applied to the whole paragraph.

This text was selected, then underlined.

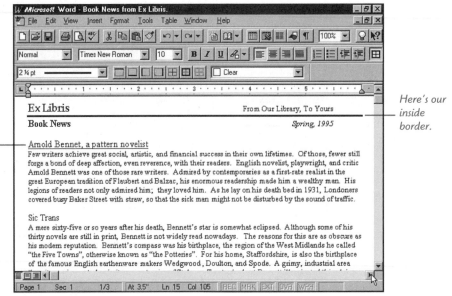

Here's our inside border.

I don't want a border all the way across the page

Suppose you have a paragraph that extends only part way across the page. You want a border under it, but you don't want a border that extends beyond your text. You could use the Underline button on the Formatting toolbar, except that it gives you the choice of a single thin line under your text, period. Some choice.

 TIP **You *can* change the underline style from the Font dialog box.** Select the text you want underlined, then choose F̲ormat, F̲ont. Click the Fo̲nt tab in the Font dialog box that pops up, and choose an underline style from the U̲nderline drop-down menu. Click OK when you're done.

For more variety, apply a border with your choice of line styles to the paragraph, then adjust the right indent marker to trim the border to fit your text. Figure 14.5 shows you how to do that.

When you release the mouse button, you'll see that the border extends only to the right indent marker, as shown in figure 14.6.

Drag the right indent marker to the left to fit the border to the text.

Fig. 14.5

Cutting a border down to size is a simple drag operation.

Click the paragraph, then click the border style or styles you want.

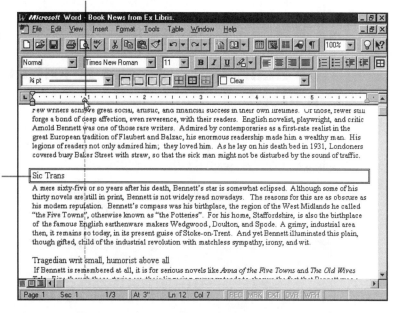

Fig. 14.6

Dragging the right indent marker keeps your borders from extending too far.

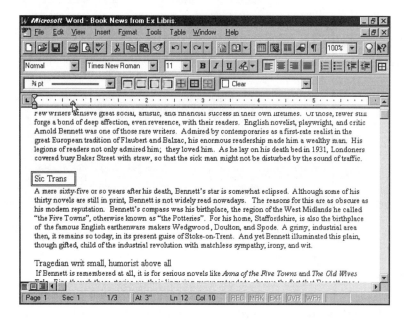

If you apply a right border to a short paragraph, the border will look very lonely sitting by itself at the right margin. Just drag the right indent marker to position the border next to the paragraph's text. See figure 14.7 for a right border dragged alongside a paragraph.

Too many borders can result in a border incident

Although you have to select paragraphs to apply inside borders, you needn't bother when you apply the other border styles. Just click a paragraph and click a border style on the Borders toolbar.

It's so effortless that you might be tempted to overdo it. As you can see in figure 14.7, too many borders can spoil the document.

Fig. 14.7
Click a paragraph, click a border style. What could be easier? But this is a little too much of a good thing.

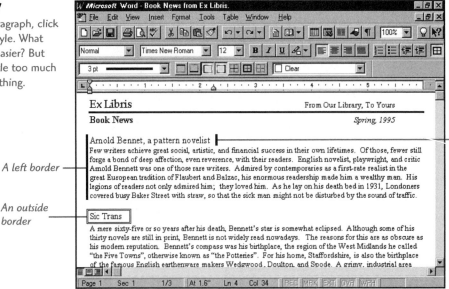

A left border

An outside border

A right border, positioned next to the short paragraph by dragging the right indent marker.

 If your document starts to look like the one in figure 14.7, select the paragraphs with borders and click the No Border button on the Borders toolbar. That instantly erases unwanted borders.

Q&A *How do I break out of this box?*

When you add a border and press Enter at the end of the paragraph to start a new one, the border also extends to the new paragraph. Right, left, and outside borders expand, and bottom borders get shoved down one line. To avoid that, start the new paragraph first, then apply the border to the previous paragraph. If you've already applied a border and you want a new, borderless paragraph, click the No Border button to clear the border, start the new paragraph, then reapply the border to the previous paragraph.

Not-so-dark shadows

Here's a dramatic way to emphasize a paragraph; cast a shadow around it. To get a shadow effect, click the paragraph you want to format, then select Format, Borders and Shading, Borders.

In the Paragraph Borders and Shading dialog box that appears, click Shadow. If you want your paragraph to cast a wider shadow, choose a thicker line style from the Style list, as shown in figure 14.8.

Fig. 14.8
Use the From Text edit box to adjust the distance between the text and the border, measured in points.

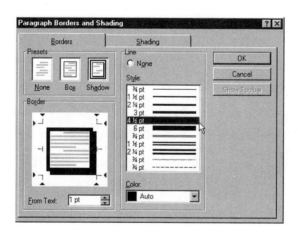

Figure 14.9 shows a paragraph with a shadow border.

Fig. 14.9
Shadows create a nifty effect, but I find that a little shadow goes a long way.

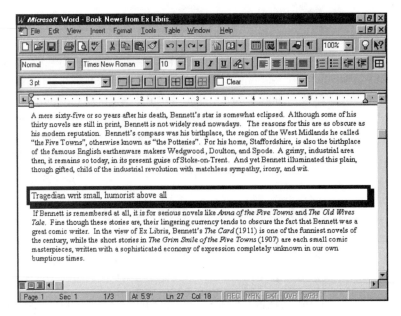

Shading and color make paragraphs jump off the page

Color printers are pretty common nowadays. If you have one, or if your e-mail system can handle colors, Word makes it easy to splash color on your borders. Click Format, Borders and Shading for the Paragraph Borders and Shading dialog box (refer to fig. 14.8). Choose the Borders tab, then click the Color drop-down arrow for a choice of border colors. Click the Shading tab and the Foreground and Background drop-down arrows to choose colors for the paragraph itself.

Even if you don't have a color printer, a combination of shading and a border makes a paragraph stand out:

1 If you don't have the Borders toolbar displayed already, click the Borders button on the Formatting toolbar, then click the paragraph you want to format.

2 Click the Shading drop-down arrow on the Borders toolbar. That gets you choices ranging from clear to solid black, with various shades of gray in between.

3 Select the shading percentage you want. Shading is applied by filling the background of the paragraph with little dots. The percentages refer to how densely the dots are packed. The higher the percentage, the darker the shading.

4 Click the Line Style drop-down list and choose a thicker line, then add Top and Bottom borders. You'll wind up with a paragraph that looks like figure 14.10.

Fig. 14.10

It's fun to experiment with attention-getting effects, but writers always like to think that their words speak for themselves.

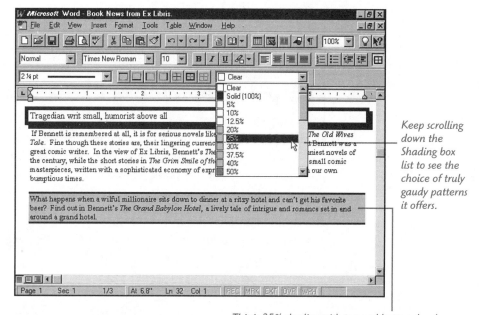

Keep scrolling down the Shading box list to see the choice of truly gaudy patterns it offers.

This is 25% shading with top and bottom borders.

If you select 80% or more shading and your font color is set to Auto (click Format, Font to check the font color in the Font dialog box), Word automatically switches the font color to white. White text on a dark background makes for a startling effect, but the text might be difficult to read. Try formatting the text in boldface to improve readability.

Q&A *My text looks white on the screen, but it prints as black. Can't I print white text against a shaded background?*

You can. Some printers just need a little help first.

1 Click Eile, Print. In the Print dialog box, click Properties for the Properties dialog box.

2 Click the Font tab in the Properties dialog box, and select the Print True Type As Graphics option.

3 Click OK in each dialog box, and your document should print with white text against a shaded background.

This paragraph looks like a sidebar

The shaded paragraph in figure 14.11 stands out from the rest of the document, in part due to its formatting, but also because the content isn't part of the narrative flow. Passages like that are called **sidebars**, and you see them scattered throughout this book. They're handy for presenting relevant, but ancillary, information.

The Borders toolbar can whip up a quick sidebar (refer to fig. 14.10), but if you want a sidebar you can easily move around the page, and around which you can wrap text, try a Word Frame.

To create a sidebar in a frame:

1 Click Insert, Erame. If you're not in Page Layout view, Word either switches you automatically, or asks if you want to be switched. If the latter, click Yes. You want Page Layout view because although you can see graphics in Normal view, you can't see the frame around the graphic.

2 The pointer turns into a cross-hair. Position the cross-hair at the upper left of where you want your sidebar, and drag to the lower right corner. When you release the mouse button, the frame pops up with the insertion point inside it.

3 Type your text inside the frame. All the lines automatically wrap at the frame's right margin. Use the Font button on the Formatting toolbar to change fonts and font sizes.

4 If you need to make the frame bigger or smaller, click anywhere around the frame's border to pop up the frame handles. Drag a handle to expand or shrink the box, as shown in figure 14.11.

Fig. 14.11
To add or edit the text, just click inside the frame to make the insertion point reappear.

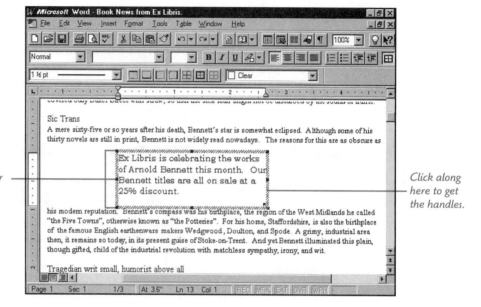

Drag any handle to make the box bigger or smaller.

Click along here to get the handles.

5 Use the Borders toolbar to add and format borders and shading. Sidebars like the ones in this book are often formatted with a top border, or with top and bottom borders. Take your pick from the Borders toolbar.

6 If you want your document body text to wrap around the sidebar, click the frame, then click Format, Frame for the Frame dialog box shown in figure 14.12.

Fig. 14.12
The Frame dialog box offers plenty of options; the one you're most likely to use is Text Wrapping.

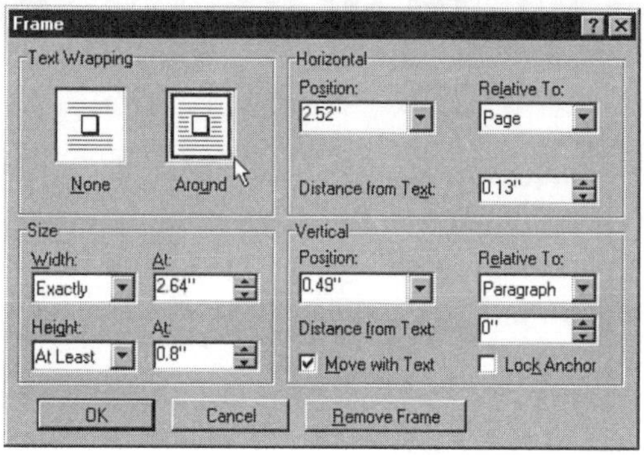

7 Click Around under Text Wrapping, then click OK to close the dialog box. Now you can drag your sidebar anywhere in the document, and your text will wrap neatly around it.

Click anywhere outside the frame to get rid of the frame handles and that fuzzy frame border. To move the sidebar around the document, point at an edge; your pointer is joined by a four-headed arrow. Now drag the frame anywhere you want to.

When you're through typing, formatting, and dragging, you'll wind up with something that looks like figure 14.13.

Fig. 14.13
Sidebars are easy to create, and they're handy for squeezing in extra information.

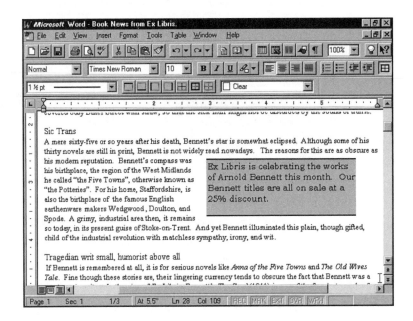

Less is more: use white space for readable documents

Word provides many ways to jazz up documents. Borders, shading, graphics—they're all great gadgets. But at the end of the day, you want a document that's a pleasure to read. After you've experimented with Word's fancy effects, you might find that adding a little white space gives you a more readable document.

The default right, left, top, and bottom margins that Word provides are probably fine for most uses. But if you want more white space around your document, just drag the margin boundaries at either end of the rulers.

 TIP **If margin exactitude is required, double-click the margin** boundaries to pop up the Margins dialog box. That lets you set your margins within hundredths of an inch.

Adding more white space within the text of the document is like drawing open a window shade; you let in a little light. Here are two quick things you can do to add more white space:

- Add a blank line after all your paragraphs, including headings and subheadings. Press Enter at the end of the last line in the paragraph.

- Increase **line spacing** (the blank space between the lines) from a single line to 1.5 lines. Select the paragraphs in which you want more white space, then click Format, Paragraph, Indents and Spacing for the Indents and Spacing dialog box. Click the Line Spacing drop-down arrow and select 1.5 Lines.

 TIP **If you set line spacing at 1.5 lines at the beginning of a new** document, you don't have to bother selecting the paragraphs first. If you've already written the document and you want line spacing of 1.5 lines for the whole thing, click Edit, Select All, then change the spacing.

Figure 14.14 gives you an idea of how these two simple tricks can make your documents easier to read.

Need a typesetter? It's you!

Many good page-design artists and typesetters feel that the best-designed page is one in which the design elements are invisible. Not that they don't want the reader to read what's on the page. The idea is to make a readable page in which the reader is unaware of all the hard work that went into making it so.

Theirs is a specialized craft, with all the trappings of specialties—arcane jargon and painstaking technique. Word puts some of those techniques in the hands of the non-specialist. Once you get a handle on the jargon, using the features is a snap.

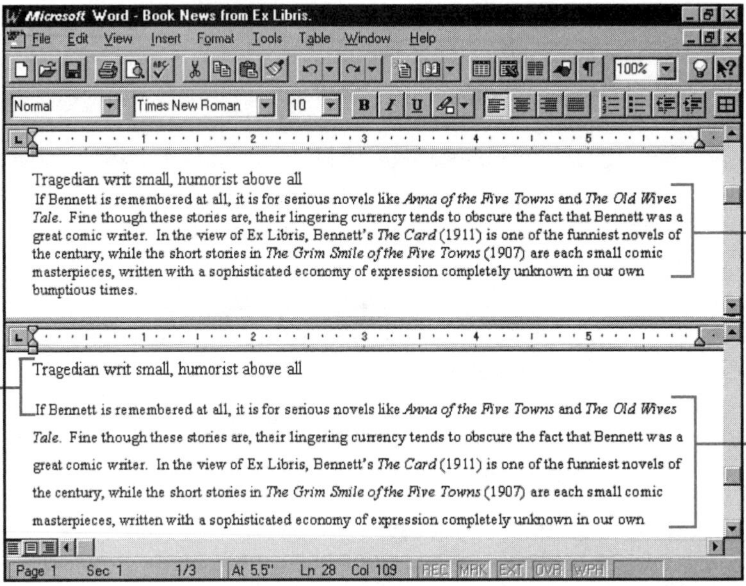

Fig. 14.14
A split-screen view
of the same two
paragraphs.

*These lines are
single spaced.*

*Adding a blank line
after a heading opens
up the page.*

These lines are spaced 1.5 lines apart.

Look closely, and you kern see extra spacing

No, that's not a typo up there. **Kerning** is the typesetter's trick of adjusting the spacing between letter pairs to compensate for the different shapes of letters. Computers don't necessarily do that, which can result in extra space between certain letters. It's especially noticeable in large font sizes, as you can see in figure 14.15.

 Plain English, please!

Kerns are the projecting parts of letters like J, in which the curved part on the bottom sticks out. Typesetters working with metal type have to make sure that there's enough space between two such projecting bits, hence **kerning**. Lacking the finesse of human typesetters, computerized fonts don't always distinguish between letters that require extra space and those that don't. AV can nestle close; tj needs more room. Depending on the computer font, no distinction is made between the letter pairs, which is why you get the extra space.

Fig. 14.15

Certain letter pairs in different fonts are prone to kerning problems.

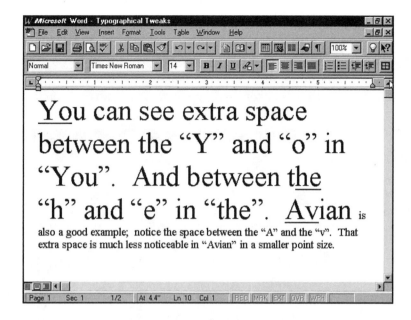

If you're working with large font sizes, in a title for example, and these spacing problems bug you, Word gives you two ways to fix the problem.

Automatic kerning works with proportionally spaced TrueType fonts such as Times New Roman. If that's what you've got, try automatic kerning first:

1 Select the characters whose spacing you want to adjust.

2 Click Format, Font, Character Spacing for the Character Spacing dialog box.

3 Click the Kerning For Fonts check box and click OK.

If you're starting a new document and you plan to work with large font sizes, click the Kerning For Fonts check box before you begin typing. Set a value for Points And Above that includes the font size you're using, and you'll avoid kerning woes altogether.

Character spacing, for the typographical perfectionist

Automatic kerning doesn't work for all fonts, and the adjustment it makes is very slight. If you'd prefer to take matters into your own hands, use the Spacing option under the Character Spacing tab to force the issue.

Select the characters whose spacing you want to adjust and click F**o**rmat, **F**ont, Cha**r**acter Spacing for the Character Spacing tab of the Font dialog box. Click the **S**pacing drop-down arrow and select Condensed. Now click the down arrow in the **B**y edit box to bring the selected letters closer together one tenth of a point at a time, as shown in figure 14.16.

Fig. 14.16

The Preview window shows your letter pair drawing closer together as you increase the value in the By edit box.

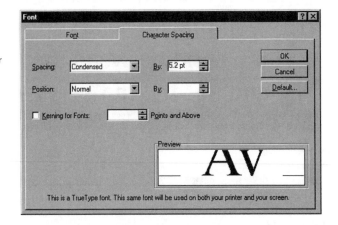

A famous American typographer named Frederic W. Goudy once said, "Anyone who would letterspace black letter characters would steal sheep." Letterspacing is what Word calls character spacing. Black letter fonts are the kind used in *The New York Times* logo, often called Gothic (to the irritation of the typographically correct).

Whatever Goudy meant by that remark, you don't need to learn a lot of arcana to use Word's typographical tweaking features. If you want to letterspace/character space black letter/Gothic characters, go right ahead. Goudy never got a chance to use Word, and he's past caring anyway; he died 50 years ago.

15

Picture This! Documents with Graphics

In this chapter:

- **Where do I find Word's artwork?**

- **How do I insert this image in my document?**

- **I need to move and resize a picture**

- **Can I wrap text around a graphic?**

- **How do I put text inside a picture?**

- **I want a picture from another program in my document**

A pick-me-up for dull documents, pictures can spice up even lively text. And if words, not pictures, are your bag, it's no problem. Word puts artwork within reach of non-artists . ▷

Where art is concerned, everyone's a critic. Take Michelangelo's *David*. It's probably the most famous statue in the world; people travel to Florence just for a glimpse of it. *David* inspires a hush in even the loudest tourist, but that's not always been the case.

When Michelangelo first unveiled his statue, one early critic looked up and shook his head. "The nose—too big," said the art expert. Since this particular expert happened to be the head of the Florentine Republic, Michelangelo grabbed his chisel, climbed to the top of his masterpiece, and started tapping away. He tapped hard enough to make a noise, but not so hard as to alter his creation. At the same time, he dropped a little marble dust from his hand. The critic looked up at the unaltered nose, nodded, and said, "Now you've got it right!"

Artwork you stick in a Word document probably won't inspire any reverential hushes. On the other hand, if any important critics (the boss, for example) object to your work, Word makes it easy to do alterations. And you can silence even the toughest critic with a simple dodge that Michelangelo couldn't have dreamed of: just click the graphic, press Delete, and insert something else.

Where is Word's artwork, and how do I view it?

You don't have to be a great artist to insert pictures in a Word document. In fact, you don't have to be an artist at all. Word comes with a gallery of **clip art** images—small pictures and decorations that you can put right in your documents. Use clip art for logos, posters, or simply to jazz up a report.

When you installed Word, you also installed a folder packed with clip art images called—no surprises here—Clipart.

For a quick preview of Word's clip art collection, click Insert, Picture. That pops up the Insert Picture dialog box, with a list of Word's clip art files. Click the Preview button in the Insert Picture dialog box and select any of the files on the list, as shown in figure 15.1.

Click the Preview button for a thumbnail preview of the selected file.

Fig. 15.1
The Insert Picture command automatically tracks down graphics files and lists them in the dialog box.

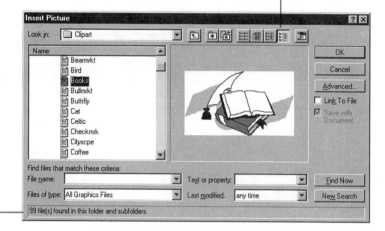

If Find doesn't find your clip art images, it'll tell you so here.

TIP **If your clip art images wound up in a folder other than the** WinWord/Clipart folder, the Insert Picture dialog box might come up with a 0 file(s) found message. Click Advanced in the Insert Picture dialog box and make sure the Search Subfolders box is checked. Then click the Find Now button. If you still can't find your clip art, try this: click the Up One Level button on the Insert Picture dialog box toolbar. Click it again if you have to. It might take a little while, but Find will search your entire disk for graphics images and display their file names in the Name list.

Scroll down the Name list of graphics files and select each one in turn for a preview. If you see an image you like, double-click the file name. That pops the image right into your document at the insertion point.

What do I do with this image?

You can pop a clip art image into an existing document, or into a new file. Either way, it's easy to move and resize the inserted image.

To insert a clip art image into a document, resize it and move it into position:

1 Position the insertion point where you want your image to appear (you don't have to be precise about location, because you can move the graphic around later) and select Insert, Picture.

2 That gets you the Insert Picture dialog box (refer to fig. 15.1). Double-click any of the image file names in the Name list to stick the image into your document, as shown in figure 15.2.

Fig. 15.2

Clip art images imported via the Insert Picture dialog box are inserted at, well, the insertion point.

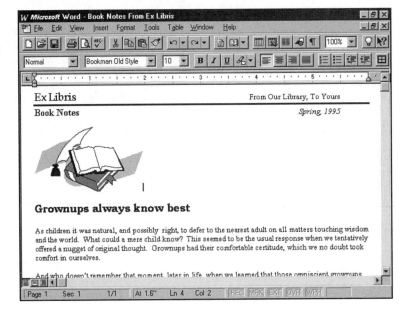

3 Just like text inserted into a document, inserted images push existing text aside to make room. If you find that your document's spacing and alignment are out of whack after you insert a picture, resize and move it. Click the image once to pop up the object **handles** (those black squares around the image).

4 Point at any of the handles and the pointer turns into a double-headed arrow. Now drag to resize the image, as shown in figure 15.3.

5 To move the image, click it to pop up the handles, then point at the image and drag. The pointer is joined by a little rectangular frame, as shown in figure 15.4.

6 Release the mouse button, and the inserted, resized image pops into the new location.

Fig. 15.3
Click a clip art image once to pop up the moving and resizing handles.

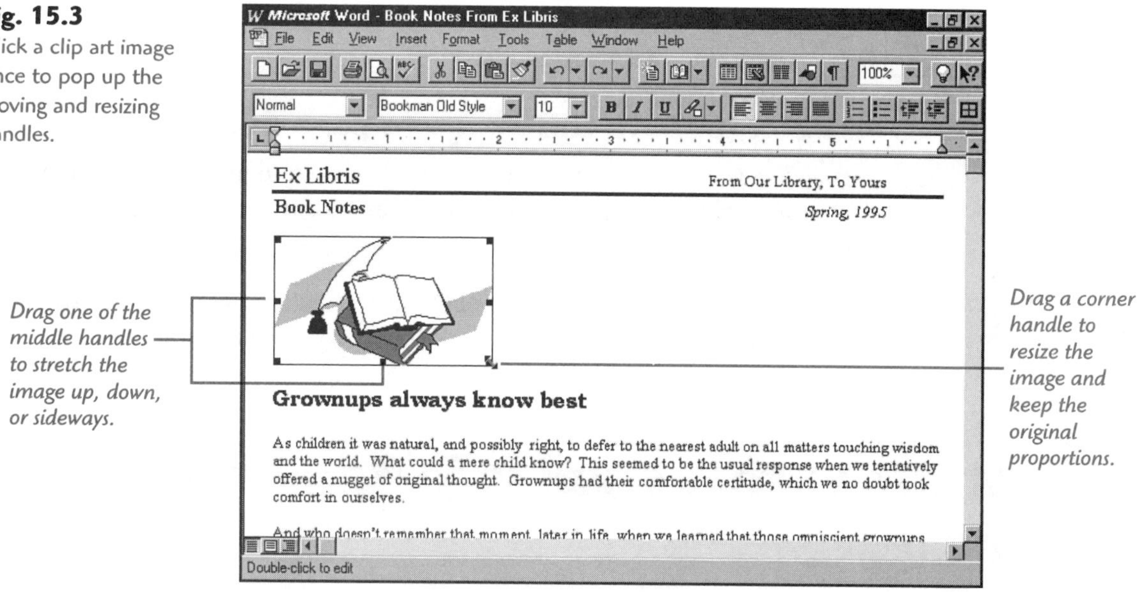

Drag one of the middle handles to stretch the image up, down, or sideways.

Drag a corner handle to resize the image and keep the original proportions.

Look closely as you drag; you'll see an outline of the insertion point, showing you where the image will be moved.

Fig. 15.4
The image won't actually move to the new location until you release the mouse button.

The pointer is joined by this outline of a frame.

Point anywhere at the image and drag to move it.

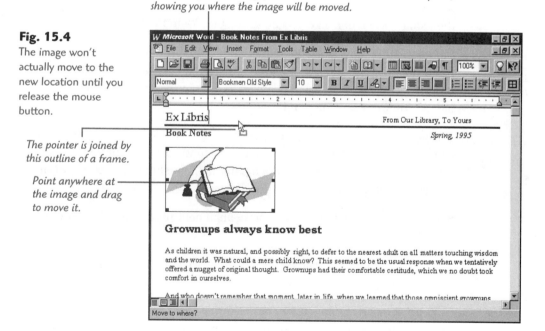

After all this, you might decide against inserting that graphic after all. To get rid of it fast, click the image once to pop up the handles. Then press Delete to instantly excise it from the document.

Really indecisive? Click the Undo button on the Standard toolbar to get just-deleted graphics back again.

I need to move this image to page 50!

Dragging is a convenient way to move things around in a Word document, but for long-distance moves, use the Cut and Paste buttons on the Standard toolbar.

Click the image to select it, then click the Cut button. Move the insertion point to the new location, click the Paste button, and the graphic pops into place.

Want to put that graphic in its place? Frame it

You *can* nail an unframed picture to the wall, but you probably wouldn't. Hanging the picture exactly where you want it would be a chore. And taking it down and moving it someplace else would be a nuisance (to say nothing of the damage the nail is likely to do to the picture in the first place).

Pictures "hung" in a Word document aren't too different. Put them in a frame, and they're easier to position and move. And frames in Word have one big advantage over the kind given as gifts by aesthetically challenged in-laws; they're easily hidden from view.

If your inserted graphic is giving you spacing and alignment trouble, a frame can help: Word frames let you wrap text around a graphic. In figure 15.5, a graphic was inserted at the end of a paragraph, pushing the last line of the paragraph out of whack.

Sticking the graphic in a frame will fix alignment problems fast. To put an inserted graphic in a frame:

1 Click the graphic. The handles pop up to let you know it's been selected.

2 Click Insert, Frame. If you're in Normal view, a dialog box pops up with the message Do you want to switch to page layout view now? Click Yes. You can only see frames in Page Layout view.

Fig. 15.5
Inserting graphics images in body text can do odd things to text alignment.

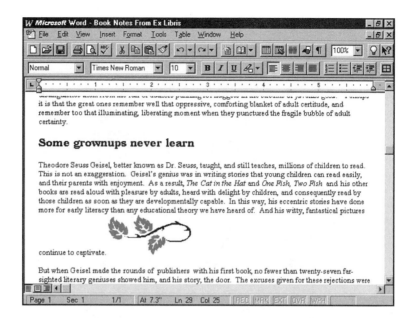

3 The frame, shown as a cross-hatched border around the graphic, appears. Now right-click the graphic to pop up the shortcut menu shown in figure 15.6.

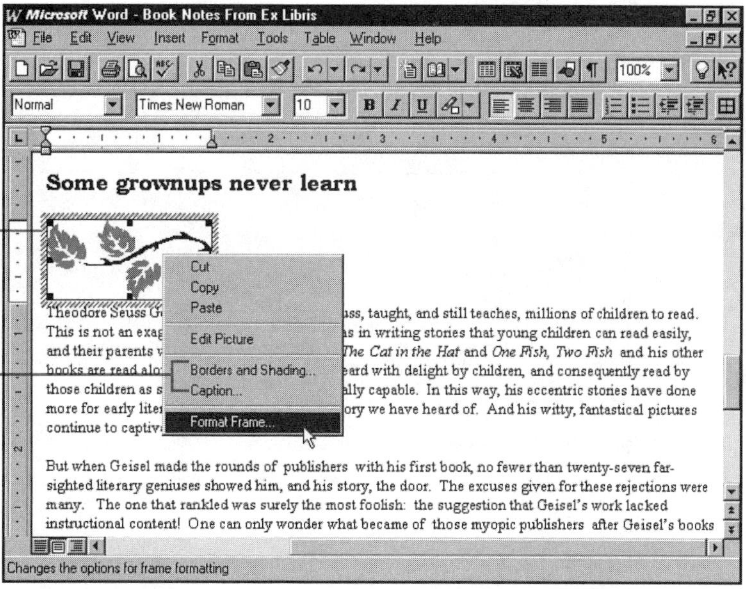

Fig. 15.6
Right-click the graphic itself for this shortcut menu; if you right-click the frame border, you get a different menu.

The cross-hatched border indicates the frame.

Add borders, shading, or a caption; just select from the menu.

4 Choose Format Frame from the shortcut menu for the Frame dialog box. Click the Around option under Text Wrapping in the Frame dialog box.

5 Now click the Horizontal Position drop-down arrow in the Frame dialog box and select Left, as shown in figure 15.7.

Fig. 15.7

You can also drag framed graphics into position, but the Position options in the Frame dialog box align graphics with precision.

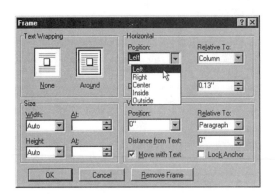

6 Click OK in the Frame dialog box. The graphic snaps into place along the left margin, with the paragraph's body text neatly wrapped around it, as shown in figure 15.8.

Fig. 15.8

Text alignment problem solved, thanks to a formatted frame.

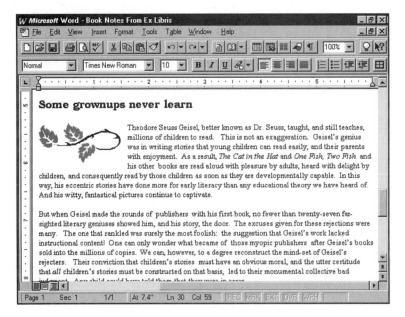

Click anywhere outside the graphic to get rid of the cross-hatched frame border and handles. If you return to Normal view, the text wrapping around the frame won't be displayed, although the formatting itself is unaffected. To see exactly how your text and graphics will appear on the page, do your editing in Page Layout view.

How do I edit this graphic?

The graphic artists responsible for creating the images in Word's clip art library spent a lot of time putting those pictures together. In seconds, you can disassemble, rearrange, color, and completely redo their good work. Why would you want to do that?

- You might want a red bull, not the stock black one.

- Maybe you'd like to pluck one element out of a clip art image and discard the rest of the picture.

- If the graphic you insert lies along the horizontal plane, it's easy to rotate it to the vertical for a margin decoration.

- Even non-artists can add their own lines and shading to customize clip art images.

To edit any inserted clip art image, double-click it. Double-clicking a graphic pops up Word's built-in drawing program, Microsoft Word Picture. You switch automatically to Page Layout view, and the Drawing toolbar appears at the bottom of the editing window, as shown in figure 15.9.

Pull apart the old picture to get a new one

The graphic in figure 15.9 is actually composed of many different objects. Each of those objects can be resized, moved, deleted, or copied. Click anything in the picture; one of the books, for example, or the quill pen. Handles pop up around the selected object, and you can do whatever you want to it.

Figure 15.10 shows the image disassembled, with its component objects dragged outside the picture boundary.

Click Close Picture when you're finished editing.

Fig. 15.9

The surrounding document disappears from view. It's still there, just hidden.

Adding, moving, or deleting objects can change the picture's size; click Reset Picture Boundary to fit the boundary to the changes.

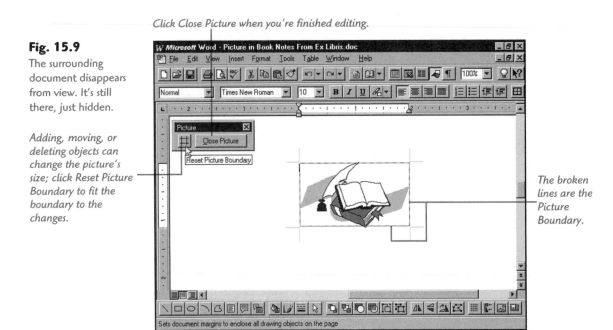

The broken lines are the Picture Boundary.

Click an object to select it; the handles pop up.

Use the toolbar buttons to cut, copy, and paste.

Fig. 15.10

This should appeal to the kid in anyone—pulling clip art apart is like tearing up an old coloring book.

Drag an object out of the picture boundary, and it'll be left out of the picture.

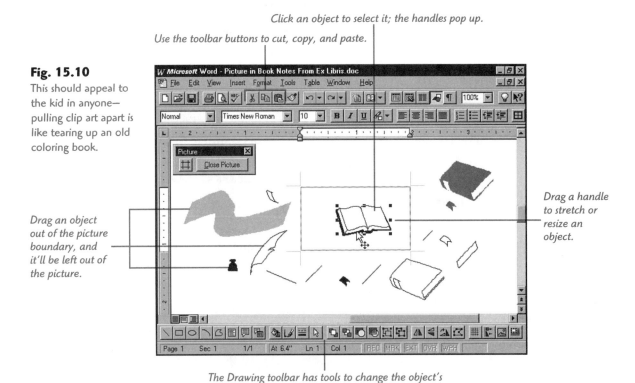

Drag a handle to stretch or resize an object.

The Drawing toolbar has tools to change the object's fill color, orientation, and other attributes.

TIP **To select filled objects, like the inkwell in figure 15.10, just click** anywhere in the object. Select unfilled objects, like the feather, by clicking anywhere along their exterior lines.

Any object left outside the picture boundary will be left out of the picture itself when you return to the document. That's handy if you're not sure whether you want to keep one element of the image or not. Instead of deleting it right off the bat (press Delete to do that), just drag it outside the boundary and leave it until you make up your mind.

I want this image behind my text

Once disassembled, use the bits and pieces of a clip art image any way you like. One handy use: putting an image behind your text. You might want to create a **logo**, for example, with a company name on top of a picture. You might also want a **watermark**, a light image behind your text. With a Word text box and a clip art image, you can do both.

To put text inside a picture:

1 Click Insert, Picture for the Insert Picture dialog box, and double-click the clip art file you want to use.

2 Double-click the image itself. That pops up Microsoft Word Picture, the built-in drawing program (refer to figs. 15.9 and 15.10).

3 Use the whole picture, or delete (or drag out of the picture boundary) the objects in the image that you don't want.

 TIP   **If you're extracting several objects from a clip art** image, click the first object, then Shift+click each additional object. With several objects selected at the same time, click the Group button on the Drawing toolbar. That groups the objects together in one unit, which makes it easier to move and resize the whole thing. To break the grouped objects up again, click the group to select it, then click the Ungroup button on the Drawing toolbar.

4 Click the Text Box button on the Drawing toolbar. The pointer turns into a cross-hair. Position the cross-hair at the upper-left corner of where you want the text in the graphic, and drag down to the lower-right corner. That puts a text box right inside the picture.

5 You might want to change the text box fill to match the fill color of the object under it. To do that, right-click the text box border for the shortcut menu and select Format Drawing Object, as shown in figure 15.11.

Fig. 15.11
Choose the same fill color for the graphic and the text box, and the marriage of the two will look seamless.

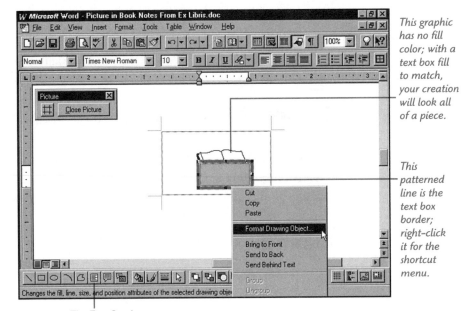

This graphic has no fill color; with a text box fill to match, your creation will look all of a piece.

This patterned line is the text box border; right-click it for the shortcut menu.

The Text Box button

6 In the Drawing Object dialog box that pops up, select None under Color, as shown in figure 15.12.

Fig. 15.12
You can also change the graphic's fill color to match the text box fill.

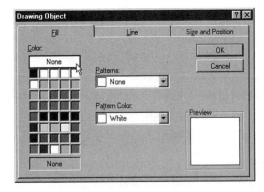

7 Click OK in the Drawing Object dialog box. The insertion point is inside the text box; type your text, and use the Formatting toolbar to change fonts and attributes.

Q&A *I don't see the insertion point inside the text box!*

It's there, but it may be hidden within the text box border. Press the spacebar or Tab key to bring it out in the open. Or click the text box border and drag a handle to expand the box. A bigger box might be easier to work with, and it also exposes the insertion point to view.

8 When you're finished typing and formatting the text and editing the graphic, click <u>C</u>lose Picture to return to your document. You'll wind up with something that looks like figure 15.13.

Fig. 15.13
Instant logos like this can be created with a clip art image and a text box.

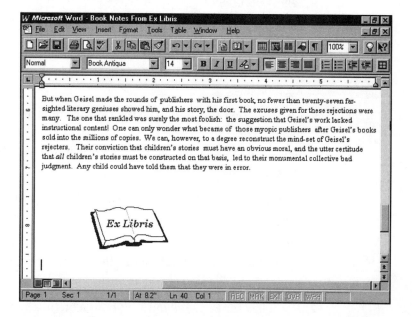

I already have text, and I want a picture behind it

When you hold a sheet of good-quality paper up to the light, you'll see a design stamped into the paper. That's a watermark. Put text on the sheet of paper, and the design will show, faintly, behind the text. You can create a similar effect in Word.

To make a watermark:

1 Click <u>I</u>nsert, <u>P</u>icture and double-click the image you want to insert in your document.

2 For the text to be legible with the picture behind it, you'll probably have to lighten the image. Double-click the inserted image to pop up Microsoft Word Picture.

3 Shift+click each object inside the picture to select them all, then click the Group button on the Drawing toolbar.

4 Right-click the grouped image, and select Format Drawing Object.

5 Under <u>C</u>olor in the Drawing Object dialog box, select a light or medium-light shade of gray and click OK.

6 Click <u>C</u>lose Picture to return to the document.

7 Back in the document, click the image to select it, then click the Cut button on the Standard toolbar.

8 Click the Drawing button on the Standard toolbar to pop up the Drawing toolbar.

9 Click the Text Box button on the Drawing toolbar. Position the cross-hair, and drag to create a text box right over your text. If the box is filled in with a shade of gray, click F<u>o</u>rmat, Drawing <u>O</u>bject for the Drawing Object dialog box.

10 In the Drawing Object dialog box, select None under <u>C</u>olor and click OK (refer to fig. 15.12).

11 Click the Paste button on the Standard toolbar to paste the picture *inside* the text box. You'll notice that the text behind the picture is hidden from view.

12 Now click the Send Behind Text button on the Drawing toolbar to put the picture behind the text, and you're done.

Figure 15.14 shows the finished watermark.

Pink elephants? It wasn't necessarily that last martini...

Once you know your way around the Drawing toolbar, you'll find it easy to modify clip art images to suit yourself. For example, Word's clip art library includes a brooding, faintly menacing elephant. But what if you prefer your elephants in dignified striped trousers, wearing a thoughtful pair of spectacles?

Fig. 15.14

It takes a few steps to do it, but it is possible to create a watermark in Word.

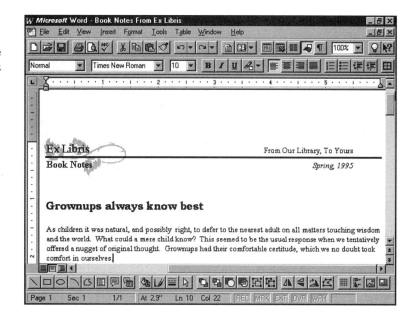

Nothing could be simpler. To customize a clip art image:

1 Select a graphic from the Insert Picture dialog box and double-click it to pop up Microsoft Word Picture.

2 Remember that each clip art image is made up of several discrete objects. Right-click an object inside the picture boundary to select it and pop up the shortcut menu. In figure 15.15, I right-clicked the elephant's legs.

3 Select Format Drawing Object from the shortcut menu. That pops up the Drawing Object dialog box. Change the Color, Pattern, and Pattern Color of the selected object, as shown in figure 15.15.

4 Select and edit other objects within the picture in the same way.

5 Now use the Drawing toolbar to create your own objects. You'll find it easier to draw your objects outside the picture boundary. To draw the pair of spectacles shown in figure 15.16, I used the Line Style button to draw a heavier line, the Line tool to draw a straight line, and the Ellipse tool to draw the lenses.

TIP To draw a circle with the Ellipse tool, click the tool, then Shift+drag the cross-hair.

Fig. 15.15
Not sure if you've selected the object you wanted? Check the Preview window in the Drawing Object dialog box.

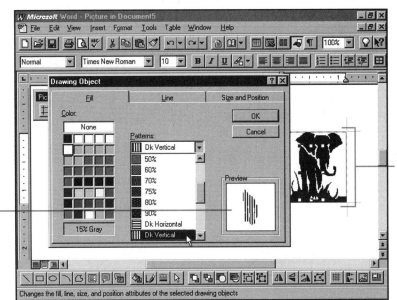

The selected object is shown in the Preview window.

This is the selected object inside the picture boundary.

Fig. 15.16
Professional graphic artists have little to fear, but you can create serviceable artwork with Word's drawing tools.

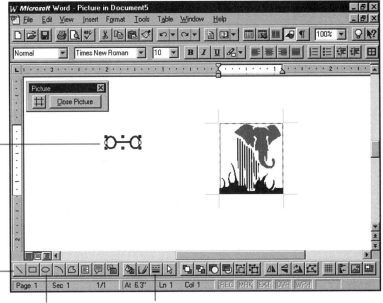

It's easier to do your drawing outside the picture boundary.

The Line tool lets you draw straight lines; just click it and drag the cross-hair.

Click the Ellipse tool and Shift+drag to draw a circle.

Click the Line Style button for a heavier line.

6 Once you've created your drawing, Shift+click each of the different objects in the drawing to select them all, then click the Group button on the Drawing toolbar.

7 Now drag the grouped object into position on the graphic, and click Close Picture to pop the image into your document. The result is shown in figure 15.17.

Fig. 15.17
Babar's long-lost older brother?

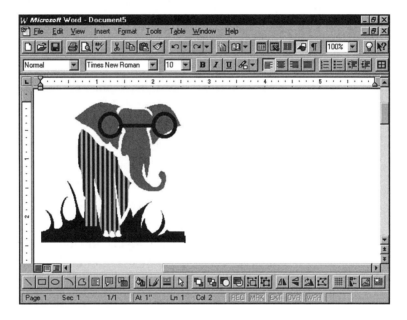

How do I insert graphics from other programs?

Handy though it is, Word's clip art collection is limited. Chances are, you'll have other programs lurking on your hard drive with more extensive image collections.

If you want to stick an image from another program into a Word document, you have a few choices for how to go about it. The simplest way of getting artwork from another program into Word:

1 Select the object in the other program.

2 Click the Copy button in that program to copy the object to the Windows Clipboard.

3 Switch to Word, and click Edit, Paste Special.

4 In the Paste Special dialog box, choose Paste, As Picture, then click OK.

The object pops into Word, and you can frame it, edit it with Microsoft Word Picture, move it, or resize it, just as you'd do with Word's own clip art images.

You can also click the Paste button on the Word toolbar to pop a copied image into Word. Or use the Insert, Picture command to select a graphics file from a different program. Those choices introduce a few more complications:

- If the program you copied the graphic from supports OLE, Object Linking and Embedding (it probably does), pasting with the Paste button inserts the graphic as an embedded object. That takes more memory. And if you double-click the object to edit it, you'll run the original program with all *its* editing tools to do so. That takes even more memory, which might lead to the odd crash.

- The Insert, Picture command converts a graphic from another program into Word's graphics format. That will work fine most of the time, but, depending on the graphic's original format, you might run into a hiccup or two in the conversion process. Editing the converted graphic may be a snap; it could also prove problematic. You really won't know until you try it.

CAUTION **Always save your Word document before you import graphics from** another program. Most likely, all will go well; in the event that it doesn't, you won't lose your work.

Part V: Organizational Tools

16

Hate Outlines?
Outline View May
Change Your Mind

● In this chapter:

- ● **Do I really need an outline?**

- ● **OK, how do I create an outline from scratch?**

- ● **Collapse? Expand? Explain!**

- ● **I need to convert this outline to a document**

- ● **How do I squeeze an outline out of this document?**

- ● **Outline looks terrible? Fix it fast**

Although outlining is the best way to organize a document, writing an outline has always been more of a chore than a pleasure. Word makes the procedure painless and quick . . ❯

When most of us sit down to write an outline, we have in mind a sketch of the final draft, the bare-bones of a document, to be fleshed out whenever we can get around to it.

H.G. Wells wasn't most of us. The author of *The Time Machine, The Invisible Man,* and *The War of the Worlds* also wrote *The Outline of History,* nothing less than a popular account of the human species. No mere sketch, Wells envisioned his *Outline* as a kind of blueprint for a future world state. Three-quarters of a million words later, Wells' completed *Outline* was a huge success. No world state materialized, but *The Outline of History* helped make its author a rich man.

Although Wells wrote with pen and ink, he'd have enjoyed using Word's outlining tools. A Word outline is a convenient way to organize documents of all kinds, even if they don't run to hundreds of thousands of words. Outlines let you display or hide as much or as little detail as you like. They clarify your thinking as you write, and help to tighten your document when you're finished. Outlines are also easy to use, whether you're writing a humble report, or trying to sort out human history.

Why bother with an outline in the first place?

Outlines are like dental checkups—we know they're important, we know they're good for us, but we don't have anything to do with them unless we have to. If somebody hands you a writing assignment, you probably want to plunge right in. If deadlines are tight (aren't they always?), who wants to take the extra time to prepare an outline? It's just an extra step, taking time that might as well be spent writing the actual document.

Here's some good news: outlines in Word don't require an extra step at all. With Word, the outline *is* the document. And just like that visit to the dentist you've been shirking for the last six months, an outline can spare you a lot of future pain.

Take a look at the following page, "Anatomy of a Word Outline," to see what outlines are all about.

Anatomy of a Word outline

Think of a Word outline as a document arranged in a hierarchy of topics and subtopics. Each topic is formatted in a different heading style, according to its importance in the context of the document. A topic in the Heading 1 style is more important than a topic in the Heading 2 style, and so on. You decide on the importance of your topics and subtopics, and Word applies the heading styles automatically.

The Heading 1 style is applied to your main topics.

The little square indicates body text.

These are subtopics in the Heading 4, 5, 6, and 7 styles.

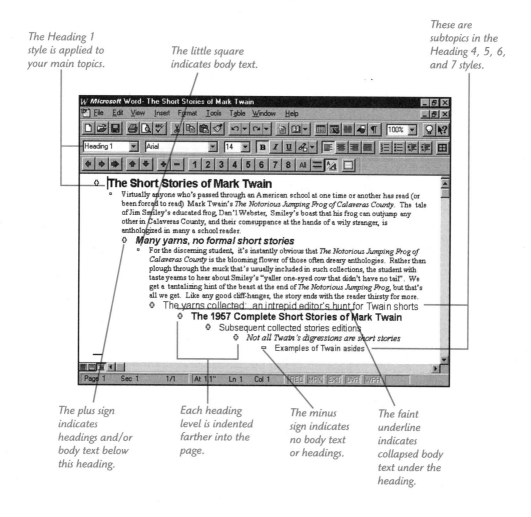

The plus sign indicates headings and/or body text below this heading.

Each heading level is indented farther into the page.

The minus sign indicates no body text or headings.

The faint underline indicates collapsed body text under the heading.

So why should you use an outline? Here are some advantages:

- Outlines force you to break your document down into topics, with headings and subheadings describing each topic. Outline headings are easily moved, promoted, and demoted. That helps you organize your material and present it in a coherent way.

- Word outlines are very flexible. You can convert a heading into body text, or body text into a heading, with a click of the mouse.

- It's easy to get lost in a tangle of words, even in a simple memo. Outlines let you see your way clearly, by hiding or displaying as much cluttering detail as you care to deal with. Shove your body text out of sight, and your topics jump right off the page. That makes it a lot easier to see the big picture of your document.

Create an outline from scratch...

Word makes it a snap to create a new outline. And if you've written a report and the boss says "Send me an outline," don't groan. It's just as easy to convert an existing document into outline form, with no retyping needed.

To create an outline:

1 Click the Outline View button down at the lower left corner of the Word window. The Outline toolbar pops up, the Styles box displays the Heading 1 style, and a fat minus sign appears in the left margin.

2 Type your first heading and press Enter at the end of the line. That'll be your first main topic, but you're not committed; if you decide to make it a subtopic later, it's easy to change things around.

3 Now type the first subtopic heading. It also gets the Heading 1 style, just like the first heading. Since you want it to be a subtopic, click the heading, then click the Demote button on the Outline toolbar. That makes it a Heading 2 style heading. Figure 16.1 shows the outline so far.

4 Press Enter to go to the next line and type your next heading. It also takes the heading style of the previous heading; if it's a lower-level topic, click Demote again to make it a Heading 3 style heading.

5 Type the rest of your topic headings. Click the Promote or Demote button and press Enter after each one. When you're done, you'll have a hierarchy of topic headings organized from level 1 on down. An outline, in other words, as shown in figure 16.2.

Close-Up: the Outline toolbar

 To get to the Outline toolbar, click the Outline View button at the bottom of the Word screen.

Promote
Changes a heading to a higher level.

Show Headings
Click any of these numbered buttons to display only that heading level and the levels above it.

Demote
Changes a heading to a lower level.

Demote to Body Text
Converts headings to body text.

All
Displays all the headings and body text in the outline

Move Up
Moves a selected heading up one line.

Show First Line Only
Toggles a display of either the first line of each paragraph of body text or all the text.

Move Down
Moves a selected heading down one line.

Show Formatting
Toggles the display of heading styles.

Expand
Displays all the items under a selected heading.

Master Document View
Pops up a toolbar to control the collapsing and expanding of large documents.

Collapse
Hides the lowest-level item displayed under a selected heading.

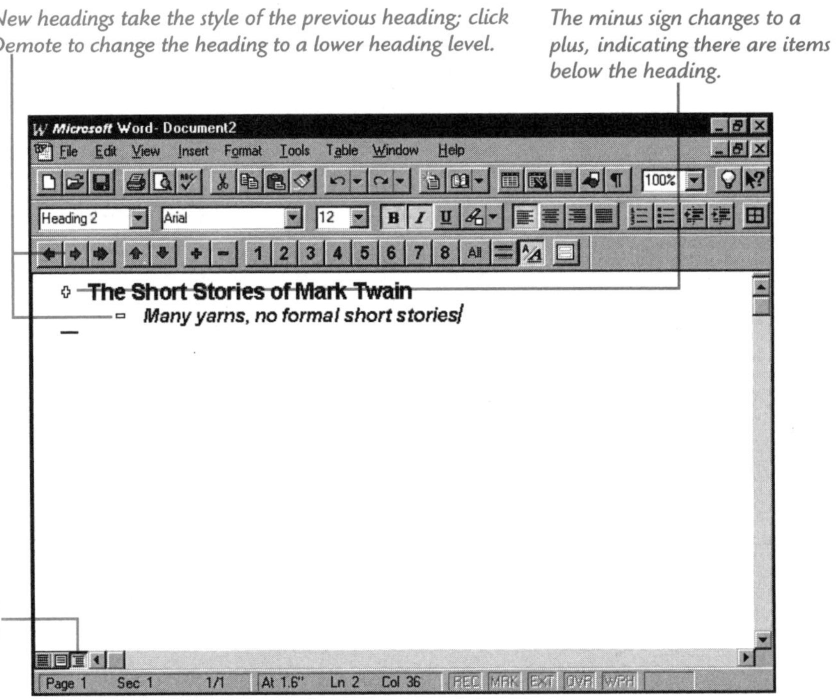

New headings take the style of the previous heading; click
Demote to change the heading to a lower heading level.

The minus sign changes to a
plus, indicating there are items
below the heading.

Fig. 16.1

As you build your
outline, you promote
or demote headings
depending on their
relative importance.

The Outline
View button

Fig. 16.2

If you change your
mind about the
importance of any of
the headings, click the
heading, then click the
Promote or Demote
button.

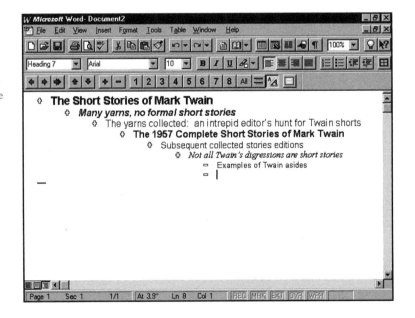

Want to promote a level 4 heading to level 2? Just click the heading and click the Promote button twice. To demote it back to level 4, click the Demote button twice.

I need to reorder these topics

Outlines show you the structure of the document, without the confusing detail of the document itself. That makes it easier to reorganize your work. An outline, like the girders supporting an office building, is the skeleton of the finished document. And just as in an office building, it's much easier to move a girder or two around *before* all the plumbing, wiring, and walls are added.

 To move a heading up or down within the outline, just click the heading, then click the Move Up or Move Down button on the Outline toolbar.

Figure 16.3 shows a Heading 4 level topic moved up one line above a Heading 3 level topic.

Fig. 16.3

When you move outline items up or down, they swap places with the items above or below them.

You don't have to select a heading to move it up or down; just click it. It's automatically selected when you click the Move Up or Move Down button.

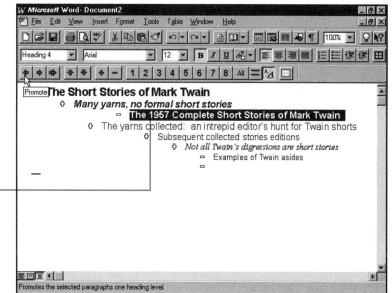

Once you move the outline item, you can promote or demote it, and promote or demote the item whose place it took, to restore the outline's order.

CAUTION **Don't click the plus sign next to a heading to select it for a move.** When you do that, not only that heading but *all* the headings and the text under the headings are selected. Move the heading, and everything under it moves too (unless that's what you want to do, of course).

Where are my outline heading numbers?

You'll notice something about Word outlines right away: they don't have that progression of numbers and letters we were all taught to use. Those I's, A's, 1's and so forth were always a pain to keep straight (mine would usually get hopelessly out of sequence), but Word makes it easy to keep them in order.

Word not only lets you add those numbering schemes to your outlines, it lets you choose a scheme that suits you. Once you've finished typing your headings, click Format, Heading Numbering, for the Heading Numbering dialog box shown in figure 16.4.

Select any of the outline numbering schemes.

Fig. 16.4

Instant outline numbers and letters that are always in sequence make outlines painless.

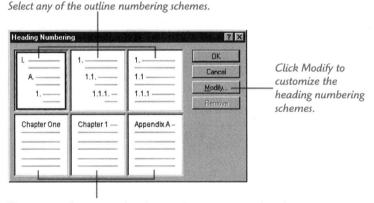

Click Modify to customize the heading numbering schemes.

These options format your headings as chapter or appendix titles.

Select any of the three outline numbering formats in the Heading Numbering dialog box and click OK. The selected numbering scheme is applied to the outline. Each heading level gets the correctly sequenced number or letter, as shown in figure 16.5.

To get rid of heading numbers, which you'll want to do if you convert your outline headings to document headings, click Format, Heading Numbering for the Heading Numbering dialog box. Select Remove, then click OK.

Fig. 16.5
Word automatically assigns numbers and letters in the order of the heading levels.

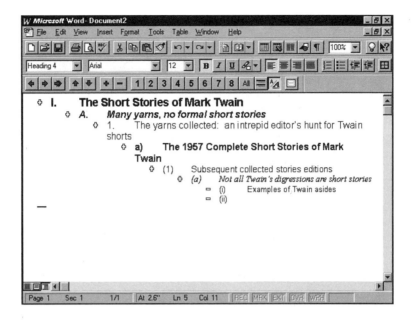

What happens if I move numbered headings around?

If you decide to move your outline headings up or down after you've numbered them, you'll see that the heading number style is linked to the heading level. For example, if your level 7 heading is numbered (i), it'll retain that numbering level even if you move it up or down in the outline.

The heading is automatically renumbered to keep the heading numbers in sequence. So if you move a heading numbered (i) below another heading numbered (i), Word renumbers the heading you moved to (ii).

TIP It'll probably be less confusing to remove the heading numbers before you start shuffling headings around. Make your moves, then reapply the numbers when you're done.

Surprise! Your outline is also your document

You need a formatted, numbered outline, something like the one in figure 16.5? Typing, promoting and demoting, then ordering and numbering headings is all you need to do. But maybe you're responsible for the document as well as the outline. If you've finished your outline headings, you've also finished your document headings.

Those outline headings *are* document headings. Just add body text, and the document is done. To add body text to your outline headings:

1 If you've numbered your headings, click Format, Heading Numbering, Remove, OK to get rid of the numbers. They can be applied again if you need to.

2 Click the Normal View button to switch to Normal view.

3 Position the insertion point at the end of a heading, press Enter to start a new line, and type your text. Use any paragraph formatting you like— tabs, indents, borders, whatever. Treat your former outline just like an ordinary document (it is an ordinary document).

4 Body text finished? Save the document and go home.

Figure 16.6 shows our existing outline headings, stripped of heading numbers, in Normal view and with body text added.

Fig. 16.6

Suddenly our outline looks like a regular document. Just click the Normal View button to switch out of Outline view.

Paragraph formatting you add in Normal view, like indents or tabs, isn't displayed in Outline view. But it isn't removed, only hidden.

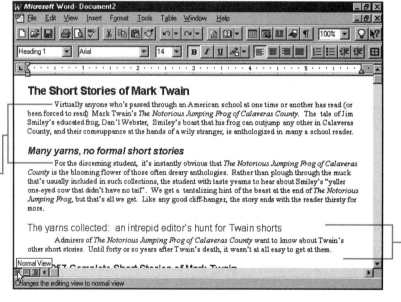

Position the insertion point after a heading in Normal view, press Enter, and type your body text.

Q&A *Why can't I just add body text in Outline view?*

You can. It's just easier to type body text in Normal view because you can see your paragraph formatting.

Use outline tools to tighten the final document

Outline view is handy for launching a writing project, as we've seen. Once you've got the document written, Outline view is just as useful for polishing the structure of the document.

Use the outline collapse and expand tools to see more or less document detail, and you'll have more control over the document's organization. Suppose you've written your body text, and now you'd like to display only your document headings again.

To hide body text and display only headings in Outline view:

1 Click the Outline View button to switch to Outline view.

2 Click a heading with body text under it. Don't select the heading; just put the insertion point anywhere within the heading.

 3 Click the Collapse button on the Outline toolbar. All the body text under that heading and the headings below it is hidden, as shown in figure 16.7.

  To redisplay the body text you've just hidden, click the Expand or All button on the Outline toolbar.

I don't want to see these headings

When you put the insertion point in a heading and click Collapse, you hide the body text below the heading, as we just did. But maybe you want to hide both the body text *and* the headings below a particular heading level.

There are two quick ways of hiding both headings and body text:

 • To display only a particular heading level and the levels above it, click one of the numbered buttons on the Outline toolbar. For example, to see only level 3 headings and above, click the Show Heading 3 button on the Outline toolbar.

- An even faster way is to position the pointer over the plus sign next to that level 3 heading, and it turns into a four-headed arrow. Now double-click; all the headings and body text below the level 3 heading are hidden, as shown in figure 16.8.

Fig. 16.7
When the trees of your document are hidden by a forest of text, put the text out of sight with the Collapse button.

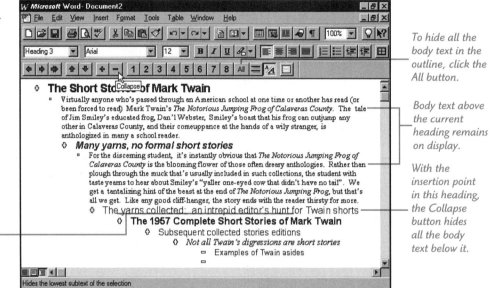

To hide all the body text in the outline, click the All button.

Body text above the current heading remains on display.

With the insertion point in this heading, the Collapse button hides all the body text below it.

The faint underline indicates body text under this heading.

Fig. 16.8
Double-click an outline's plus sign to speedily hide the outline items below it.

Double-click the plus signs, and all the outline items below them will be hidden.

The pointer turns into a four-headed arrow when you place it over the outline symbol.

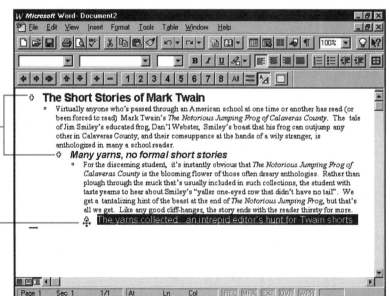

To redisplay the outline items you've just hidden, double-click the outline symbol again.

Can't I just see my headings and some of my body text?

When you want to hide or display text and headings, a Word outline gives you a lot of flexibility. That's good, because it lets you control precisely what you see. It can also be mildly confusing, because there are so many options. Just play around with it; since you're not making any changes to the document itself, you can hide, display, and hide again until you're comfortable with all the controls.

Here's one more outlining trick: suppose you want to see all your headings and the first line of each paragraph of body text? That's a handy way of getting a bird's-eye view of a document's structure without losing sight of all the detail.

Just click the Show First Line Only button on the Outline toolbar. Figure 16.9 shows you how it looks.

Fig. 16.9

Now you can see the trees, and some of the undergrowth too.

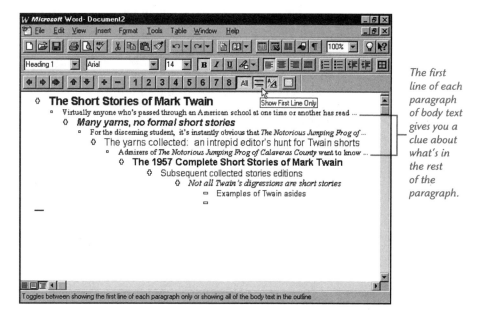

The first line of each paragraph of body text gives you a clue about what's in the rest of the paragraph.

Q&A *I just moved my outline heading up, but the body text below it got left behind!*

If you move headings around in an outline, you can wind up with orphaned body text, deserted by the parent heading when you moved it up or down. To avoid this, collapse the body text under the heading first, then move the heading. Collapsed body text accompanies a heading wherever you move it.

I need to turn this document into an outline

After hours of toil, your document is finally finished. You reach out a hand shaky with exhaustion and make the fateful phone call:

You: "It's ready. Want me to send it up?"

The boss: "Can't read the whole thing now. Just send me the outline." Click.

You (talking to yourself, never a good sign): "I didn't do an outline. I didn't have time to do an outline. If that no-good so-and-so wants an outline, why then—"

Don't say it. With Word, you can craft an instant outline from an existing document. The fact that it's an afterthought is entirely between you and your conscience; no one else need ever know.

To turn an existing document into an outline:

- If you've used Word's built-in styles for headings (Heading 1...8 in the Style box) in your document, just click the Outline View button. Your outline is finished with one click. Add heading numbering if you want to, and send the outline on its merry way.

- Chances are, your document is a mix of body text, bolded headings, italicized subheadings, and so on. Now that you know your way around the outline tools, it's easy to turn that jumble of formatting into an outline. Click the Outline View button. Word ignores all your own paragraph formatting, and treats the whole document as body text. Use the Promote, Demote, and Demote to Body Text buttons on the Outline toolbar to turn selected text into outline headings and body text. A few minutes of work will see that pesky outline completed.

Text that you promote to headings in Outline view is formatted with those heading styles, even when you switch back to Normal view. If you like the formatting of your original document, save the document first, then switch to Outline view and make your promotions and demotions. Click File, Save As, and save the outline under a different name.

On the other hand, converting your document headings to the Word heading styles automatically gives your document a consistent, polished look. Going through the exercise of turning a document into an outline just might leave you with a better-looking document. That's another bonus of using Word's outline tools.

How do I change this outline formatting?

If the default heading styles don't appeal to you, just modify the styles. See Chapter 12 for details on how to change document styles.

Or take the express route to outline formatting makeovers. With the insertion point anywhere in your outline, click Format, Style Gallery to pop up the Style Gallery dialog box. Your outline is shown in Normal view in the Preview window, as shown in figure 16.10.

Fig. 16.10

Use the Style Gallery for instant outline formatting changes.

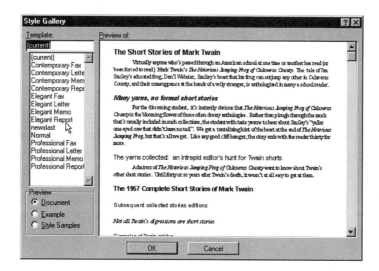

Even though you're previewing the outline in Normal view, it'll revert back to Outline view when you leave the dialog box. Now choose a new format from the Template list in the Style Gallery dialog box, then click OK. The outline is instantly reformatted in the styles of the new template. Figure 16.11 shows our outline formatted in the Elegant Report template style.

Fig. 16.11
Remember that when you reformat an outline, you're also reformatting the document.

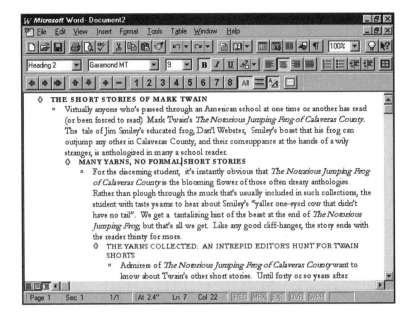

I need to print this outline

Outline printing works like document printing, with a few twists:

- Those plus and minus outline symbols won't print. Ditto for the little squares indicating body text. Those symbols only display on the screen.

- You print as much outline detail as you have displayed when you click the Print button on the Standard toolbar. If you want to print only your headings, collapse the body text first, then click the Print button.

- Heading numbering does print; if you want heading numbering in the print job, just add it to the outline before printing.

17

Mastering Big Documents Is No Mystery

● **In this chapter:**

- Do big documents go in one file, or many smaller files?

- What are master documents, and when do I use them?

- I want to turn a long document into a master document

- How do I create a new master document?

- All these documents would be more convenient in one file

A long report in a dozen parts, or a dozen different files? With a master document, you can consolidate them in one big file! . . . . ➤

What do stereotomy (cutting solids into sections), Epicurus (the ancient Greek philosopher), and fruit vendors have in common? Nothing much, unless you happened to be fiction's first great detective, C. Auguste Dupin. Before Sherlock Holmes saw action, Edgar Allan Poe's Dupin followed those three clues to the perpetrator of *The Murders in the Rue Morgue*. And with that, the modern detective story was born.

Those unwieldy, biceps-testing mysteries and thrillers we lug to the beach are outsized descendants of Poe's compact tale. If you've ever fallen asleep over one and had it land on your chest, you might have been tempted to take the stereotomist approach to big books: cut them up into more manageable pieces.

That's exactly what Word master documents let you do to big documents. You can break up a long file into handier smaller files. What's more, you can put them back together again. Just try doing that with the latest best-seller.

Do I keep my work in one big file, or many little ones?

Painting the back porch? Chances are, you'll start with the railings, then do the steps, and so on. Any big chore is more manageable when you break it up into smaller parts, and big writing jobs are no different. Most of us tackle long reports or book-length documents one part or chapter or section at a time. That makes the job seem much less overwhelming. You also organize your material better when you focus on each section separately.

You *could* keep all your chapters or sections in one long document in Word. It's easier to keep the parts of a big document in separate files:

- Spell checking, finding and replacing, and even file saves all go more quickly in a smaller file.

- You'll want to print a single chapter every once in a while, not the whole document. That's not as easy to do if your chapter is buried inside a big document.

- Coworkers or editors may need to see a chapter or a section, not the whole document. It's easy to copy a file to floppy disk, or send it on the network. It's much more work to extract a chunk of big document first, before copying or sending it.

- If you're working on a single chapter and the rest of the document is unchanged, you don't want to have to back up the whole document just to preserve the changes in one section of it. If your chapter's in its own file, you can just back up the file.

Keeping your document parts in separate files is efficient, but there are some drawbacks to the strategy. There'll be times when you do want to work on the whole document instead of each part. You might want to print the whole document, or make global replacements. And pagination can be a chore when you've got loads of small files that are all part of a bigger document.

Master documents combine, then divide, smaller files

So what should we use for a long document, one long file, or many smaller ones? We'd rather have both at once: the parts of a large document in separate files, that we could combine into one large file whenever necessary. And when we needed to, we could break up the large file into its component parts again. Then recombine them when the urge struck.

That's exactly what we get with a **master document**. A master document is like an outline of a large document, akin to the outlines we looked at in Chapter 16. In a master document, the outline items are themselves smaller files, called **subdocuments**. Each subdocument is a section of the large document. When you expand the master document, you get your entire large file to edit or print. Collapse it again, and you can work on each subdocument individually.

The following page shows a master document containing five subdocuments. Each subdocument is a section of a book manuscript.

Master big documents with master documents

Use the Outline toolbar to create the master document.

This little lock indicates that the subdocument is locked—no changes allowed, unless you unlock it again.

This level 1 heading is the document title.

Master Document view toggles between Outline view and Master Document view.

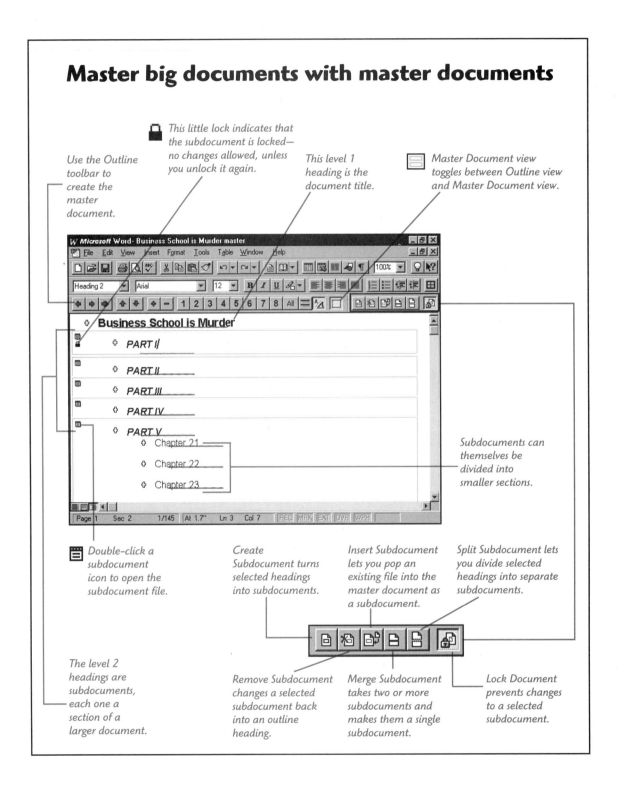

Subdocuments can themselves be divided into smaller sections.

Double-click a subdocument icon to open the subdocument file.

Create Subdocument turns selected headings into subdocuments.

Insert Subdocument lets you pop an existing file into the master document as a subdocument.

Split Subdocument lets you divide selected headings into separate subdocuments.

The level 2 headings are subdocuments, each one a section of a larger document.

Remove Subdocument changes a selected subdocument back into an outline heading.

Merge Subdocument takes two or more subdocuments and makes them a single subdocument.

Lock Document prevents changes to a selected subdocument.

You can create a new document as a master document, or take an existing long document and turn it into a master document. You can even combine many existing document files into a single master document. We'll take a look at all three possibilities.

Like an electronic paper clip, master documents let you clip together a stack of document files. Pull the files out to work on them, then clip them together again when you're done. Master documents are just as easy to use as paper clips, with the advantage that no amount of use will bend them out of shape.

How do I create a master document for a new writing job?

Any writer embarking on a big writing project has to settle one question at the outset: where do I start? Plenty of writers throw up their hands and give up, unable to get past that point. Word master documents ensure that this calamity need never befall you. With a new master document, you always get your writing job off to a good start.

Suppose, for example, that we're planning to write a book in twenty-five chapters, divided up into five parts. Each of those five parts is going to be a subdocument, with five short chapters in each subdocument. Instead of staring at a blank screen, wondering what the heck to write, we'll get off to a solid start with a master document.

Master documents start with an outline

To create a master document for a new long document, you begin by creating an outline. Make it as detailed as you like. As long as you use Word's outline tools to format your headings and subheadings, the master document will come out perfectly.

To outline a new document:

1 Click <u>V</u>iew, <u>M</u>aster Document. That switches you to Master Document view and pops up the Outline and Master Document toolbars.

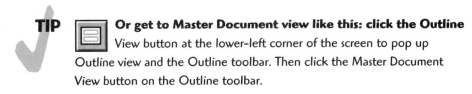

TIP **Or get to Master Document view like this: click the Outline** View button at the lower-left corner of the screen to pop up Outline view and the Outline toolbar. Then click the Master Document View button on the Outline toolbar.

2 Type your document title. This will be the title for the long document itself. You don't have to have a title at all, but it's always a good beginning.

3 Press Enter to go to the next line, and type the first section heading. It's going to be our first subdocument. We'll call it **Part I**.

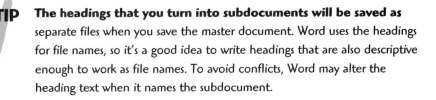

TIP **The headings that you turn into subdocuments will be saved as** separate files when you save the master document. Word uses the headings for file names, so it's a good idea to write headings that are also descriptive enough to work as file names. To avoid conflicts, Word may alter the heading text when it names the subdocument.

4 Click the Demote button on the Outline toolbar to demote the heading to Heading 2 level. Figure 17.1 shows the master document so far.

Fig. 17.1
Creating a master
document is just like
creating an outline.

This subheading
under the document
title will be the first
subdocument.

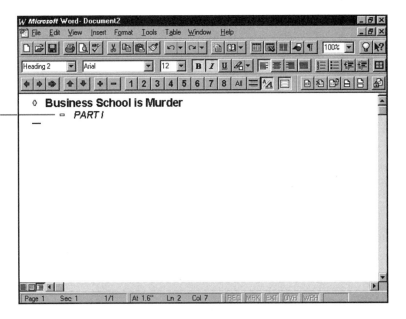

5 Now type the first subheading under Part I. We're calling it **Chapter 1**. Press Enter at the end of the line and type the next subheading, **Chapter 2**. Repeat the procedure for all the subheadings in Part 1, through Chapter 5.

6 We want to demote those subheadings under Part I to Heading 3 level, so we'll take care of them all at once. Position the pointer over the minus sign next to Chapter 1, and it turns into a four-headed arrow. Click to select the subheading, Chapter 1.

7 Put the pointer over the minus sign next to the last subheading in Part 1, Chapter 5. Shift+click the four-headed arrow to select all the subheadings under Part I, as shown in figure 17.2.

Fig. 17.2

Click the first subheading, then Shift+click the last subheading in a section to select them all.

The pointer turns into a four-headed arrow when you position it over the outline symbols.

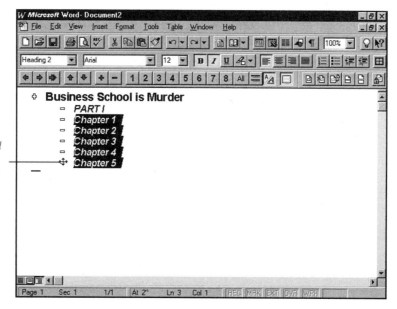

8 Click the Demote button on the Outlining toolbar to demote all the selected subheadings to Heading 3 level.

9 Type the next subdocument heading, **Part II**. Click the Promote button on the Outline toolbar to make it a Heading 2 level heading. Type the subheadings, Chapters 6 through 10, select and demote them, and repeat for Parts III, IV, and V. When you're through, it'll look something like figure 17.3.

Fig. 17.3
One more benefit
of using master
documents: you're
forced to write an
outline before you start
writing the document.

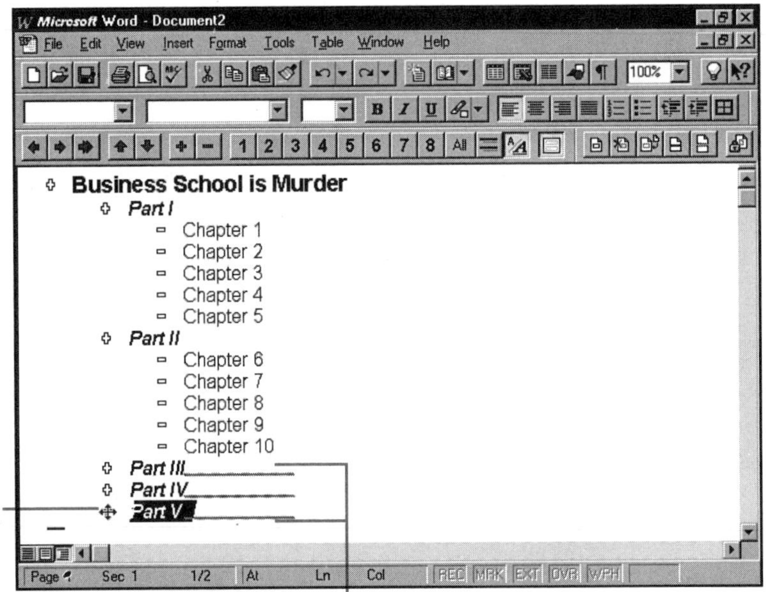

*To collapse outline items
under a heading, double-
click the plus sign with the
four-headed arrow.*

W *Microsoft* Word - Document2

File   Edit   View   Insert   Format   Tools   Table   Window   Help

100%

- **Business School is Murder**
  - *Part I*
    - Chapter 1
    - Chapter 2
    - Chapter 3
    - Chapter 4
    - Chapter 5
  - *Part II*
    - Chapter 6
    - Chapter 7
    - Chapter 8
    - Chapter 9
    - Chapter 10
  - *Part III*
  - *Part IV*
  - *Part V*

Page 1   Sec 1   1/2   At   Ln   Col   REC MRK EXT OVR WPH

This text is collapsed so you can see all the headings.

Turn outlines into master documents with a click or three

Once the outline is completed, turning it into a master document is a snap. There's only one decision to make: what heading level to use as subdocuments. In the example in figure 17.3, we only have one Heading 1 level heading, so the choices are between the Heading 2 and Heading 3 level headings.

Either one works; it's just a question of how many subdocuments you want to work with. Word will create separate document files for each heading we turn into a subdocument, based on the first heading in the selection. If you really wanted twenty-five different files, you'd make the first selected heading a Heading 3 level head. In this case, five separate files seems like plenty, so we'll make our first selection a Heading 2 level heading.

To create a master document from an outline:

1 Select all the headings that you want to turn into subdocuments. Click the first heading that you want for a subdocument, then Shift+click the last heading. Figure 17.4 shows the selected headings.

If you find the subheadings confusing, click the Collapse button to put them out of sight.

If you wanted subdocuments for each chapter, you'd make the first Heading 2 head your first selection.

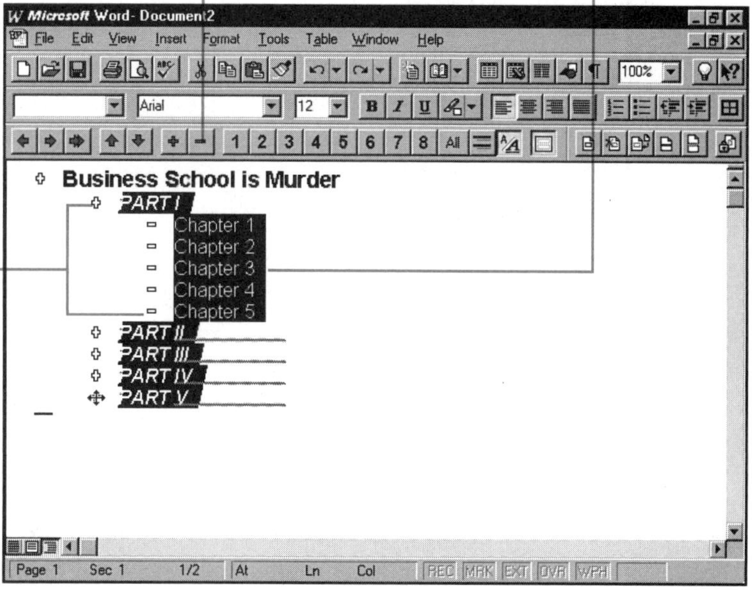

Fig. 17.4

These selected Heading 2 heads will become subdocuments, with the Heading 3 heads below them as subheads in the subdocument files.

Selecting the Heading 2 headings also selects the Heading 3 subheads, which become subsections in each subdocument.

2 With the outline headings selected, click the Create Subdocument button on the Master Document toolbar. Since a Heading 2 level head was the first heading in the selection, Word creates a subdocument for every Heading 2 head it finds within the selected text, as shown in figure 17.5.

Fig. 17.5
The Heading 2 level heads in the selected text created the subdocuments.

These subdocument icons appear automatically; double-click one to open the subdocument.

The subheads are within each subdocument.

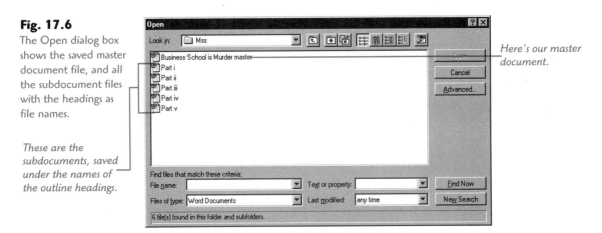

Word adds a border around each subdocument.

What happens when I save my master document?

With the master document created, all you have to do is save it (of course, there's still that little matter of actually writing the document). Click the Save button on the Standard toolbar and give your master document a name. When you click <u>S</u>ave in the Save As dialog box, Word saves the master document, and all the subdocuments too. Each subdocument gets the heading text as a file name, as shown in figure 17.6.

Fig. 17.6
The Open dialog box shows the saved master document file, and all the subdocument files with the headings as file names.

These are the subdocuments, saved under the names of the outline headings.

Here's our master document.

So what do I do with this master document?

Now we've got our document outlined, divided up into handy subdocuments, and named and saved. Just add text and call it a day. To add the text, double-click any of the subdocument icons in the master document. That opens the subdocument, and you can start typing. Format the text any way you like; the subdocument is an ordinary Word file, so treat it accordingly.

Figure 17.7 shows a windowed view of the master document and an open subdocument.

Fig. 17.7

A mere five chapters to write, and they're probably due tomorrow. At least the chapter headings are done.

Double-clicking the Part 1 subdocument icon...

...popped open the Part 1 document.

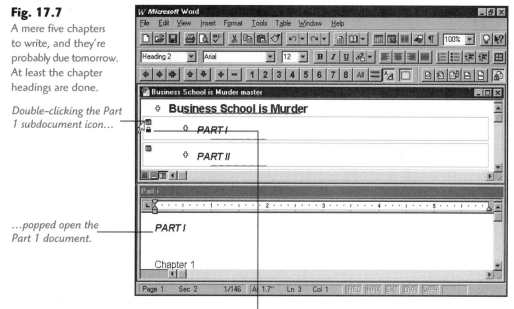

The padlock in Master Document view appears when you open the subdocument.

When you open a subdocument for editing, a padlock appears in the subdocument in Master Document view (refer to fig. 17.7), indicating that the master document subdocument is locked. You can edit all you want in the open subdocument file, but you can't make changes to the corresponding master document subdocument. If you want to do that, close the subdocument file first.

TIP **Text that you type in the subdocument also appears in the master** document. If you add additional subheadings in a subdocument, format them with the built-in Word heading styles (Headings 1...8). Formatted this way, the headings will show up in the master document *as* headings. That preserves the structure of your outline. To get the built-in headings, click the Style Box drop-down arrow on the Formatting toolbar.

What else should I know about master documents and subdocuments?

Although subdocuments are ordinary Word document files, they're linked to the master document. Because of that, there are a few things to keep in mind:

- If you want to delete a subdocument, do it from the master document, not the Windows Explorer or My Computer. Otherwise you'll get an error message from Word when you try to open a master document containing subdocuments that Word can't find.

- Double-click the subdocument icon in the master document and use the Save As dialog box to move or rename subdocuments. Moving or renaming subdocuments with the master document closed results in error messages when you try to reopen the master document.

- Editing changes you make within a subdocument automatically update the subdocument in the master document. The reverse is also true: make changes to the subdocument from the master document, and when you open the subdocument, you'll find those changes in it as well.

How do I turn this long document into a master document?

There's nothing quite like finishing a big writing project. Fiction or nonfiction, book or report, for a writer "The End" is the most satisfying phrase in the language. But for most of us, The End is just the beginning: of rewriting, editing, and revising.

Converting a single big document file into a master document can help make the revisions phase of a writing project less arduous. Breaking up an existing document makes it easier to focus on problem areas one at a time. And if you have cowriters on the project, it's sometimes handier to send revised subdocument sections back and forth, rather than the entire document.

It's easy to turn an existing file into a master document:

1 Open the document and click <u>V</u>iew, <u>M</u>aster Document.

2 Your document is displayed in Outline view. If you already have headings styled in the Heading 1 through Heading 8 styles, your outline is already done and you can skip down to step 5.

3 If you used your own formatting for headings, they appear as body text. Click the heading, then click the Promote and Demote buttons on the Outline toolbar to format them in the various heading styles, as shown in figure 17.8.

Fig. 17.8

Converting an existing document into a master document starts with an outline.

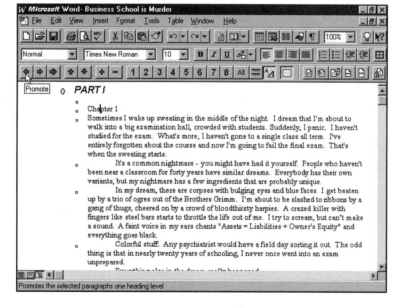

4 Work your way through the entire document, applying Word's heading styles to your headings. If you don't like the way they look, modify the heading styles (see Chapter 12 for details on how to do that).

TIP **The fast way to track down headings in a long document? Click** Edit, Find for the Find dialog box. Type the first few letters of your next heading in the Find What text box (type **chap** if you're looking for chapters, for example). Then click Find Next. When you get to your heading, don't close the Find dialog box. Click in the document, but outside the dialog box, then click the Promote or Demote button. That promotes or demotes the heading, and leaves the Find dialog box popped up. Click Find Next again to go to the next heading, and repeat.

5 With all your headings properly promoted or demoted, it's decision time. Which heading level do you want at the beginning of each subdocument? Whichever heading you choose, Word will dump all the text between those heading levels into each subdocument you create. Here, we're going to create subdocuments at each Heading 2 level heading.

6 Click the Show Heading 2 button on the Outline toolbar. That collapses all the text in between each Heading 2 heading, as shown in figure 17.9.

Decide what heading level you want at the beginning of each subdocument, then click the corresponding Show Heading button.

Fig. 17.9
This step is not essential, but it's a lot easier to see what you're doing when only the critical headings are in view.

Clicking Show Heading 2 displays only the Heading 2 level heads (the faint underline tells you the text is collapsed).

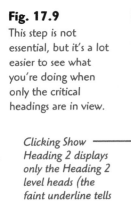

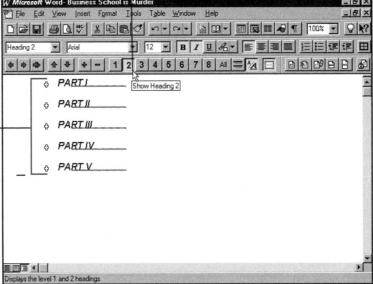

7 Position the pointer over the plus sign next to the first displayed heading and click to select it.

8 Now position the pointer over the plus sign next to the last displayed heading, and Shift+click to select them all, as shown in figure 17.10.

Fig. 17.10
Use the Shift+click combination to select each heading in turn.

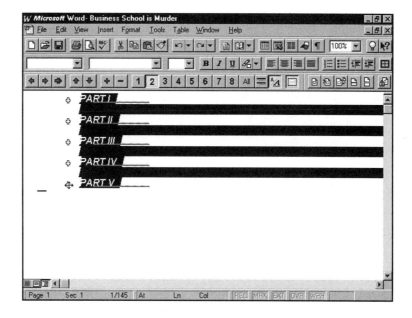

9 With all the headings selected, click the Create Subdocument button on the Master Document toolbar. The selected headings are enclosed in boxes, and the subdocument icons pop up beside each one, as shown in figure 17.11.

All the text in between each Heading 2 head in figure 17.11 is now dumped into separate subdocument files. The subdocument files are named after each heading, as in Part I.

To open each subdocument, double-click the corresponding subdocument icon. To view the entire document, click the Normal View button down at the lower left corner of the screen.

Fig. 17.11
Eureka! The long
document is broken
up into handy sub-
documents, easing
editing chores.

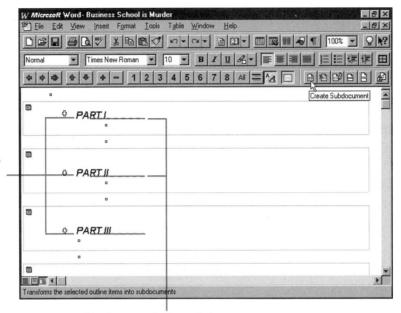

The headings are also
the subdocument file
names.

The document body text in between
each heading is in a subdocument.

Q&A ***I changed the master document's template, and now
all the formatting in my subdocuments has changed!***

The more you look at a master document, the more inclined you might
be to change the way it looks. The F<u>o</u>rmat, Style <u>G</u>allery command, for
example, can give your master document a radically new appearance.
That's fine, but the master document's template overrides the subdocuments' formatting. If you change the master's template, the change is also
applied to the subdocuments.

I want to print my master document

Here's one good reason to use master documents: they let you control exactly how much or how little of a document you print. You can print the whole document, or just bits and pieces of it, with ease:

- To print the entire document, click the Normal View button, then click the Print button on the Standard toolbar.

- If you want to print a subdocument, double-click the subdocument icon in the master document to open the subdocument file. Click the Print button, and only the open subdocument will print.

- To print several subdocuments, click the Open button on the Standard toolbar. Click the first subdocument you want to print to select it, then Ctrl+click each additional subdocument. Press the right mouse button and select Print from the shortcut menu. Click OK in the Print dialog box to print the selected subdocuments.

- To print selected sections of a long document, use Master Document view and the Outline toolbar to display or hide as much of the document as you want to print. Click the Print button on the toolbar to print only the displayed text.

How do I turn these different files into a single master document?

You've been slaving away for weeks on a long document. You've dutifully saved each section or chapter of the opus in separate files, named Chapter 1 or Section 2, or something similar. Now that you've accumulated a collection of such files, you're beginning to wish the document was in one file after all. Maybe you need to make a global replacement or two, or print the whole document.

If a heap of separate files is a nuisance, use Word's electronic paper clip to gather them together. Just create a new master document, in which the subdocuments are your separate files.

To gather different files together in a master document:

1 Click <u>V</u>iew, <u>M</u>aster Document to switch to Master Document view.

2 Click the Insert Subdocument button on the Master Document toolbar. That pops up the Insert Subdocument dialog box shown in figure 17.12.

Fig. 17.12

The Insert Sub-document menu looks a lot like the Open dialog box. Just like its twin, it lists all your Word files.

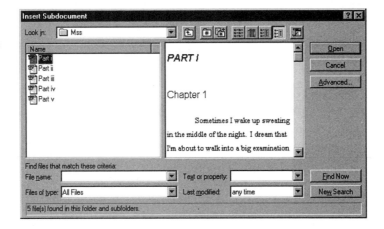

3 Double-click any file listed in the Insert Subdocument dialog box, and the file is popped into the master document as a subdocument.

4 Files inserted into master documents keep their existing file names. Add as many files as you like, then save the master document with its own file name.

If you insert a file as a subdocument and change your mind, just click the Undo button on the Standard toolbar.

CAUTION **Remember that the master document template overrides the** formatting in subdocuments. If your master document is formatted in a template different from your inserted subdocument's template, the subdocument gets the master document's formatting.

Running a Tight Ship: Managing Your Files

● **In this chapter:**

- Avoiding file overload: creating new folders

- Can I really create a list of the folders I use the most?

- Where did I put that file? How to find lost documents

- I need a system for organizing my files!

- Moving, copying, and renaming files

With Word's simple file management tricks, you'll spend more time writing and less time trying to unearth misplaced documents . . . . ▶

I t's an annual taxpayer's ritual. Each spring, you spend countless hours digging out the receipts, invoices, and canceled checks you tossed in drawers and shoe boxes during the last 12 months. And each spring you promise yourself that from now on you're going to keep your financial papers organized.

Your Word files are a lot like your personal paperwork. They're made up of many different kinds of documents—some big, some small, some important, some not, but too often tossed carelessly into whatever folder is available as you hurry from one task to the next.

Your computing life doesn't have to be that way. After all, you have a computer to make life simpler, not create more chaos. Why not let your computer do the work it's designed for?

Word for Windows 95 has a host of features whose purpose is to help you organize your documents. You can create folders; move easily among your folders; delete, move, and rename files; and find files by file name or by content.

Good file organization starts with good folder management. Once you learn how to create folders and subfolders, you'll begin to see how you can use those folders to develop a file-saving system. Who knows? It might even give you some ideas on how to prepare your financial records for next April.

Folder finesse

On most computers, Word is set up to save your files in a folder called Winword. But putting all of your documents in one folder is like tossing all your papers into one file drawer—convenient but sloppy. A much better strategy is to create subfolders by subject as you need them.

Since every computer is set up differently, you'll have to decide for yourself where you're going to put what folders for what documents. Later, we'll talk more about how to organize the documents on your hard drive. But for now, let's keep life simple and use the Winword folder as our base of operations.

 Plain English, please!

A **folder** is Windows 95's term for what previous versions of Windows and MS-DOS called a directory.

Why wouldn't I use Windows 95's Explorer for my file and folder management?

Word's Open and Save As dialog boxes are designed to handle simple, routine file and folder management. Explorer has more functions, and it gives you better options for moving and copying files (for example, the ability to drag and drop). If you're familiar with Explorer and have to do extensive file management tasks, Explorer is probably the better option.

Creating a new folder

Your Winword folder will probably contain several folders already, such as Letters, Macros, and Startup. Let's assume you want to create a fourth folder called Expense Reports.

 From the Save As dialog box, click the Create New Folder button. The New Folder dialog box appears like the one shown in figure 18.1. New Folder is highlighted in the Name text box; type the name of the folder you want to create and click OK.

Fig. 18.1
To create a new folder, type its name in the Name text box and click OK.

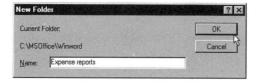

 TIP **You can create folders within folders. For example, the folder** Letters might in turn contain a folder for each month of the year. The second folder is often called a **subfolder**.

 When I create a folder, can I only use it for Word documents?

Word is not actually creating the folder, it's instructing Windows 95 to create it. Thus, your folder is available to all of your programs. Also, you can manage folders created in Word with Windows Explorer.

Moving to a folder

You move to your new folder by double-clicking it.

To return to the previous folder, click the Up One Level button to the right of the Save In text box.

 TIP Click the Details button on the Save As dialog box toolbar to get more information on the files in a folder. Word tells you if the item is a folder, Word document, or other item; when you last modified the folder or file; and, for files, the size.

Playing Favorites: creating a list of favorite folders

Urban rail commuters can usually choose between two types of transportation—the regular train, which stops at every station, or the express train, which goes straight to their destination.

 The Save As dialog box has its own express train: the Favorites list. Click the Look In Favorites button on the Save As dialog box toolbar. Click a folder on the list, and Word goes directly to the folder, no matter where it is on your hard drive. The Favorites list can also include files, which you can open without first going to the proper folder.

Figure 18.2 shows a typical Favorites list, consisting of a file and two folders.

Fig. 18.2
For quick access to your most used folders and documents, use the Favorites list.

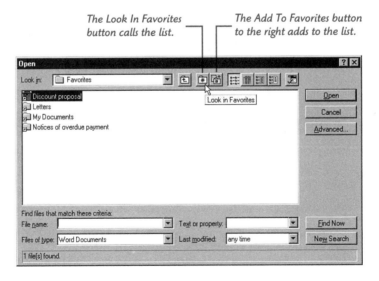

Your Favorites list is empty until you add folders and files to it. To add an item to your Favorites list, go to the appropriate folder and click the Add To Favorites button on the Save As dialog box toolbar. A small selection box pops up, giving you two options:

- Add Look In Folder To Favorites adds the folder that appears in the Look In text box to your list.

- Add Selected Item To Favorites adds the item you've selected in the list box. You can select any item, including documents and folders.

List limitations

Favorites is a folder that contains shortcuts, called **links**, to the files and folders you see. (You can identify a shortcut by the little boxed arrow in the lower left-hand corner of the icon.) If you use the shortcut menu to delete an item in the Favorites list, you delete the link, not the actual file or folder. Similarly, copying or moving an item copies or moves the link, not the file or folder the item represents.

 CAUTION **Be careful that you don't accidentally save a file into the Favorites** folder. You might mistake it for a link and accidentally delete it. Keep actual files in regular folders.

Changing your startup folder

When you run Word, it always starts you in the same folder—a real inconvenience if you want to begin your work somewhere else. It's easy to change this startup folder to one of your own choosing.

Select Tools, Options from the menu bar and click the File Location tab. Highlight Documents in the File Types selection box, then click Modify.

A Modify Location dialog box appears, similar to the Open dialog box. Move to the folder you want as the default. Its name appears in the Folder Name text box. Then click OK.

Finding files

As long as you have only a handful of documents in a few folders, finding your files won't be hard. You can click folders and the Up One Level button to move around until you see the document in the Open list box.

But as you create new folders, and subfolders within folders, and subfolders within subfolders within folders, the day will come when you'll start to lose track of your files. Before long, you'll be wandering around your hard drive like a bewildered shopper in a mall, searching every shelf of every aisle for that old report your boss suddenly wants a copy of.

Word devotes a number of features to helping you find files. But first, let's digress a bit and talk about disk drive organization.

Before you reach for the silver bullets and garlic cloves, be assured that this will not be a technical discussion of sectors, file allocation tables, and other such technical trivia. We'll keep the material simple and talk only about matters that relate directly to finding your documents.

How your drive is organized

It's much easier to find a store at the mall if you have a general idea of the mall's floor plan. You'll likewise have an easier time finding folders and files if you understand how they're placed on your hard drive.

The easiest way to get a sense of how your folders are structured is to click the Look In text box in the Open dialog box. Word shows you a tree similar to the one shown in figure 18.3.

To simplify matters for now, we're going to forget about Desktop and My Computer and assume that the hard drive (labeled Vol10-03-93 (C:) in fig. 18.3) is at the top of tree. Cascading from C: is a series of folders that eventually lead to the current subfolder, called Notices Of Overdue Payment.

 TIP **On most computer systems, the floppy drive is drive A:, the hard** drive, C:, and the CD-ROM drive, D:. If you're on a network, the network drives will have other letter designations.

The tree reveals how the folders and subfolders are nested within one another. MSOffice contains Winword, which contains Letters, which contains Notices Of Overdue Payment.

Fig. 18.3
Click the Look In text box to see how your folders are organized.

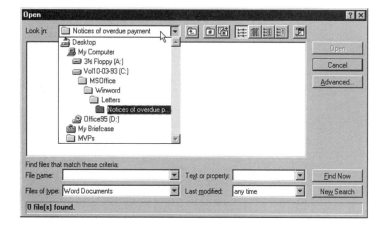

Clicking the Up One Level button takes us to the Letters folder. As figure 18.4 shows, Notices Of Overdue Payment is one of three folders in Letters. Moving up another level would show that Letters is in turn one of five folders in Winword.

Fig. 18.4
Notices Of Overdue Payment is one of three folders nested in the Letters folder.

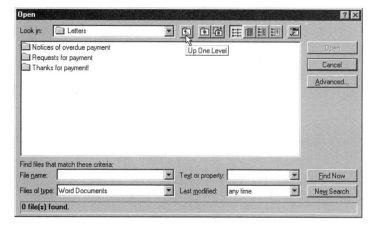

C: worthy

Eventually, if you go up enough levels, you'll get to the C: drive (see fig. 18.5).

Fig. 18.5
At the top of the
folder heap is C:, to
which all folders
belong.

To return to our shopping mall metaphor, C: is the mall's main atrium. Along with MSOffice are a variety of other "stores," which variously contain programs (1-2-3, Word for Windows 2 and 6, PKZip), groups of programs (games, utilities), and system files (DOS, Windows). Most of these folders have nested folders similar to those inside MSOffice.

If your computer is new, you probably don't have many folders in C:. But if you're a compulsive organizer, folders will start multiplying like the dust bunnies under your bed. A modest 380-megabyte drive might hold thousands of files in hundreds of folders.

Obviously, clicking folders and the Up One Level button to root around your hard drive looking for a file is impractical. In fact, it's a complete waste of time when you can automate the search with Word's file-finding features.

Finding a file anywhere on your drive

Here's a simple example of how to search your entire drive for a specific file. In this case, the search is for an e-mail message whose file name includes the word "jazz":

1 Open the Open dialog box (see fig. 18.6) and select the C: drive from the Look In text box.

2 Because the file might not have a .DOC extension, choose All Files in the Files Of Type text box.

Fig. 18.6
Start a file search in the Open dialog box by entering a file name or part of a file name in the File Name text box and choosing what types of files to look for.

3   Click the Commands And Settings button and select Search Subfolders.

4   Type the search string (such as **jazz**) in the File Name text box.

5   Click File Now. Word searches the hard drive for all file names that include "jazz" and presents a list.

6   Click the Preview button to display the contents of the files and show what folders they're in (see fig. 18.7).

Fig. 18.7
When Word is done with its search, it shows you a list of all the files that match the search criteria.

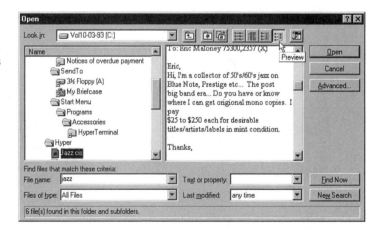

TIP **Searching your entire hard drive can take several minutes. If you** know the file is somewhere in a certain set of folders, start your search from the top folder of the tree.

Finding a file by its contents

A few years ago, Ed's mom sent him e-mail that included a quotation Ed now wants to use in a speech to the local literary club. But there's a problem—Ed can't remember the name of the file it's in.

Almost all of us have lost information this way. In such an instance, a file name search is futile. But Word has a solution: it can search the *contents* of your files.

A content search is almost identical to a file name search. The only difference is that you leave the File Name text box empty and put the text you want to find in the Te*x*t Or Property text box.

In figure 18.8, for example, Word lists all files in the Hyper folder that include the string "murder."

Fig. 18.8
Word lets you search for documents that include a specific string, which you type in the Text Or Property text box.

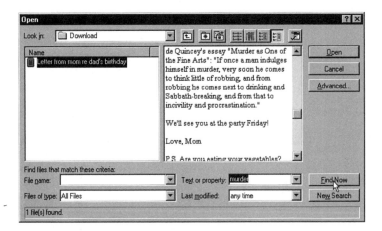

TIP **You can sort your file names by size, type, or date modified. Select** Sorting from the Commands and Settings menu.

Q&A *I did a content search, and it took more than half an hour! Is there any way I can speed up my searches?*

You can take a couple of steps to make your searches go faster. First, don't search the entire drive unless you have to. If you know the file is in a certain tree of folders, search only those folders. And second, avoid using All Files in the Files of Type text box.

CAUTION   **Don't forget to turn off Search Subfolders when you're done with** your search. Otherwise, Word will search all of your subfolders the next time you use the Open dialog box.

Barking up the right folder tree

Throughout this chapter, we've touched on how a hard drive organizes folders and files. We've also mentioned the importance of not putting all of your documents in the Winword folder.

But we haven't answered an important question: how do you decide what folders to create and where to put them?

This is not the place for a long discussion of file organization. However, because drives are as large as they are these days, you need a plan you can put into effect from the moment you save your first document.

Here is an overview of the two most popular models for file organization: Grouping files by subject and grouping them by file type.

Organizing files by subject

When you organize files by subject, you create a folder for each subject and folders for different parts of the subject.

For example, let's say you sell widgets for the Wellworthit Widget Company. For each client, you've got a variety of reports, correspondence, and proposals.

You might begin by creating a folder called Clients in drive C:. In that folder, you create subfolders for each client. And in each of those subfolders, you create subfolders for the type of document. The resulting tree would look something like this:

```
--Drive C:
  --Clients
    --Carbo
      --budgets
      --letters
      --proposals
      --reports
    --Fisk
      --budgets
      --letters
      --proposals
      --reports
    --Lee
      --budgets
      --letters
      --proposals
      --reports
    --Rice
      --budgets
      --letters
      --proposals
      --reports
```

Mixing file types

When you organize by subject, you often mix file types. For example, in the tree above, the folder Proposals might include Word documents and Excel budget spreadsheets. This technique is becoming more practical as programs are able to use data of different formats.

Pros and cons of organizing files by subject

The advantage of this type of disk organization is that you can manage your files by subject. You can move, copy, and delete files and folders with minimum effort.

Also, while your documents are in many different folders, you can still manage them as a group by using the file-finding commands in the Open dialog box. For example, if you want to copy certain documents to a floppy disk, you search the drive for all document files, and then select and copy the ones from the resulting list.

The disadvantage is that not all programs you use will have Word's ability to manage files. For example, if you're using a spreadsheet program that's a few years old, you might not like having your spreadsheet files scattered all over your hard drive.

Organizing files by type

When you organize your files by type, you set up folders to hold the data files for each of your programs.

The tree below shows a file structure for the Wellworthit Widget Company. Main folders have been set up for spreadsheets, Word documents, and databases. Each main folder has subfolders for different subjects:

```
--Drive C:
  --Excel spreadsheets
    --Clients
      --Carbo
        --budgets
    --Expense reports
  --Word documents
    --Clients
      --Carbo
        --letters
        --proposals
    --Meeting notes
  --Databases
    --Clients
      --Active list
      --Old list
      --Prospects
    --Vendors
    --Distributors
```

Pros and cons of organizing files by type

The upside of organizing by file type is that you can copy, back up, and delete all of your documents more easily. Your documents are also a little easier to find—you don't have to swing from tree to tree to find the files you want.

On the other hand, you might have files for a project scattered among several folder trees, so deleting or backing them up as a group can be inconvenient.

Besides their obvious jobs of saving and opening files, respectively, the Save As and Open dialog boxes can handle routine tasks such as copying, moving, deleting, and renaming files.

The important commands are packaged neatly in a shortcut menu (see fig. 18.9), which you get by selecting the file you want to work with and clicking the right mouse button.

TIP **You can use the shortcut menu to copy, move, and delete folders** the same way you do files.

Fig. 18.9

For common file management commands, select a file in the Open dialog box and click the right mouse button.

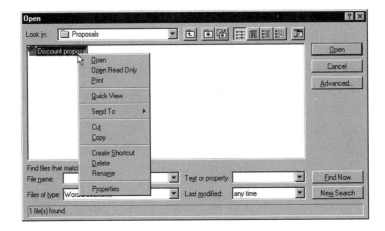

How to copy files

Word's copy functions lack many amenities, such as the ability to drag and drop a file. But the shortcut menu's Copy command can't be beat for quickly and efficiently copying a file to another folder.

Highlight the file you want to copy and choose Copy from the shortcut menu. Ignore the fact that absolutely nothing seems to happen, and go to the folder you want to copy the file to. Click the right mouse button on an empty part of the list box. Choose Paste from the shortcut menu, and a copy of the file appears.

TIP **To copy a file to a floppy disk, choose Send To on the shortcut** menu and select the floppy drive.

How to move files

You move files the same way you copy them, only you use Cut instead of Copy.

Highlight the file you want to move and choose Cut from the shortcut menu. Go to the destination folder and click the right mouse button on an empty part of the list box. Click Paste.

How to delete files

To get rid of a file, choose Delete from the shortcut menu. Word asks you to confirm the deletion, then tosses the file into the Recycle Bin.

TIP You can copy, move, and delete several files at a time. Just select the files you want, then click the right mouse button on any of the highlighted files to get the shortcut menu.

How to rename files

To rename a file, select the file name in the Open or Save As dialog box. Click the file name; it changes to a mini-text box with an insertion point. Type a new file name or edit the existing file name by pressing an arrow key and deleting and inserting text as you would in any text box.

CAUTION You can rename items in your Favorites list. However, be aware that you're renaming only the shortcut to a file or folder, not the file or folder itself.

Part VI: Expert Topics for Non-Experts

Document Signposts: Tables of Contents and Indexes

● **In this chapter:**

- **Do I have to use Word's heading styles?**

- **I need a quick table of contents**

- **What happens if my document page numbers change?**

- **Can I really create an instant index?**

- **I want to add more entries to my index**

Just as road signs help us find our way around town, indexes and tables of contents help readers, and writers, find their way around documents . . . . ➤

magine trying to find your highway exit without those big green road signs.

From flickering neon to shimmering constellations, signs show us where to go and what to do. Long before neon was even a bad idea, Constantine I, Emperor of Rome, was about to fight a crucial battle. According to the famous story, a glowing cross appeared in the sky, with the words "in hoc signo vinces"—"In this sign, conquer"—under it. Constantine's men duly painted crosses on their shields and won the battle.

Long documents, like highways and battles, sometimes need to be sign-posted. That's the job of indexes, cross-references, and tables of contents. They act like signs in a Word document, telling readers where to go to find things. What's more, Word indexes and tables of contents are a snap to create—no assistance from a higher power is needed.

Heading styles make fast tables of contents

Word's built-in heading styles are the backbone of the outlines and master documents we looked at in Chapters 16 and 17. You also use heading styles to generate speedy tables of contents.

Tables of contents help your readers find what they need. Like a summary outline, they display only headings and page numbers, and that makes them handy for your own reference as well. Tables of contents are also navigational tools. Double-click a page number in a table of contents, and you go right to that page in your document.

If you've already applied the built-in heading styles to your document, you're all set to create a table of contents. Otherwise, consider going through your document and applying the heading styles before generating a table of contents.

If you use the built-in heading styles, Word tables of contents automatically track down all the headings in your document. Then they display the heading text, with the corresponding page number, in a neat table.

Plain English, please!

A **style** is a collection of formatting commands that have been named and saved. The Heading 1 style is Arial 14-pt. bold, for example. See Chapter 12 for more information on creating, modifying, and applying styles.

Figure 19.1 shows Word's built-in heading styles as they're applied to a document.

Click the Style box drop-down arrow to display the heading styles.

Select a heading style to apply it in the document.

Fig. 19.1
With Word's built-in heading styles in your documents, you can generate tables of contents with ease.

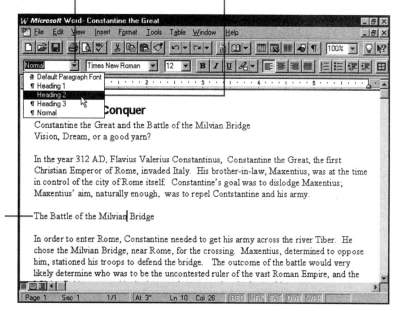

Click the heading where you want the style applied.

 TIP **If you're working with new text, don't forget about Word's** automatic headings. Type a heading at the left margin, then press the Enter key on the keyboard twice in rapid succession to format the heading in the Heading 1 style. To automatically apply heading styles 2 through 9, press Tab once for Heading 2, twice for Heading 3, and so on. Type the heading, then press Enter twice. Make sure your heading starts with a capital letter and contains no punctuation. Otherwise, automatic headings won't work.

For instant tables of contents, just add mouse clicks

There's nothing more frustrating than laboring over a long report, turning it in, and then having a reader come back to you with "Why didn't you cover x, y, and z?" You *did* cover those topics; the careless reader simply missed the crucial passages. With a table of contents, even the sloppiest reader knows where to look for the information he seeks.

Format your document with Word's built-in headings. Then, to add a table of contents:

1 Put the insertion point where you want the table of contents to appear. A blank line at the very beginning or the very end of the document is a good choice.

2 Click Insert, Index and Tables, Tables of Contents. That gets you the Tables of Contents tab of the Index and Tables dialog box shown in figure 19.2.

Fig. 19.2
Even though these are instant tables of contents, the options in the dialog box let you add custom touches.

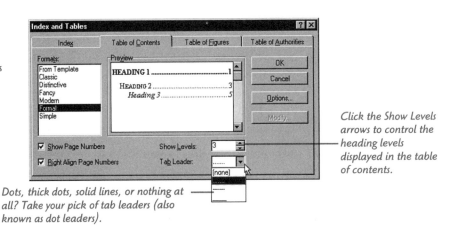

Click the Show Levels arrows to control the heading levels displayed in the table of contents.

Dots, thick dots, solid lines, or nothing at all? Take your pick of tab leaders (also known as dot leaders).

3 Click any of the formats on the list in the Formats box, then view the result in the Preview window.

4 Tab leaders are the dots, lines, or spaces that separate headings from page numbers. Click the Tab Leader drop-down arrow and choose one of the options, or don't do anything and use the selected format's default tab leader.

TIP **Use the Tab Leader options to modify the canned table of contents** formats. If, for example, you like the look of the Fancy format but you want tab leaders, click the format, then select one of the tab leader choices.

5 How detailed do you want your table of contents to be? Click the Show Levels arrows to decide what heading levels to display in the table.

6 Once you've made your choices, click OK in the Index and Tables dialog box. Your table of contents appears at the insertion point, as shown in figure 19.3.

Fig. 19.3
Word tables of contents handle all the page numbering and formatting issues for you.

Word found all the document headings and their page numbers.

IN THIS SIGN, CONQUER..1

CONSTANTINE THE GREAT AND THE BATTLE OF THE MILVIAN BRIDGE 1
   Vision, Dream, or a good yarn?...1
THE BATTLE OF THE MILVIAN BRIDGE 1
THE ACCOUNT OF LACTANTIUS..2
   Constantine's Vision...3
THE ACCOUNT OF EUSEBIUS...4
   Was it only a dream?..5
THE POLITICS OF CONVERSION 6
   Roman Persecution...7
COUNCIL OF NICAEA..8
SHOE ON THE OTHER FOOT..9
   Persecution of the Pagans...9

These are tab leaders.

Page 1   Sec 1   1/9   At 4.1"   Ln 17   Col 1

If you decide you don't want a table of contents after all, just get rid of it. Select the entire table, either by dragging through it with the mouse or with the Shift+arrow key combination, then press Delete.

What happens to my table of contents if I change my page numbers?

Word tables of contents do a great job of finding your headings and their page numbers. But what if you create your table, and then move text around? You might also add or cut an entire section of the document. Those changes will alter the pagination in your document, but the table of contents won't reflect the new page numbers.

Not until you tell it to show the new page numbers, that is. To speedily update the page numbers in a table of contents:

1 Click anywhere in the table of contents. Word colors the table in gray shading to show it's been selected.

2 Press F9. That pops up the Update Table of Contents dialog box shown in figure 19.4.

Fig. 19.4
The Update Table of Contents dialog box brings your table page numbers up to date after editing changes.

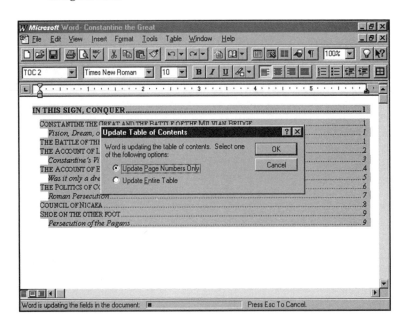

3 Select Update Page Numbers Only in the Update Table of Contents dialog box, then click OK. Word updates the page numbers in the table to reflect the new page numbers of the headings in the document, including any headings you've added or cut.

CAUTION **If you select the Update Entire Table option in the Update Table** of Contents dialog box, Word updates the heading page numbers and restores the table's formatting to the default for whatever table format you chose. If you've added your own formatting to the table of contents, it'll be wiped out.

I have my own heading styles, and I want a table of contents

Sturdy individualists who refuse to use canned headings aren't left out in the cold when it comes to creating tables of contents (although using canned heading styles is a bit easier). If you've created your own heading styles, you can use those to generate a table of contents without too much fuss.

For example, suppose you've created three heading styles and called them Custom 1, Custom 2, and Custom 3. To create a table of contents based on your own styles:

1 Put the insertion point where you want the table of contents to appear.

2 Click Insert, Index and Tables, Tables of Contents for the Tables of Contents tab of the Index and Tables dialog box (refer to fig. 19.2).

3 Click Options. That pops up the Table of Contents Options dialog box shown in figure 19.5.

Fig. 19.5

You can create tables of contents based on your own styles; it's just a little extra work.

Word's built-in styles are selected by default.

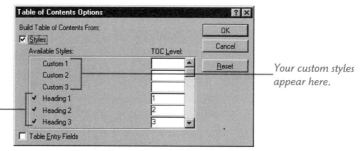

Your custom styles appear here.

4 Deselect the built-in heading styles by deleting the numbers in the TOC Level edit boxes. You'll notice the check marks by the built-in styles in the list of Available Styles disappear.

5 Enter TOC Level numbers of your own in the edit boxes next to your custom styles. Type a **1** for your first level heading, a **2** for the second level, and so on. It should look like figure 19.6.

Fig. 19.6
Once you assign TOC levels to your own heading styles, you can generate a table of contents based on those styles.

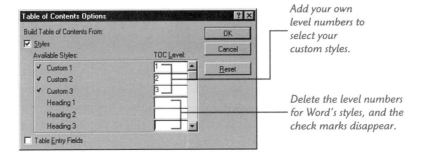

Add your own level numbers to select your custom styles.

Delete the level numbers for Word's styles, and the check marks disappear.

6 Click OK in the Table of Contents Options dialog box.

7 Make your selections in the Table of Contents dialog box, then click OK to generate the table of contents.

Research assistant on vacation? Index your own document

For some people, creating an index is truly effortless. University professors with graduate students at their beck and call, or law partners with a team of paralegals standing by, simply summon the hapless victim and say "Do me an index please" (we hope they say please). For the rest of us, indexes are a little more work. If you're using Word, the extra work really is only a little.

There are two steps to creating an index:

- Go through your document marking the text you want to appear in the index.

- Select a format and generate the index based on the marked text.

Word automatically lists any marked text with its corresponding page number in an index. The index pops up in its own two-column section at the end of the document.

TIP **Want your index to appear in the table of contents? Title the** index, and apply one of the heading styles to the title. Click the table of contents, press F9 to update it, and the title of your index appears with the correct page number.

First, mark your index entries

The hard labor involved in creating an index is deciding what to put in it. And even that's not too much of a sweat; all you do is select the text. Important names, recurring topics, key theories, they're all candidates for inclusion in an index.

To select and mark text for an index:

1 Select the first text you want in the index and press this combination of keyboard keys: Alt+Shift+X.

2 The Mark Index Entry dialog box pops up, with the selected text displayed in the Main Entry edit box, as shown in figure 19.7.

Fig. 19.7
If you want to edit the index entry text, make your changes in the Main Entry edit box.

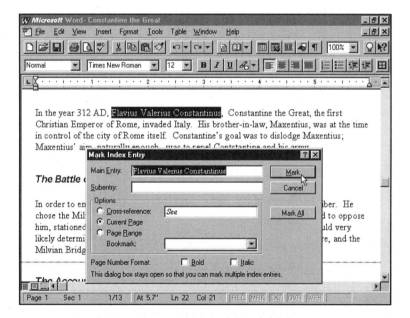

3 Click Mark in the Mark Index Entry dialog box. If it's text that recurs throughout the document, click Mark All to mark every occurrence of the text.

4 Word displays the XE index entry code next to the selected text. That's one of Word's normally hidden codes, which are scattered (though out of sight) throughout your documents. Click anywhere outside the dialog box, and select the next text you want in the index. The Mark Index

Entry dialog box stays open, and you can scroll the document and select text while it's popped up.

Q&A *I selected my next index entry, but the Mark button in the Mark Index Entry dialog box is still grayed out!*

Click the Main Entry edit box. You have to do that for every index entry you select.

5 With the next text selected, click the Main Entry edit box. The text appears in the box, and you can make any necessary changes to it there.

6 Click Mark or Mark All. Click outside the dialog box, select the next text, click the Main Entry edit box, then click Mark or Mark All again.

7 Continue to select and mark all the text you want in the index.

8 When you've marked all the index text, click Close in the Mark Index Entry dialog box.

Generate the index from the marked text

Once all your text is marked, generating the index is easy. To create an index of text entries you've already marked:

1 Click Insert, Index and Tables, Index for the Index tab of the Index and Tables dialog box.

2 Select a format for the index from the list of Formats (Modern is a good choice). The Preview window gives you an inkling of how the index will look, as shown in figure 19.8.

Fig. 19.8
The index formats automatically add an index heading letter above each alphabetical group of entries.

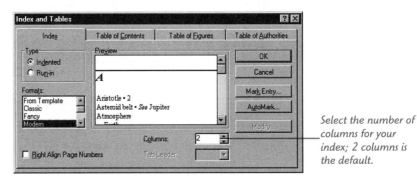

Select the number of columns for your index; 2 columns is the default.

3 Click OK, and the index appears at the end of the document in its own section.

Word automatically alphabetizes your index entries and displays them in columns, with their corresponding page numbers. Figure 19.9 shows a completed index in Page Layout view.

Click the Show/Hide button to hide Word's formatting codes.

Fig. 19.9
If your readers still can't find their way around a document after you've added a TOC and an index, tell them to wait for the movie.

Word automatically alphabetizes the entries and supplies these headings for each letter.

Switch to Page Layout view to see the index's columnar format.

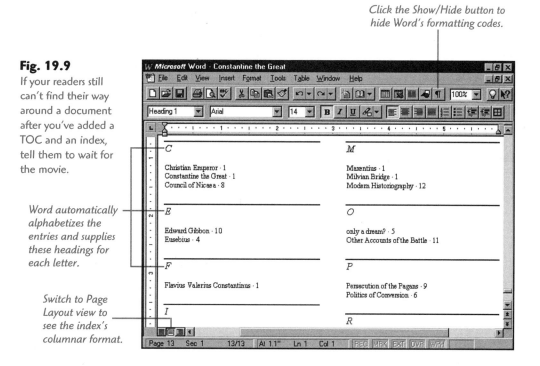

How do I add entries to an existing index?

It's easy to miss entries as you scroll through a document marking text. No need to redo the index—once you've created your index, you can easily add anything that's been missed.

Press Shift+Alt+X to pop up the Mark Index Entry dialog box. Select the additional text, click <u>M</u>ark, and repeat until you've added all the new entries. Click Close in the Mark Index Entry dialog box, put the insertion point in the index, then press F9.

Your index is automatically updated to include the new entries.

20

Text as Art, Numbers as Pictures: Graphs and WordArt

● In this chapter:

● **What is WordArt, and where do I find it?**

● **These WordArt special effects are attention-getters!**

● **How can I make a quick graph?**

● **What kind of graph should I use?**

● **This graph needs a complete makeover**

With WordArt and Microsoft Graph, documents need never be boring—even if the content doesn't exactly scintillate . . . . ⊙

Personal computers do remarkable things with text and numbers. Colorful images, exotic fonts, startling graphs—they're all just a mouse click or two away. So why are so many documents so boring?

Content has something to do with it. Invoices, tax forms, and the latest corporate decree might all be terminal cases. Like Ogden Nash's ruminant—"The cow is of the bovine ilk/One end is moo, the other, milk"—some documents are what they are, and there's not much you can do about it.

But if your document has a flicker of life, Word has a couple of tricks to fan the flicker into a flame. Microsoft Graph takes boring rows of numbers and turns them into colorful pictures. WordArt stretches and bends text into arresting shapes. A cow may be just a cow, but a dull document is easily made into something a little livelier.

Shake up your fonts with WordArt

If the sight of dinner companions swirling and sniffing their wine provokes an irresistible urge to order a beer, you'll love WordArt. Nowadays, font experts seem to be as thick on the ground as wine swirlers. And learned chatter about descenders and ascenders (those parts of a character that go above or below the line) might make you want to grab a font and give it a good shake.

That's exactly what WordArt lets you do. WordArt takes fonts and stretches, shadows, and shapes them. Use it to create logos, posters, and banners. WordArt is also great for getting a rise out of the office font connoisseur.

Figure 20.1 shows you what a WordArt object looks like.

Where do I find WordArt (and other interesting little programs)?

WordArt is one of a collection of programs that comes bundled with Word. In computer jargon they're called **applets** (as in "little applications"), and you get to them by clicking Insert, Object, Create New. That pops up the Create New tab of the Object dialog box shown in figure 20.2.

Fig. 20.1
When ordinary fonts won't do, get some attention with a little WordArt.

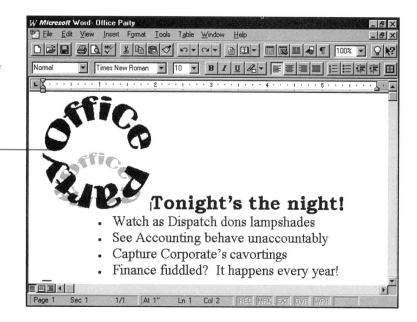

WordArt objects are inserted into Word documents, just like pictures or any other objects.

Fig. 20.2
Some of the object types are actually applications you run to create objects; others require programs like Excel or Quattro Pro.

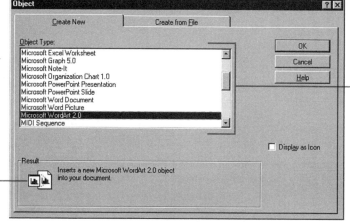

Double-click the object types to insert objects, or to run applications to create objects.

The Result box is a bit misleading—some of these object aren't inserted until you create them!

Q&A Why don't I see WordArt in the Object Type list?

WordArt might not have been installed when you installed Word. If you don't see it in the Object dialog box's Object Type list, close Word and insert your Word (or Office if you're using Microsoft Office) program disk number 1 or CD. Run Setup, click the Add/Remove button in setup and work your way through the dialog boxes to add WordArt.

The Object dialog box is a gateway to a host of other applications. Click items on the Object Type list, and the Result box (refer to fig. 20.2) tells you what sort of object will be inserted.

 Plain English, please!

Objects can be graphs, maps, pictures, spreadsheet tables, even Word documents. An object is anything in your computer that can be edited, moved, or inserted into an application. Why are they called objects? Probably because "things" would have sounded a bit vague.

The Result box in the Object dialog box is not always accurate. Objects aren't necessarily inserted into your document until you create them. Double-click Bitmap Image in the list of Object Types, for example, and you'll actually run Windows Paint, the drawing program that comes with Windows.

On the other hand, if you double-click Microsoft Excel Chart, you really do insert an Excel chart. But before that can happen, Excel has to be installed on your computer. The bottom line on the Object dialog box:

- Some of the items on the Object Type list require you to have other software installed, like Excel or Quattro Pro.

- Other items run applications that come bundled with Word or Windows. For example, double-click Microsoft Drawing. That runs Microsoft Drawing from within Word. Create your object, then close Microsoft Drawing to pop the object into your document.

 Q&A *I've been experimenting with the Object dialog box, and now Word doesn't respond to the keyboard or the mouse! What do I do?*

Get a cup of coffee. Inserting objects can be a slow affair, and Word might just be working on your last command. If nothing happens for more than a minute or two, press Ctrl+Alt+Delete. The Close Program dialog box pops up. If Microsoft Word is listed as Not Responding in the Close Program dialog box, select Microsoft Word and click End Task. That shuts down Word, but you lose any unsaved work. If Word isn't described as Not Responding in the Close Program dialog box, click Cancel and wait another minute or two. Word is still working, it's just working slooowly.

CAUTION   **Always save your current Word document before experimenting** in the Object dialog box. Running other applications from within Word, or inserting created objects into Word documents, strains your computer's memory and system resources. That can cause Word to crash. If you've saved your work first, you can laugh, or at least smile weakly, at the occasional crash.

Make a poster with WordArt

There you are minding your own business, trying to put a dent in your work, reasonably content with life in general. Then you get one of those phone calls from upstairs. "We need a poster for the office party. Oh, and we need it by four o'clock."

"Do it yourself" is on your lips, but you're a good soldier. You hold your fire and fire up WordArt instead. To create a poster with WordArt:

1 Click Insert, Object, Create New for the Create New tab of the Object dialog box (refer to fig. 20.2). Scroll down the Object Type list and double-click Microsoft WordArt 2.0.

2 That pops up the Enter Your Text Here dialog box and the WordArt toolbar; type your text, as shown in figure 20.3.

Fig. 20.3

Type whatever you want in the Enter Your Text dialog box, but try to keep it short—verbosity spells trouble in WordArt.

Insert Symbol pops up a palette of special characters to insert in your text.

Click Update Display after you make changes to your text.

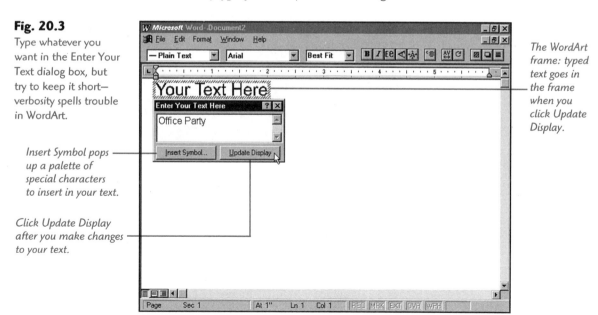

The WordArt frame: typed text goes in the frame when you click Update Display.

3 Click Update Display, and the text you typed appears inside the WordArt frame.

4 Now the fun starts: click the Shape box drop-down arrow to pop up the palette of shapes shown in figure 20.4.

Fig. 20.4

Here's one reason to keep your WordArt text short: some of these shapes will make long messages unreadable.

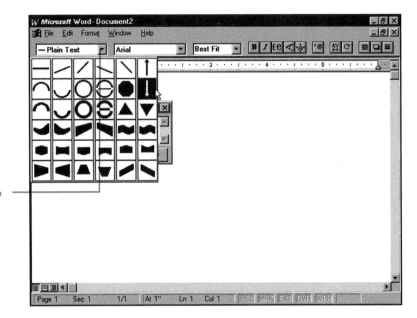

Click the Shape box drop-down arrow for a palette of shapes to transform your text.

5 Click any of the shapes in the Shape box, and your text turns into silly putty, stretching and bending into the selected shape. You can turn your text into a doughnut, cascade it to the left or right, arrange it in a wave, or stand it on end from top to bottom.

6 Click the WordArt toolbar buttons to change fonts and add all kinds of special effects. Figure 20.5 shows the effect of clicking the Stretch button on the toolbar.

7 In the end, you might settle for something conservative, like shaping text top to bottom, standing characters on their side, adding a silver shadow, and changing the font and font size. That's what I did in figure 20.6.

8 When you're happy with your WordArt creation, click anywhere outside both the frame and the Enter Text dialog box to close WordArt and pop the WordArt object into the current document.

Close-Up: the WordArt toolbar

The WordArt toolbar buttons are the building blocks of WordArt objects: mix and match, and just have fun!

 *Click **Bold** to make text bold.*

 *Click **Italic** to make text italic.*

 ***Even Height** makes upper and lower case letters the same height.*

 ***Flip** turns characters on their sides.*

 ***Stretch** stretches characters to the frame borders.*

 *Click **Alignment** to align text left, right, or center within the frame.*

 ***Character Spacing** pops up a dialog box that lets you adjust the space between letters.*

 *Click **Special Effects** to rotate text at a different angle.*

 *Click **Shading** for the dialog box shown here. Add shading and change the color of the characters and the background.*

 *Click **Shadow** for a choice of shadow styles and colors.*

 ***Line Thickness** pops up a dialog box with a choice of border styles.*

 *Select another font in the **Font** box.*

 *Click to change the font size; **Best Fit** fits the text to the frame.*

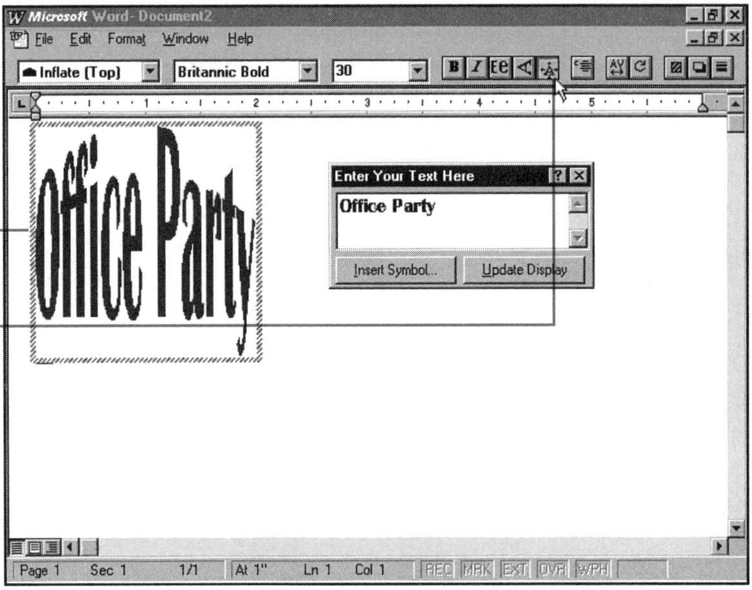

Fig. 20.5
Stretched text, like a stretch limo, gets attention, though possibly not the sort you want.

No need to select WordArt text before formatting it; any text you typed is changed when you click the toolbar buttons.

Fig. 20.6
The possibilities are limited only by how much time you have to spare.

Click the Shadow button to pop up the Shadow dialog box, then take your pick of shadow styles.

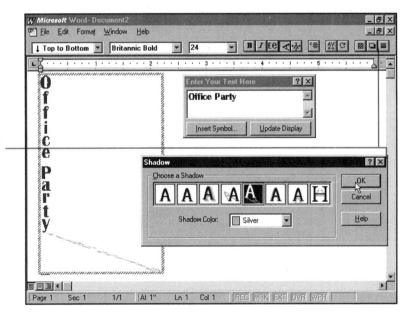

Experimentation is the ticket with WordArt. Try the different effects on for size, and have a little fun doing it. That, after all, is the best revenge for being saddled with assignments like creating the office party poster.

Q&A *I want to format the WordArt frame, but nothing happens when I click it. What do I do?*

You can't format the WordArt frame. It should resize automatically when you change font sizes and WordArt shapes. If you want to add a border or shading, add them to the WordArt object itself with the toolbar buttons.

TIP **If you're having trouble positioning the WordArt object in your** document, click the object to select it. The handles pop up; choose <u>I</u>nsert, <u>F</u>rame to put a frame around it in the document. Now drag the frame anywhere you like.

How do I edit an inserted WordArt object?

Once you stick WordArt in your document, it's easy to make further changes. Just double-click the object to return it to the WordArt editing window.

And if you decide to get rid of the WordArt object entirely, click it once to select it, then press Delete.

Can I make charts in Word?

Numbers tell stories just as words do. Annual reports, marketing studies, and similar documents rely on numbers to make their point. To a trained eye, numbers might speak with the eloquence of words; but for the rest of us, there isn't a lot of poetry and drama in tables of numerical data.

Charts make those numbers come alive. Since Word makes creating charts a snap, use them whenever your document includes numerical data. Charts can supplement your data, or even replace it.

 Plain English, please!

Chart or graph, which is it? Either, or both. The terms are interchangeable. Microsoft Graph has a Chart Type button to let you change chart types, so I call them charts. If you prefer to call them graphs, feel free.

Use Word's built-in chart for fast results

Word has a ready-made sample chart built right into the program. Just enter your own numbers and labels, and you've got an instant chart.

Suppose we're preparing a billing report for a small accounting practice. We want a chart that shows the billings generated by each of the four partners in the first quarter of 1995.

To put Word's sample chart to work on your own data:

1 Click Insert, Object for the Object dialog box. Click Create New, and on the Object Type list, double-click Microsoft Graph 5.0.

2 Graph's sample data and chart pop up, together with the Graph toolbar, as shown in figure 20.7.

Column charts like the one in figure 20.7 display data along two or more arms, called **axes**. The axes correspond to the columns and rows of the datasheet:

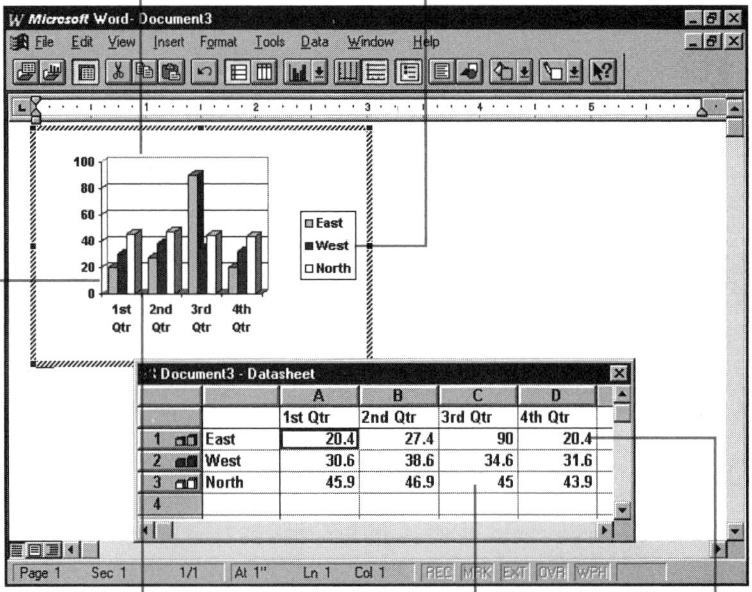

The y axis shows the data series in the rows of the datasheet.

The chart legend is the key to the chart.

Fig. 20.7
The labels and numbers in the datasheet produce the chart. Just drag the data sheet window out of the way to see the chart.

3D charts like this one have a z axis to display data series values.

The x axis shows the categories in the datasheet columns.

The values in each cell are data points.

The data in each row is a data series.

- The vertical y axis represents **data series**, those numbered rows of data in the datasheet. That's why it's also called the series axis. In a column chart, a group of columns of the same color is the graphical way of showing a data series.

- A 3D chart has a second vertical axis, called the z axis, which displays the values in the rows of data in the datasheet. Each value in a row is represented by a single column in a column chart. That's called a **data point**.

- The horizontal x axis represents the categories in the datasheet. In figure 20.7, the categories are each of those lettered columns in the datasheet. The category labels appear at the top of each column in the datasheet, and also along the x, or **category axis**, on the chart. In figure 20.7, the categories are 1st Qtr, 2nd Qtr, and so on.

3 The sample chart reflects the data and the labels in the sample datasheet. All we need to do is enter our own data in the rows and columns of the datasheet. Type the numbers or text in each cell, right over the sample data, then press Enter, Tab, or an arrow key. Every press of the key updates the chart, as shown in figure 20.8.

Fig. 20.8
Enter your own labels and values in the datasheet to create your own chart.

The graph columns adjust to reflect the new data.

The x axis labels change to show the new column headings.

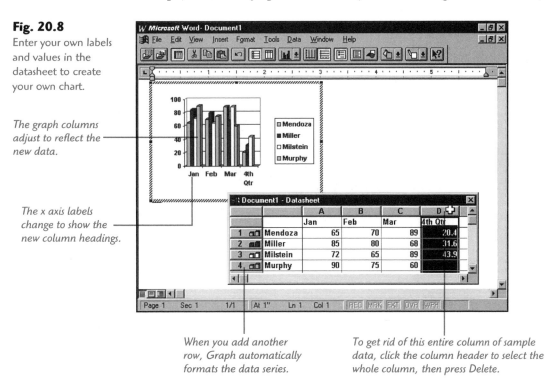

When you add another row, Graph automatically formats the data series.

To get rid of this entire column of sample data, click the column header to select the whole column, then press Delete.

4 To format the numbers and text in the datasheet, drag through the cells you want to format and right-click for the shortcut menu. If you want to display your numbers with dollar signs, for example, drag through the cells to select them, right-click, and select Number from the shortcut menu. The Number Format dialog box pops up, as shown in figure 20.9.

Fig. 20.9

The Number Format dialog box looks more confusing than it is; just choose a category and click one of the format codes.

Look at the Sample to see how your numbers will look.

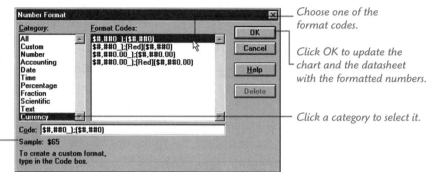

Choose one of the format codes.

Click OK to update the chart and the datasheet with the formatted numbers.

Click a category to select it.

5 Now that our numbers are formatted, we need to tell the reader what the numbers mean with chart and z axis titles. Click the chart, and the datasheet drops out of sight (we haven't lost it, it's just hidden from view).

6 Click Insert, Titles for the Titles dialog box. Click the Chart Title and Values (Z) Axis check boxes, as shown in figure 20.10.

Fig. 20.10

Chart titles tell readers everything they need to know about the chart.

The chart title will go here.

The z axis title will go here.

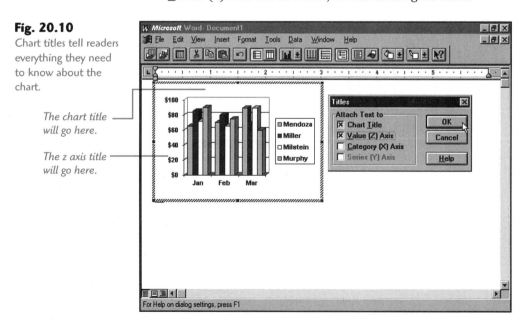

Q&A *How come the Titles choice on the Insert menu is grayed out?*

You have to select the chart before inserting chart titles. Click the chart, and then click Insert, Titles.

7 Click OK in the Titles dialog box. The z axis title is already selected. Type your title, then click the chart title to select it. Click it again (don't double-click; this maneuver calls for two distinct clicks), and type your chart title, as shown in figure 20.11.

Fig. 20.11
With informative titles and labels, the reader knows at a glance what the chart is all about.

Click View Datasheet to toggle the datasheet display.

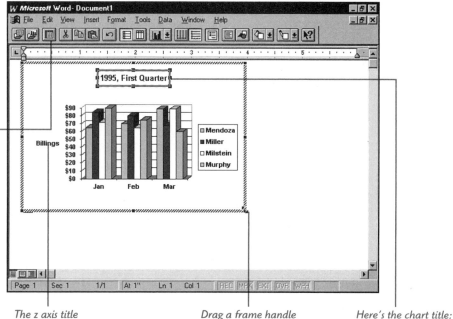

The z axis title

Drag a frame handle to resize the chart.

Here's the chart title; click to select it.

 TIP **To align a z axis title parallel with the z axis, select the chart, then** right-click the title to get the shortcut menu. Choose Format Axis Title on the shortcut menu; that pops up the Format Axis Title dialog box. Click the Alignment tab in the Format Axis Title dialog box, then click your choice of Orientation options. Click OK when you're done.

8 With your own data and titles, the sample chart is now *your* chart. Click anywhere outside the chart to pop it into your document.

9 Once the chart is in your document, click it, then select Insert, Frame to put a frame around it. Click Format, Frame for the Frame dialog box, and choose a text wrapping option.

To edit the chart further, double-click it to return to Microsoft Graph 5.0.

This chart's not my type: formatting tips and tricks

Modified with your own data, Word's sample chart is perfectly acceptable. But if acceptable isn't good enough, you don't have to settle for it. A few clicks can completely transform Word's canned chart.

Changing the chart type is the most radical transformation you can make. It's also the easiest. The default type is a 3D column chart.

To change the chart type, double-click the chart if it's already in your document. That returns you to Microsoft Graph 5.0. Now click the Chart Type drop-down arrow on the Graph toolbar for a palette of chart types. Click any one of them to change your chart type, as shown in figure 20.12.

Fig. 20.12
The Chart Type button gives you a fast chart makeover, but not all charts are suitable for all types of data.

The Chart Type button changes to show your last selected chart type.

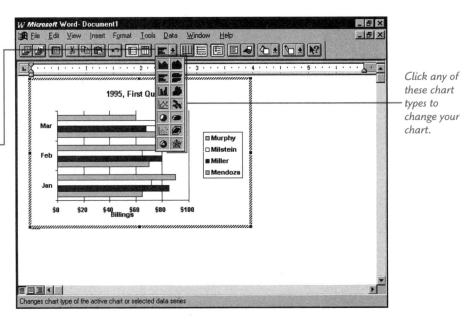

Click any of these chart types to change your chart.

What chart type should I use?

With all the available chart types, you're probably wondering what type is best. Some chart types work for certain types of data, some don't. To see all the available chart types, click Format, Chart Type to pop up the Chart Type dialog box shown in figure 20.13.

Fig. 20.13
Word has a chart for every type of data, and each chart type has several subtypes to choose from.

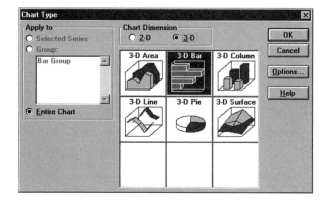

Double-click any one of the chart types in the Chart Type dialog box to instantly transform your chart. Click the 2D option button in the Chart Type dialog box to view the 2D charts, as shown in figure 20.14.

Fig. 20.14
3D charts are more dramatic, but 2D charts are just as informative as their 3D cousins.

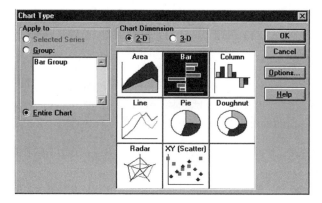

The difference between 2D and 3D charts is mostly aesthetic. In either case, the best choice of chart depends on your data:

- **Bar charts** like the one in figure 20.12 show comparisons among different items in one period of time, or changes in different items over several periods (annual sales and expenses for one year or several, for example).

- **Pie charts** are used to show the relationship between the parts and the whole. Pie charts only show one data series (different budget items as parts of the total budget, for example).

- **Line charts** show changes over time for one item or several (your stock's performance over the past six months against the Dow, for example).

- **Area charts** show changing values over time, like line charts, and proportional relationships, like pie charts.

- **Scatter charts** are often used in statistics to show the strength of the relationship between single values and a mean value.

- **Radar charts** illustrate differences between each data series, and between many data series simultaneously. They're sometimes used in complex project management applications.

- **Doughnut charts** are like pie charts; they show the relationship of the parts to the whole. The difference is that doughnuts show multiple data series. Each ring of the doughnut corresponds to a different row of data on your datasheet.

Chart interior makeovers with a click or two

Ever move your furniture around for a change of pace? You can do the same kind of thing with the interior of your chart. Everything in the chart—axes, titles, legends, data series, and points—can be altered to suit.

No matter what the alteration, the basic principle is the same: click the object in the chart to pop up the handles. Then either drag the object to move it, or right-click for the shortcut menu and choose a formatting option. Change the colors of your bars, the fonts of your titles, or the appearance of the chart background.

Figure 20.15 shows a selected data series and the shortcut menu that pops up when you right-click the selected object.

Click any of the columns to select the data series, right click for the shortcut menu, then change the patterns or colors.

Click these buttons to toggle Vertical and Horizontal grid lines on and off.

Fig. 20.15
Click an object to select it, then make any changes you want from the shortcut menu.

These are the chart walls. Click the walls or floor to select them, then right-click for the shortcut menu.

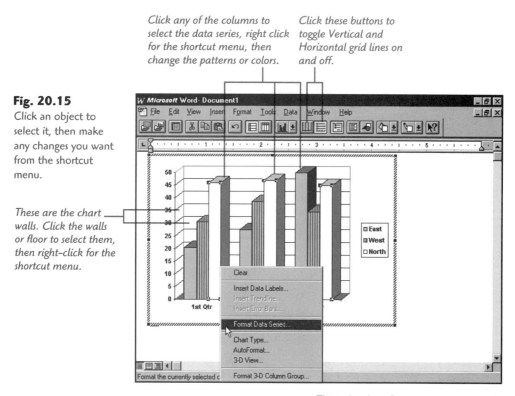

This is the chart floor.

Take a slice out of your pie

Here's a nifty chart interior alteration: if you have a single data series, select a pie chart with the Chart Type button. If one of the slices of the pie is a mere sliver, it'll be hard to see.

If that's the case, draw the slice out of the pie:

1 Click the pie to select the data series. The data series handles pop up.

2 Click the slice you want to pull out of the pie, and the data point handles appear.

3 Now drag a data point handle to slip the slice out of the pie, as shown in figure 20.16.

Fig. 20.16
Pie charts are more appetizing if you can see all the slices.

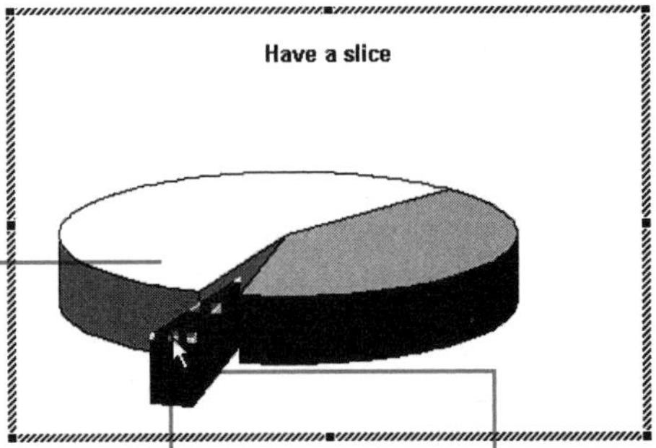

Have a slice

Click anywhere in the pie to get the data series handles.

Drag a data point handle to slide the slice out.

Click the slice for the data point handles.

21

Customizing Word

● In this chapter:

- **How do I change what I see on the screen?**

- **Adding and removing toolbar buttons is more like a snap**

- **I need a toolbar for what *I* do in Word**

- **What's a macro?**

Does your desk look like it's been hit by a hurricane? Or maybe it's as tidy as a Swiss village. Whatever your work habits, you can make Word as comfortable as your own desktop. . . . .

Build to suit" suggests the property-for-sale ads. Three words that say a lot about the way we like to rearrange our surroundings to please ourselves.

Historian Kevin Starr tells the story of a handful of alterations-minded Californians. In 1853 they stumbled on a three thousand-year-old redwood tree, over three hundred feet high and nearly a hundred feet around. Unimpressed, they spent weeks chopping the giant down. The polished stump became a dance floor. The fate of the hollowed-out trunk? A bowling alley.

One big benefit of the computer age: make any alterations you want, and they stay on your screen. Word has all kinds of options for adjusting the program to your tasks and preferences. You can also restore the original settings if you don't like your alterations. When you build Word to suit, the only lasting impact is on your work habits.

Window work: fit the editing window to the job

Some writers type happily on crowded trains or planes. Marcel Proust preferred an isolated room lined with cork. Word accommodates itself to either style; crowd the screen with tools, or work in a completely bare editing window. Your chore might dictate your choice. If you're writing a long, plain-text document, clear the screen of everything but text to see more of your work. For a document loaded with graphics, keep your tools at your fingertips.

Change your views

To see more document and fewer tools, click View, Full Screen. Everything disappears from the screen except your document and the Full Screen button, as shown in figure 21.1.

To restore the toolbars, menu bar, and all the other screen elements, click the Full Screen button or press Esc.

You can still apply Word's formatting commands in full-screen view. Just use the keyboard shortcuts. Press Ctrl+B, for example, to apply boldface to text (check out the tear-out card in the front of the book for a list of keyboard shortcuts).

Fig. 21.1
It's still Word, but full-screen view looks like a sheet of typewriter paper, about right for a novel or long report.

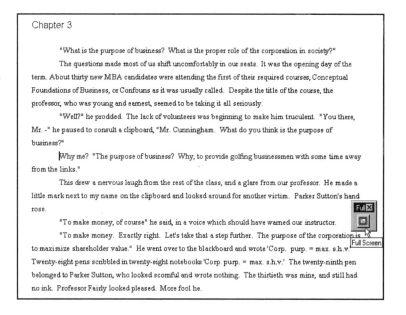

Chapter 3

"What is the purpose of business? What is the proper role of the corporation in society?"

The questions made most of us shift uncomfortably in our seats. It was the opening day of the term. About thirty new MBA candidates were attending the first of their required courses, Conceptual Foundations of Business, or Confouns as it was usually called. Despite the title of the course, the professor, who was young and earnest, seemed to be taking it all seriously.

"Well?" he prodded. The lack of volunteers was beginning to make him truculent. "You there, Mr. -" he paused to consult a clipboard, "Mr. Cunningham. What do you think is the purpose of business?"

Why me? "The purpose of business? Why, to provide golfing businessmen with some time away from the links."

This drew a nervous laugh from the rest of the class, and a glare from our professor. He made a little mark next to my name on the clipboard and looked around for another victim. Parker Sutton's hand rose.

"To make money, of course" he said, in a voice which should have warned our instructor.

"To make money. Exactly right. Let's take that a step further. The purpose of the corporation is to maximize shareholder value." He went over to the blackboard and wrote 'Corp. purp. = max. s.h.v.' Twenty-eight pens scribbled in twenty-eight notebooks 'Corp. purp. = max. s.h.v.' The twenty-ninth pen belonged to Parker Sutton, who looked scornful and wrote nothing. The thirtieth was mine, and still had no ink. Professor Fairly looked pleased. More fool he.

If you like to see all your tools, make the tools easier to see. Click View, Toolbars to pop up the Toolbars dialog box. Click the Large Buttons check box, and your screen will look like figure 21.2.

Fig. 21.2
If you're working late on a heavily formatted document and your eyes start to protest, bigger buttons might help.

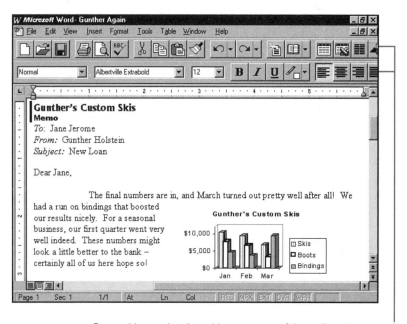

One problem with enlarged buttons: part of the toolbar drops out of view.

Open or split windows to shed light on documents

Not too many writers regret the passing of the typewriter, but those technological relics did have one advantage over their modern descendants: you could still see the top of your page when you typed your way down to the bottom. Even in full-screen view, Word only displays about half a page at a time.

You can compensate for this minor nuisance by either splitting the screen, or by opening a new document window.

To split the screen so that you can see two parts of the current document at once:

1 Click Window, Split. The gray split bar appears across the screen, and the pointer turns into a double-headed arrow.

2 Slide the split bar up or down the screen by moving the mouse; don't drag, just slide. The split bar follows the pointer as you move the mouse.

3 When you've gotten the split bar where you want it, click to split the screen. The editing window is divided in two. Scroll the parts independently to see two different sections of your document at once, as shown in figure 21.3.

Click in either portion of the split to edit that section of the document. To get rid of the split again, double-click the split box on the vertical scroll bar (refer to fig. 21.3) or click Window, Remove Split.

Split screens are handy for displaying a document in different views—Outline, Normal, and Page Layout—simultaneously.

 TIP **If you have sharp eyes and a steady hand with the mouse, here's** the fast way to split the screen: the split box lives at the top of the vertical scroll bar in the Normal, Page Layout, or Outline view. You know you've found it when the pointer turns into a double-headed arrow. Drag or double-click the split box to split the screen. The split box is still functional when you split the screen; it just moves down the vertical scroll bar as you move the split bar (refer to fig. 21.3).

Fig. 21.3

Split-screen view is handy for long documents, or to see the top and bottom of the page at the same time.

The pointer becomes a double-headed arrow when you point at the split bar. Drag the bar to resize either window.

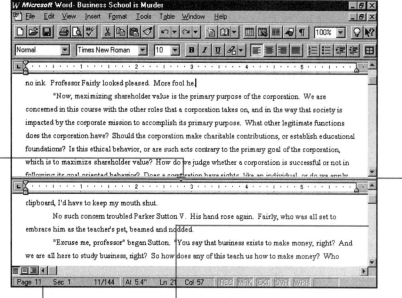

The status bar displays your position in the section of the split that holds the insertion point.

The second view gets its own scroll bar.

Double-click the split box to remove the split. When the screen is split, the split box looks like part of the split bar.

Open windows extend your view

Working on several documents at once? You can view them simultaneously in separate windows by opening each document and clicking Window, Arrange All. Figure 21.4 illustrates how viewing multiple documents on the screen may not always be helpful.

Between the ruler, the title bar, and the scroll bars, you don't get to see too much of the actual document. To put these various screen elements out of sight:

1 Before you open your documents, click View, Ruler to get rid of the ruler.

2 Click Tools, Options, View and clear the check boxes for the Horizontal and Vertical Scroll Bars.

3 Click OK in the Options dialog box, and the scroll bars drop out of sight.

Now open your various documents and arrange the windows on the screen. You'll see a little more document with the scroll bars and ruler out of sight.

Fig. 21.4
The more documents you put on the screen, the less you see of each document.

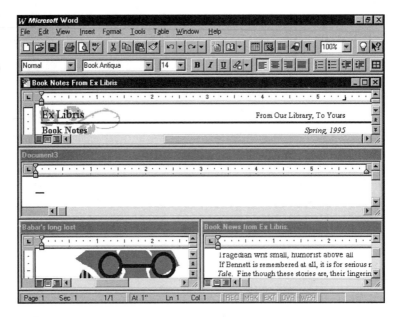

 TIP   **If you're working with several open documents, you might find it** more useful to open them in full-sized windows. Press Ctrl+F6 to flip from document to document.

Make your own toolbars

Between the Standard and the Formatting toolbars, you'll probably find that most of the tools you need are right under your nose. But maybe not all the tools you need are where you can see them. And you just may not have any use for some of the tools on the existing toolbars.

If you've ever wished you could rearrange those obscure buttons on the family VCR in a way that makes them usable, here's a feature you'll like. Word comes with a library of extra tools that you can add to the toolbars. And you can tear off tools you don't need and discard them. You can even make your own toolbar. You'd need a supply of spare parts and an electronics degree to do that to your VCR. With Word, all you need is a mouse.

Make room for me! Removing a toolbar button

We all use Word in different ways. Some might insert loads of Excel tables in their documents; others might never do that at all. Maybe those non-Excel users find themselves producing a lot of envelopes instead.

If you're in the latter camp, get rid of the Insert Excel Worksheet button on the toolbar, and put the Create Envelope button in its place.

First, to get rid of a toolbar button:

1 Click View, Toolbars to pop up the Toolbars dialog box.

2 In the Toolbars dialog box, click Customize for the Customize dialog box shown in figure 21.5.

Fig. 21.5
The Customize dialog box contains a library of fully functional buttons, arranged by category.

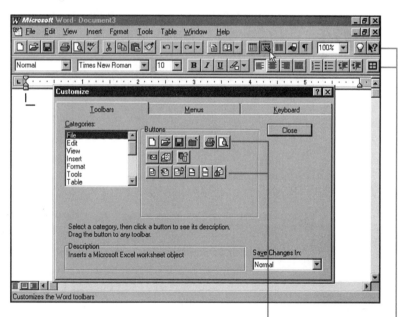

All the buttons in the dialog box can be dragged onto a toolbar.

As long as the Customize dialog box is active, any of these buttons can be dragged off the toolbars.

3 With the Customize dialog box active, any toolbar button is fair game; just drag the button off a toolbar to get rid of it (see fig. 21.6).

Fig. 21.6
If there are toolbar buttons you never use, drag them to oblivion.

Drag a button off
a toolbar, and it
vanishes when
you release the
mouse button.

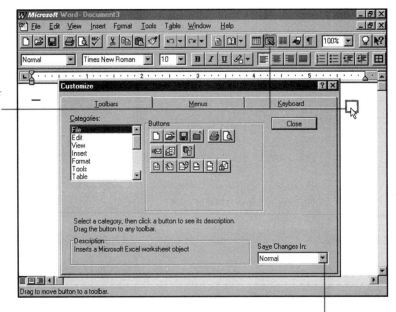

To save your toolbar changes to
a different template, click here.

4 Click Close in the Customize dialog box, and your toolbar changes are saved in the current template.

TIP **Do you want your new toolbar button available to all your** documents, or do you need it only in a particular template? If you want the button in a template other than the default, Normal template, open the other template first. Click File, New and select one of the templates in the New dialog box, for example. Then follow the steps to add and remove toolbar buttons. When you're done, click the Save Changes In drop-down arrow in the Customize dialog box and select a template (refer to fig. 21.6).

Let me in! Adding a toolbar button

To add a button to a toolbar:

1 Click View, Toolbars, for the Toolbars dialog box; then click Customize to pop up the Customize dialog box. Or take the direct route: point at a toolbar's gray background and right-click for the shortcut menu (see fig. 21.7). Choose Customize on the shortcut menu for the Customize dialog box.

2 Click any of the Categories in the Customize dialog box, and the buttons in that category appear in the Buttons box. To see what the buttons do, click one, then read the Description, as shown in figure 21.7.

Right–click between, above, or below the toolbar buttons for the shortcut menu.

Fig. 21.7
Each of these buttons really works, but not until you drag it onto a toolbar.

Click a button, and read the description here.

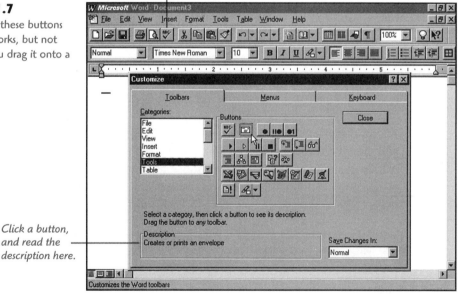

3 When you locate the button you want, drag it onto a toolbar, as shown in figure 21.8.

Here's our new button.

Fig. 21.8

Drag a button from the Customize dialog box to a toolbar, and it works as soon as you close the dialog box.

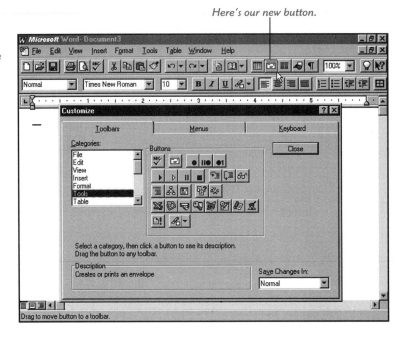

4 Once the button's in place, click Close in the Customize dialog box. You'll find that the newly added button not only works, it even has its own ToolTip.

Add or remove as many buttons as you want to the existing toolbars. If you add more buttons than there's room for on the toolbar, some of the buttons will be pushed out of sight. To see those hidden buttons, point at the toolbar background and drag the toolbar onto the editing window as shown in figure 21.9.

Once the buttons are in sight again, you can use the Customize dialog box to add, remove, or rearrange them.

TIP **To restore a floating toolbar to its docked position, double-click** the toolbar's title bar.

Fig. 21.9
If your toolbars get so crowded that you can no longer see your buttons, just drag the toolbar into view.

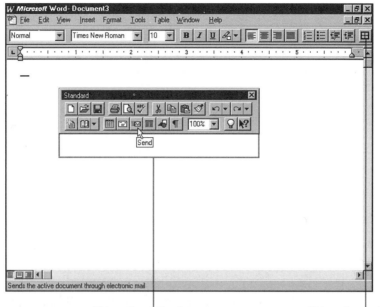

This toolbar is floating.   *This toolbar is docked.*

Q&A   ***How do I get the original toolbars back again?***

You might have so much fun dragging buttons around that you wind up with toolbars that are not as functional as you'd like. To restore the toolbars to their original state, click <u>V</u>iew, <u>T</u>oolbars, <u>R</u>eset. All your button addition and subtractions are erased, and your toolbars are back to where they started.

The Letters toolbar is born

If you often find yourself doing the same chore in Word, build a specialized toolbar to help speed your work. For frequent letter writers, here's how you'd create a Letters toolbar:

1 Click <u>V</u>iew, <u>T</u>oolbars, <u>N</u>ew for the New Toolbar dialog box.

2 In the <u>T</u>oolbar Name edit box, type a name for the new toolbar, as shown in figure 21.10.

Fig. 21.10

Make your toolbar name something you can live with; you can delete new toolbars, but you can't rename them.

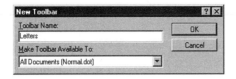

3 Click OK in the New Toolbar dialog box, and the Customize dialog box pops up. The new toolbar appears as well. Select one of the <u>C</u>ategories in the Customize dialog box, and drag buttons onto the new toolbar.

4 As you add buttons to the new toolbar, it grows to accommodate them (see fig. 21.11).

Fig. 21.11

New toolbars expand to hold as many buttons as you care to add.

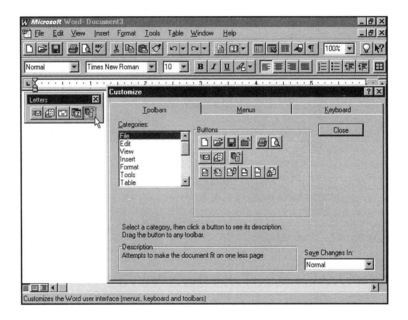

5 Click Close in the Customize dialog box when you're done, and the new toolbar is finished.

You can't delete Word's own toolbars, but you can get rid of any new ones you create. Click <u>V</u>iew, <u>T</u>oolbars. You'll see your new toolbar on the list of Toolbars. Select it, and the <u>D</u>elete button pops up on the dialog box. Click <u>D</u>elete, <u>Y</u>es to delete your new toolbar.

Macros turn Word into a robot assistant

Creating something new is always exciting. Doing the same old thing over and over again is just plain dull. Word has a great gadget to save you from the tedium of repetitive chores: **macros**. Recording a macro is like dictating a memo to a high-speed dictation expert; your every keystroke and mouse click is faithfully taken down. When you run a macro, all your keystrokes and mouse clicks are played back again, just as you performed them.

 Plain English, please!

Macro is a familiar prefix, meaning large or long; think of macroeconomics, or even macrostylous (long-styled, as in prosy authors). In computer lingo, a **macro** is a single command that executes a large number of other commands.

Use a macro for any repetitive task involving more than a couple of keystrokes:

- Text that you type often, like a company name and address.

- Formatting commands that you use and reuse. Macros are especially handy for combining often-used text and formatting commands—your company name in a particular font, for example.

- File searches, especially if you find yourself hunting for the same group of documents all the time.

- Any Word task that requires a series of steps, like setting up a page with special margins and other settings.

Macros are as simple or as complicated as the task they record. You can use a macro for a quick change of fonts and attributes, or for a complex, twenty-step page setup. Either way, there are three easy steps to creating a macro: turn the macro recorder on, perform the chore, and turn the macro recorder off.

Need a letterhead? Let a macro do it for you

Word comes with a choice of letter templates that you can use to craft good-looking correspondence. To view them, click File, New, Letters & Faxes and double-click any of the template icons. I find it faster to use my own macro for letterhead stationery. I can set up the letterhead exactly the way I want it, and with a macro, I only need to set it up once; thereafter, I just run the macro to produce instant stationery.

To create a letterhead macro (or any macro) of your own:

1 Click Tools, Macro for the Macro dialog box. Type a name and description for the macro, as shown in figure 21.12.

Fig. 21.12
Adding a description is a good idea; otherwise, you might forget what the macro is for.

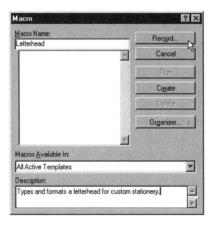

2 Click Record in the Macro dialog box, and the Record Macro dialog box pops up. You can assign a macro to a menu, a toolbar, or a keyboard shortcut from here, but for now we won't bother. Just click OK in the Record Macro dialog box.

3 The Record Macro dialog box drops out of sight, and you get the Macro Record toolbar instead. The pointer acquires a little cassette icon, to remind you that whatever actions you take are being recorded. Whatever your Word chore, perform it just as you would ordinarily.

For a letterhead like the one shown in figure 21.13, click View, Header and Footer, type your text in the header, change fonts, add an inside border, and align some of the text flush right.

Fig. 21.13

For text and formatting that you reuse all the time, macros turn the chore into a one-time job.

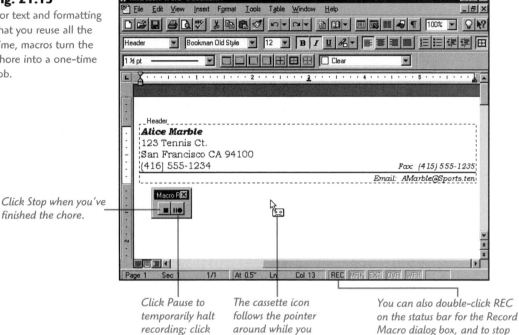

Click Stop when you've finished the chore.

Click Pause to temporarily halt recording; click again to restart recording.

The cassette icon follows the pointer around while you record the macro.

You can also double-click REC on the status bar for the Record Macro dialog box, and to stop recording a macro.

4 Click the Stop button on the Record Macro toolbar when you've finished the chore you're recording. That puts the Record Macro toolbar away, and you can go back to work.

TIP **Another way to start and stop recording a macro: double-click** REC on the status bar to pop up the Record Macro dialog box (refer to fig. 21.13). Double-click REC again to stop macro recording.

If you make a mistake while you're recording the macro, just correct it as you would ordinarily. When it's time to play back the macro, even though your errors are recorded, the corrections are recorded too. The end result should be fine.

Make sure that you perform all your repetitive keystrokes and commands while recording the macro. For example, if you click the Borders button on the Formatting toolbar to add borders during macro recording, click the Borders button again while the macro is still recording to put away the

Borders toolbar. Same thing with headers and footers. If you include either one (or both) in your macro, click View, Headers and Footers again while macro record is on to exit the header or footer.

Q&A ***I'm trying to select text while recording this macro, but I can't seem to do it with the mouse!***

That's because you *can't* select text with the mouse while recording a macro. Use the Shift+arrow key combination instead. The mouse does work for toolbar buttons and menu commands during macro recording.

Macro recorded? Run it

The only labor involved in creating macros is performing the chore you're recording. Once that's done, playing the macro is a snap.

To play back a macro:

1 Click Tools, Macro for the Macro dialog box.

2 Your newly recorded macro appears on the list under Macro Name; select the macro, then click Run. That runs the macro, inserting any text and formatting you've recorded at the insertion point.

If you recorded a letterhead macro, just run the macro any time you want letterhead stationery. That saves you a lot of typing and formatting, to say nothing of a trip to the printer.

A macro mistake! Can I fix it?

The last thing anyone needs is another of life's minor irritations. Sometimes that's just what you get with a macro. After you go to the trouble of recording it, playing back a macro might reveal a flaw or two in your creation.

If the flaws seem more like major errors, you can always delete the macro. Click Tools, Macro for the Macro dialog box, select the offending macro, and click Delete to do that. You can sort out what went wrong, then just record a new, error-free macro.

But if it's just a question of a minor bug, squash it. Word includes some handy tools for editing macros, and it doesn't take a programming expert to put them to work. Suppose that letterhead macro we just created was fine in all respects, but we got a digit wrong in the phone number's area code. It's a lot easier to fix a small mistake like that than it is to rerecord the whole macro.

To edit a macro:

1 Click <u>T</u>ools, <u>M</u>acro for the Macro dialog box, select the macro, and click <u>E</u>dit. That pops up the Macro Editing window and toolbar shown in figure 21.14.

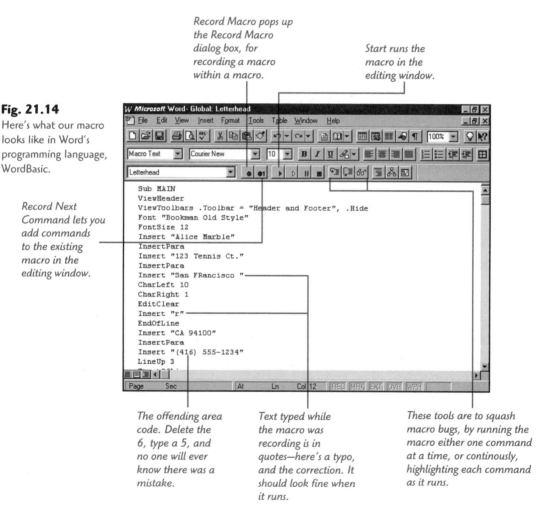

Record Macro pops up the Record Macro dialog box, for recording a macro within a macro.

Start runs the macro in the editing window.

Fig. 21.14
Here's what our macro looks like in Word's programming language, WordBasic.

Record Next Command lets you add commands to the existing macro in the editing window.

```
Sub MAIN
ViewHeader
ViewToolbars .Toolbar = "Header and Footer", .Hide
Font "Bookman Old Style"
FontSize 12
Insert "Alice Marble"
InsertPara
Insert "123 Tennis Ct."
InsertPara
Insert "San FRancisco "
CharLeft 10
CharRight 1
EditClear
Insert "r"
EndOfLine
Insert "CA 94100"
InsertPara
Insert "(416) 555-1234"
LineUp 3
```

The offending area code. Delete the 6, type a 5, and no one will ever know there was a mistake.

Text typed while the macro was recording is in quotes—here's a typo, and the correction. It should look fine when it runs.

These tools are to squash macro bugs, by running the macro either one command at a time, or continuously, highlighting each command as it runs.

2 The Macro toolbar can be used to add commands to a macro, or debug a troubled macro. For a simple text fix, we don't need it. Text that you type while recording a macro appears in quotes in the macro editing window (refer to fig. 21.14). Simply locate the text you want to change, use Backspace or Delete to clear the mistake, and type in the correction.

3 When you've corrected your macro, click <u>F</u>ile, <u>C</u>lose. At the prompt, click <u>Y</u>es to save your changes.

The <u>F</u>ind and <u>R</u>eplace commands on the <u>E</u>dit menu are handy for fixing text in the macro editing window. They not only locate mistakes and fix them, Find and Replace also ensure that you don't accidentally delete any of the WordBasic commands and punctuation. Each of those quotation marks, for example, is a vital part of the macro. If you zap one by mistake, your macro won't run properly.

What is WordBasic?

When you give commands in Word, to change fonts for example, or to save a file, you click menu choices (or toolbar buttons). That's a bit like ordering from a menu in a restaurant. Macros bypass the menus and execute commands directly, as though you went back to the kitchen and ordered your dinner directly from the chef. To do that, macros talk to the chef, er, to Word, in a language it can understand, called WordBasic. It's a variant of the programming language BASIC, or Beginner's All-purpose Symbolic Instruction Code, which was invented by a couple of Dartmouth College mathemati-cians, John Kemeny and Thomas Kurtz. Their idea was to create a computer programming language that non-experts could use. Kemeny and Kurtz knew what they were doing. Basic is still in use by millions of computer types around the world, decades after its invention. Although Basic is enough like plain English for casual users to understand, actually inventing the language required considerable expertise. How much expertise? John Kemeny, a distinguished math-ematician in his own right, got his start as Albert Einstein's assistant!

22

Mail Merge, for Homemade Mass Mailings

● **In this chapter:**

- **Just what is mail merge?**

- **I've got a letter and a dozen folks to send it to—now what?**

- **Main document? Data source? Explain, please!**

- **I'm only sending letters to Kansas**

- **How about some labels and envelopes?**

Really clever goods look hand-crafted, even when they're not. Like Word's mail merge documents—they're mass-produced, but they don't look it . . . . ❯

Ransom E. Olds' 1901 Oldsmobiles were successful—until people started driving them. Olds' cars didn't last on roads designed for the horse and buggy. Henry Ford came along and designed a car tough enough for rough roads; the only problem was producing enough of them to satisfy demand.

Ford's answer was the assembly line, thanks to which the Model T was a historic success. But eventually, the car passed into history. Its problem? Every Model T was identical; they were mass-produced, and they looked it.

Buyers began demanding cars that at least gave the illusion of individuality. And that's still true. Our cars can be identical, but we're happier if mine is red and yours is green. That's why you'll like Word's mail merge feature. You get mass-produced documents, letters by the hundreds if you want them, that look entirely personalized. Your assembly-line letters may not make history, but your readers will appreciate the personal touch, however illusory.

Why do I need mail merge?

A dozen identical letters to write, a dozen people to send them to, and you've got the makings of a really tedious chore—but not if you use mail merge. In a merge, you write a single letter in one document, enter all your recipients' names and addresses in another document, and then merge the two to produce as many personalized letters as you need. Magic? Not really. Convenient? You bet.

What happens in a merge?

Like Ford's assembly line, mail merges take the shell of the finished product, add parts as needed, then roll out the completed goods.

There are three parts to a merge:

- You enter items like your recipients' names and addresses in a handy **data form**. All the information you enter in the data form, such as last names, first names, street addresses, and so on, is saved in a table, called the **data source**. The data source supplies all the spare parts for your assembly-line document.

- Once you've entered all your data, you write the letter. The body of the letter is text formatted any way you like. But instead of typing in names and addresses, you insert **merge fields**. Just like that space on a tax form labeled LAST NAME, merge fields are labeled spaces that look like this: <<LastName>>. You choose the merge fields you need from a list, and click to insert them in the appropriate spots in your letter. The document containing the merge fields is called the **main document**. It's the shell of the final product, ready to be filled in along the assembly line.

- When you perform the merge, the spare parts from the data source, those names and addresses, are plugged into the corresponding merge fields in the main document, turning a shell of a document into the final product. Last names replace all the <<LastName>> merge fields, and so on. You get as many letters as you have names and addresses in the data source.

Use mail merges whenever you have one document to send to more than a couple of recipients. You can also use a merge to produce dozens of labels and envelopes, each one neatly addressed with the names and addresses you entered in the data source.

Figure 22.1 shows you what a typical main document and data source look like.

Plain English, please!

A **data source** is a database, an orderly list of information. Databases have their own jargon (doesn't everything?), a smattering of which you'll need to know. **Records** are like Rolodex cards; each record holds all the information for one of your letter recipients. The items of information in a record—last names, first names, and so on—are called **fields**. In a Word data source table, the rows of the table are records, and the columns are fields. The top row of the table (the **header row**) labels each column, or field.

Each column is called a
field, containing items of
data such as last names.

The data source is a table that
Word creates; each row is like a
Rolodex card of information.

Fig. 22.1
You probably won't
need to tinker with the
data source itself, but
as you step through the
mail merge, it's helpful
to know what the
jargon refers to.

The header row has the
names of each field.

These are the merge
fields. They're replaced
by the data in the
corresponding fields in
the data source.

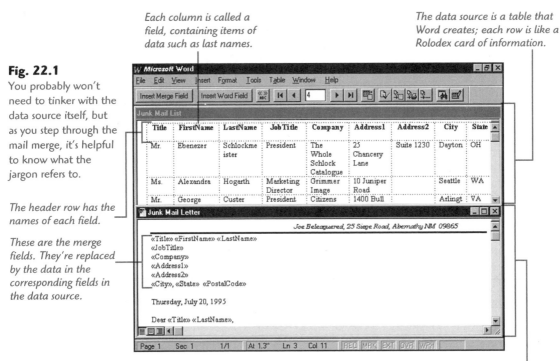

The main document holds
the body text of your letter.

Mail merges made easy

Is your mail box as crowded with junk mail as mine? Catalogues, fund-raising letters, political statements—we're bombarded with mass mailings. Mail merges give you the chance to strike back. You create your own form letter, Word fills in the blanks, and then produces a blizzard of completed letters that you can send to as many recipients as you care to.

Mail merges start with a data source

Use mail merge to send newsletters, product announcements, change of address letters, whatever you like. Another possible use for mail merge: gather a few days' worth of junk mail, clip out the senders' names and addresses, and send them all a letter asking them not to send you any more letters. If your letters are addressed to the senders by name, they might even get results.

To produce a mass mailing with mail merge, first create the data source, the file for your recipients' names and addresses:

1 In a new blank document, click <u>T</u>ools, Mail Me<u>r</u>ge. The Mail Merge Helper pops up.

2 Click <u>C</u>reate in the Mail Merge Helper for the list of options shown in figure 22.2.

Fig. 22.2
We'll tackle envelopes and labels later. For now, we want a stern letter.

3 Click Form <u>L</u>etters on the Create drop-down list, and a message from Word pops up, prompting you to choose the location of your main document. Since we started from a new blank document, click <u>A</u>ctive Window.

4 That takes us back to the Mail Merge Helper. Click <u>G</u>et Data and choose <u>C</u>reate Data Source. The Create Data Source dialog box pops up, as shown in figure 22.3.

Fig. 22.3

Remember the header row? Here's where you get to pick what goes into it.

To add a field name of your own, type it here and click Add Field Name.

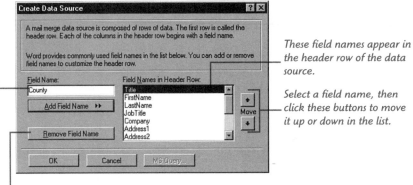

These field names appear in the header row of the data source.

Select a field name, then click these buttons to move it up or down in the list.

Select any field name you don't need, then click Remove Field Name to discard it.

5 The Create Data Source dialog box is where you decide just what items of information to put in your data source. If the names in the list of Field Names have your data covered, do nothing in the Create Data Source dialog box. But if you want to tinker with your field names, try one of these options:

- Scan the list of Field Names In Header Row. If any of the field names don't apply to your data, select them and click Remove Field Name. If you're sending letters in the U.S., for example, you might not need the Country field name.

- None of the field names on the list apply to your data? Type your own field name in the Field Name edit box, then click Add Field Name to add it to the list.

- If you want to reorder the field names, click a name, then move it up or down the list with the Move arrows.

TIP **The main document determines what data is included in your** letters, and where the data will go *in* the letter. That being the case, you don't have to worry too much about your choices in the Create Data Source dialog box.

6 Click OK in the Create Data Source dialog box, and the Save As dialog box pops up. Type a name for your data source file in the File Name edit box and click Save.

7 Another message from Word appears, with the helpful information that the data source you just created contains no data (I like to yell "I KNOW that!" at this point, but that's optional). Click Edit Data Source.

8 The data form pops up. There are edit boxes for each of the field names you included in the Create Data Source dialog box. Enter your first record, typing the data in the appropriate box. Click the box you want, or press Tab to go from box to box. Figure 22.4 shows the data form completely filled in, but you don't have to fill in every field in every record. Word ignores any blanks when it performs the merge.

These are the field names from the Create Data Source dialog box.

Fig. 22.4
It takes a few steps to get here, but the data form is a handy way to enter information.

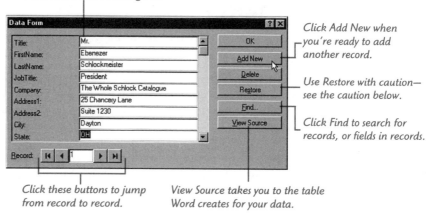

Click Add New when you're ready to add another record.

Use Restore with caution— see the caution below.

Click Find to search for records, or fields in records.

Click these buttons to jump from record to record.

View Source takes you to the table Word creates for your data.

CAUTION **The Restore button on the data form restores your entries to the** way they were when you last saved them. If you click Restore before saving a record, any entries in that record are wiped out. You "restore" the blank edit boxes! Helpful, no? If you call up an existing record, edit it, and make a mistake during the edit, use Restore to restore the original record. Restore also won't restore deleted records, by the way.

9 When you've finished typing the fields for your first record, click Add New in the data form. That saves your first record, and clears the edit boxes so you can add the next record. Enter all your records, clicking Add New for each one.

10 Once you've entered all your records, click OK in the data form. The data form drops out of sight, and you're in the main document, with the

Mail Merge toolbar parked above it. At the moment, the document is blank, but we'll change that.

Q&A *How come I don't see that data source table Word created?*

 It's there, but you don't need to bother with it. The data source lurks in the background, supplying data as needed. If you want to examine the data source, click the Edit Data Source button on the Mail Merge toolbar for the data form, then click View Source.

The next step: make your own form letter

No matter how cleverly the "personalized" name and address is slipped in, it's usually easy to spot a form letter. That stilted, unnatural language, the carefully noncommittal constructions, it's all a dead giveaway. When you get one of those magazine subscription letters that begin "You Jane E. Smythe have a unique opportunity…" you can practically see the merge code where your name was inserted.

Here's your chance to improve on the standard boilerplate. Form letters in Word are still form letters, but at least they're of your own writing. To create the mail merge form letter:

Insert Merge Field

1 Once you've clicked OK in the data form (see step 10 on the previous page), you're in a blank document with the Mail Merge toolbar displayed above it. Click the Insert Merge Field button on the Mail Merge toolbar, and a list of your field names drops down, as shown in figure 22.5.

2 There's a merge field for every one of the data source field names. Click a merge field, and it pops into the document at the insertion point. Insert a title where you want a title, and so on. If you want your data separated by a space or a blank line, be sure to press the spacebar or the Enter key after inserting the merge field. The salutation and recipient's address part of the form letter might look like figure 22.6.

Fig. 22.5
You saw them in the Create Data Source dialog box, and in the data form, and here they are again as merge fields: the ubiquitous field names.

Click any of the merge fields to insert them at the insertion point.

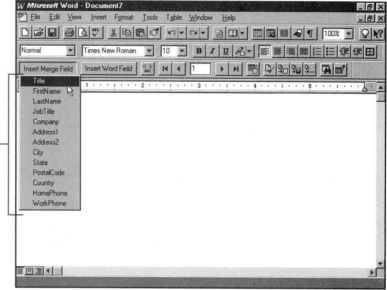

Press Enter to put merge fields on a new line, just as though you were entering text on a new line.

Fig. 22.6
Insert a merge field from the Insert Merge Field list wherever you want the corresponding data.

Insert spaces between merge fields where you'd want spaces between words in your text.

Don't forget to include punctuation between merge fields, like commas.

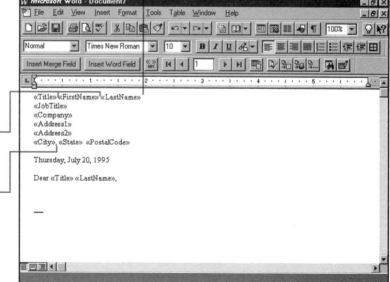

3 Once you've inserted a few merge fields, click the View Merged Data button on the Mail Merge toolbar to preview the merged document. The merge fields are replaced by data from the data source, as shown in figure 22.7.

Click View Merged Data for a preview of the merged document.

Click these buttons to preview additional records from the data source—they only work if you click the View Merged Data button first.

Fig. 22.7
You haven't committed yourself to the merge yet; the View Merged Data button just gives you a sneak preview.

The information from the data source replaces the merge fields when you view merged data.

If you need to change a record, click Edit Data Source to display the data form.

Want to find a particular record? Click Find Record to ferret it out.

Q&A   *I inserted a merge field I didn't want!*

It's easy to click the wrong merge field. Or you might decide you don't want a particular field in a particular spot in your document. Either way, click the merge field to select it. Word shades the merge field to show it's been selected; press Delete to get rid of it.

CAUTION   **Don't try to type merge fields by hand; Word will ignore any such** attempts. For merge fields to work, they have to be inserted with the Insert Merge Field button on the Mail Merge toolbar.

4 Once you've got your merge fields where you want them, type the letter body text. Insert merge fields throughout the letter if you like. Add a letterhead, save the document, and the finished form letter will look something like figure 22.8.

Fig. 22.8
Somehow a form letter always winds up sounding like a form letter, no matter how you try to disguise it.

You can use the same merge field as many times as you like.

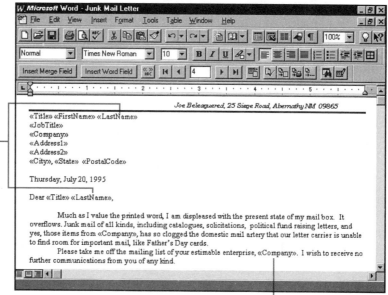

Merge fields can go anywhere in the main document, including in the body text.

Data done? Form finished?
Merge maneuvers come next

Assembling data and writing the form letter is the labor-intensive part of mail merges. The actual merge is handled by Word, so it's pretty easy. How easy?

 With your data entered, and your form letter completed, click the Merge to New Document button on the Mail Merge toolbar. Word merges your data and form letter, and gives you multiple copies of your letter with the data filled in, one copy for each record in the data source, as shown in figure 22.9.

Word gives your merged document a temporary file name, but
there's no need to save the file.

Print Preview mode,
with the Multiple
Pages button selected

Fig. 22.9

Instant custom letters.
Mail merge sure beats
retyping the same
letter a dozen times.

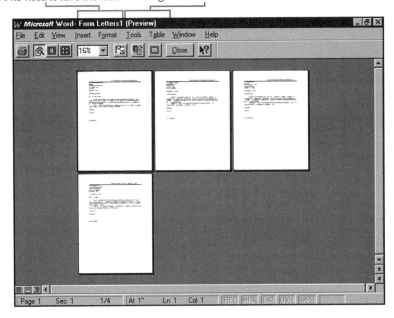

You'll want to print a sample page or two before turning your printer loose
on all the merged documents. That way you can check to make sure that all
the merge codes are in the right place, and that you haven't made any data
entry errors when you set up the data source.

To print a preview document, click File, Print. In the Print dialog box, click
the Current Page option, then click OK. That prints a single page of the
merge file; eyeball the printout carefully before sending the entire file to the
printer.

If you want envelopes or labels addressed to your recipients, read on.

TIP **There's no need to save the new document containing the merged**
letters—that just takes up hard disk real estate. Since you've saved your data
source file and your form letter, you can merge them again any time you
want to.

What if I don't want to merge all my data?

Maybe you don't want to send a letter to everyone in your data file. No problem. Click the Mail Merge button on the Mail Merge toolbar to pop up the Merge dialog box shown in figure 22.10.

Fig. 22.10
All your records are numbered, from 1 to whatever. Just enter the range of records you want to merge in the Merge dialog box.

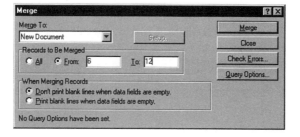

Click From in the Merge dialog box, then enter the range of record numbers you want to merge. If you have twelve records, for example, and you want to merge only the last six, enter From **6** To **12**, then click Merge in the Merge dialog box.

Can't remember which record is numbered what? Click Close in the Merge dialog box. Then click the View Merged Data button on the Mail Merge toolbar and use the Previous Record and Next Record buttons to browse your records. The record numbers appear in the Go To Record box, in between the Next Record and Previous Record buttons.

I'm only sending letters to Kansas

Merging only a range of records isn't the most refined way of orchestrating your mass mailing. What if you only want to send letters to folks in a single town or state? Or maybe you only want to send letters to doctors. Either way, you can **filter** your records to extract exactly the ones you want, and just merge those extracted records.

To filter data source records:

1 Click the Mail Merge Helper button on the Mail Merge toolbar (if the toolbar isn't displayed, choose Tools, Mail Merge).

2 In the Mail Merge Helper, click Query Options to pop up the Query Options dialog box.

3 Click the Filter Records tab in the Query Options dialog box, then click the Field drop-down arrow.

4 That gets you a list of those familiar field names we've seen in various guises. Select a field name from the list; if you're sending mail to Kansas only, choose the State field name from the dropped-down list.

5 By default, the Comparison is Equal To. In English, that means that only those records in which the State field contains exactly what you type in the Compare To edit box will be chosen. For our Kansas mailing, we'd type **Kansas** in the Compare To edit box. Figure 22.11 makes it all more comprehensible.

Click here for the other comparison operators, like Not Equal To or Less Than.

Fig. 22.11
The Query Options dialog box is a powerful search tool, and after you play around with it a little, it's pretty easy to use.

You can refine the filter further by adding additional fields and criteria.

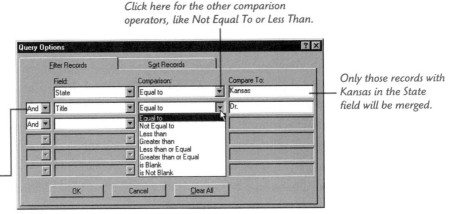

Only those records with Kansas in the State field will be merged.

6 Refine the filter still more if you want to. For letters to doctors in Kansas, leave the default And operator at the beginning of the second row, click the Field drop-down arrow in the second row, and choose Title. Still on the second row, set the Comparison to Equal To, and type **Dr.** in the Compare To edit box.

7 Click OK when you're done, then go ahead and merge. Only the records that match the criteria you've set will be merged into your main document.

How about those envelopes and labels?

We just merged our data into a form letter; it's just as easy to merge the same data into envelopes or mailing labels.

TIP   **Word gets your envelope return address from the User Info tab of** the Options dialog box. If you want to change the return address, click Tools, Options, User Info. Then type a new address in the Mailing Address box and click OK.

Envelopes by the bushel

To create mail merge envelopes:

1 Click the Mail Merge Helper button on the Mail Merge toolbar. In the Mail Merge Helper, click Create, Envelopes.

2 If you've already merged your form letters, a Word message pops up asking if you want to convert the merged document into envelopes, or open a new document for your envelopes. You'll probably want to do the latter, so click New Main Document.

3 Now we're back to the Mail Merge Helper. Click Get Data and choose Open Data Source.

4 The Open Data Source dialog box pops up. It should look familiar—it's close kin to the Open and Save As dialog boxes. Double-click the file name of your data source file.

5 That gets you another Word message box. Click Set Up Main Document in the message box.

It took a while to get here, but that pops up the Envelope Options dialog box. Here you can change the fonts or pick a different envelope size.

6 Click OK in the Envelope Options dialog box, and eureka! We've arrived at the Envelope Address dialog box.

7 In the Envelope Address dialog box, click Insert Merge Field, and select merge fields to insert in the Sample Envelope Address box, as shown in figure 22.12.

Fig. 22.12

This is just like inserting merge fields in the form letter; click a field on the list, and it pops in at the insertion point.

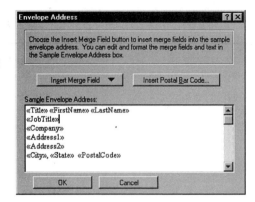

8 Don't forget spaces, blank lines, and punctuation in between the merge fields. Click OK in the Envelope Address dialog box when you're done.

9 We've come this far, and we're back to the beginning: the Mail Merge Helper reappears. But the work is done. Just click Merge in the Mail Merge Helper, and the Merge dialog box pops up (refer to fig. 22.10).

10 Choose all your records or a range of records. Click Merge in the Merge dialog box. Word merges your data into envelopes and displays them in Page Layout view. Look them over to make sure that all is right, then go ahead and print the envelopes.

If you want labels instead of envelopes, go back to step 1 and click Create, Mailing Labels. Then work your way through the same steps we took to create envelopes. Word automatically formats the labels for a variety of standard Avery label types. Just check your label package for the model number, and choose the same type of labels when you get to the Word Label Options dialog box.

23

Pony Express It's Not: Sending Data In and Out of Word

● **In this chapter:**

- **Can I open old word processor files in Word?**

- **I want my Excel chart in a Word document**

- **How do I get at PowerPoint's clip art?**

- **I can send faxes and e-mail, right from Word?**

Exchanging data between applications on your hard drive, or between offices across the continent, just isn't what it used to be. Thank goodness for that! . . . . ●

The next time you get a Federal Express delivery, spare a thought for FedEx's ancestor: the Pony Express. The daredevil riders of the famous mail service raced letters from Missouri to California—almost two thousand miles—in eight days, twice as fast as the regular mail.

Their route was no milk run. Besides rough terrain and bad weather, two- and four-legged dangers lurked at every pass. The "pony-riders'" greatest admirer was Mark Twain, who reported that there was "but little frivolous correspondence" in a Pony Express mail bag. Only important business letters justified the hefty (in 1860) five-dollar charge.

Heroics aren't required to send important letters, or any other kind of data, in and out of Word. A few quick mouse clicks, and the job is done. And it doesn't take much more time than that for Word to dispatch faxes or e-mail to anywhere, from California to Missouri and beyond. About the only danger you face exchanging data in and out of Word is missing the exchange; look away for a moment, and it's already happened.

What do I do with my old files?

Summer in Europe. Sunshine, fountains, outdoor cafes—and phrase-book-studying tourists bumping into walls. We might be among them. Without those handy phrase books, how could we convert unfamiliar words into plain old English?

Word has its own phrase books built right into the program. They're called **filters** and **converters**. Word uses them to translate files from other applications into its own terms. The translation is automatic; just open your file, and Word puts its phrase books to work. You don't have to do a thing.

Word's translation isn't perfect. Just as that French you try to speak to the cabby at the airport may not sound exactly *comme il faut*, files from other applications may look a little different when you open them in Word. Fonts, spacing, and page layouts may not turn out exactly the way you want them to. It depends on your original application, and on how heavily formatted your document happens to be:

- Documents from older versions of Word will convert to Word for Windows 95 with few, if any, changes. Just open your document.

- Documents created in other Windows word processors, like Word-Perfect for Windows, may undergo some formatting changes when you open them in Word. Chances are, the changes won't be too drastic, and you can put all the Word formatting tools to work on any necessary repairs.

Word's file translations will be close to the original, even for files in older DOS word processors. Figure 23.1 shows a file created in WordPerfect 5.0 for DOS in one window, and the same file in the Word editing window.

Fig. 23.1
The fonts changed slightly when the WordPerfect 5.0 document was opened in Word, but not much.

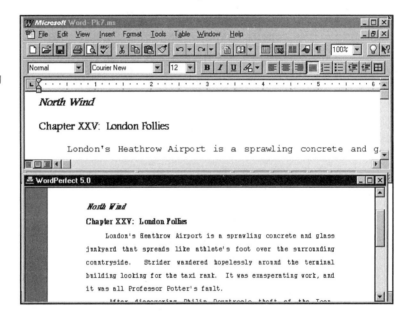

This imported file isn't behaving

If you're in France, naturally you grab a book of French phrases. Word does the same thing when you import a file from another word processor; the right converter or filter is chosen for you automatically. And just as you would if you were translating foreign words into English, Word makes some judgment calls about the best way to render a "foreign" file in Word.

Word's decisions can sometimes give odd results. Documents imported from certain versions of WordPerfect, for example, may give you a lot of trouble if you try to format them with balanced newspaper columns in Word. It's a bit like a Frenchman teaching an English course, and insisting that "a veal is a dead calf" (true story). Technically correct, but...

Although that Frenchman will probably never see the error of his ways, Word is more flexible. If your imported document seems to be misbehaving in Word, click Tools, Options for the Options dialog box. Click the Compatibility tab, shown in figure 23.2.

On the Compatibility tab:

- It's unlikely to happen, but if Word made an entirely wrong guess about the origins of your imported file, click the Recommended Options For drop-down arrow and select the appropriate file format.

- If your import is acting up, clear the Options check boxes. Then click OK to return to your document.

- Word substitutes the closest match among your installed fonts for imported documents that use fonts not installed in your copy of Windows. If you don't like the choices Word made, just click the Font Substitution button and select different proxy fonts. But you might find it easier to simply change fonts using the Word Formatting toolbar.

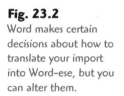

Fig. 23.2
Word makes certain decisions about how to translate your import into Word-ese, but you can alter them.

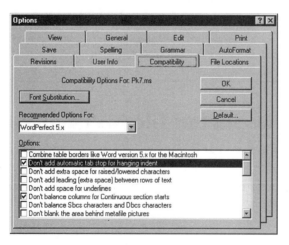

How to put a chart in your document

Word has a charting feature of its own called Microsoft Graph (see Chapter 15 for details). But if you're a serious number-cruncher, you probably use a spreadsheet program like Lotus 1-2-3, Quattro Pro, or Microsoft Excel.

When you stick a chart created in one of those programs into a Word document, you get a pretty snappy document. And sticking a chart into Word is a simple job. Select the chart in the spreadsheet program, copy it, then paste it in Word.

That's the basic idea, anyway. There are a few wrinkles that you should know about. To illustrate them, we'll take an Excel chart and pop it into a Word document.

Stick Excel charts in Word documents the fast way

There are a few things you can do to simplify inserting Excel charts in Word documents:

- Excel chart sheets are too big for Word documents. Chart sheets are what you get when you select your data in Excel and choose Insert, Chart, As New Sheet on the Excel menu bar. They're designed to fill the page, so they'd be out of scale inserted in a page of text in Word. That doesn't mean you *can't* insert a chart sheet in Word. You just have to resize the chart in Excel before shipping it over to Word.

- Embedded charts are the kind you get when you click the Excel ChartWizard button and drag through your worksheet. You probably won't have to resize an embedded Excel chart as drastically as a chart sheet before inserting it in Word. You do have to select the embedded chart with care, however. When you select the chart in Excel to copy it, just click it. Double-clicking the chart in Excel, and then copying it, causes problems if you subsequently try to resize the chart in Word.

- Do your chart editing and resizing in Excel, before you insert the chart in Word. You *can* tinker with Excel charts from within Word, but you'll find it easier to do your tinkering in Excel first.

CAUTION **Save your work before copying and pasting between applications.**
Windows 95 is much more stable than previous incarnations of Windows, especially for maneuvers like these. Unexpected things can still happen, though, and there's nothing worse than losing a morning's work because your application decides to go south on you.

To resize an Excel chart sheet and paste it in a Word document:

1 With both Word and Excel running, switch to Excel. Click your chart sheet tab to display the chart.

2 Click File, Page Setup on the Excel menu bar for Excel's Page Setup dialog box.

3 In the Page Setup dialog box, click the Chart tab and select the Custom option, as shown in figure 23.3.

4 Click OK in the Page Setup dialog box, and you'll see that your chart is surrounded by a broken-line border, labeled Chart Area in the lower right-hand corner.

5 Click the broken-line border around the chart; the border changes from broken line to patterned, and handles pop up around it. Now drag any handle to resize the chart, as shown in figure 23.4.

Fig. 23.3
Even though you're not printing the chart, you can only resize chart sheets with the Page Setup Custom option.

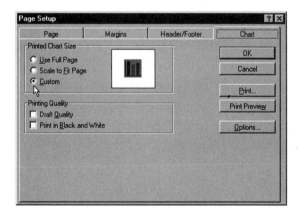

Fig. 23.4

As you drag a handle, the border changes back to a broken line. Quirky, but it works.

Remember that chart sheets aren't displayed at 100% magnification, so this chart looks smaller than it really is.

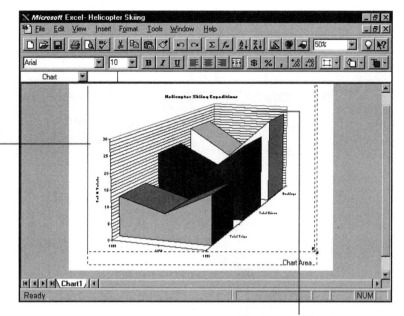

If resizing the Chart Area does odd things to your chart's appearance, click the Plot Area to select it, then drag to resize it.

TIP **To keep the chart in proportion as you resize it, drag the corner** handles.

6 You'll have to resize the chart title, legend, and axes fonts. Right-click each of them in turn and select Format Axis (or Title or Legend, depending on what you've right-clicked) on the shortcut menu. In the Format dialog box that pops up, click the Font tab, select a smaller font size, and click OK.

7 Once you've dragged the chart down to size, click the Zoom Control drop-down arrow on the Standard toolbar (refer to fig. 23.4) and select 100% so you can see your chart's actual size. Drag to resize further if you have to; you'll want the chart small enough to fit on a page full of text.

8 Got your chart resized? The handles around the Chart Area should still be displayed; if they're not, click the chart to get them back. Then click the Copy button on the Excel Standard toolbar. That copies the chart to the Windows Clipboard.

9 Now switch to Word. Put the insertion point where you want the chart and click the Paste button on the Word Standard toolbar. The chart pops right into your document, as shown in figure 23.5.

Fig. 23.5

Inserting a chart *is just like inserting text; everything around it gets shoved aside to make room.*

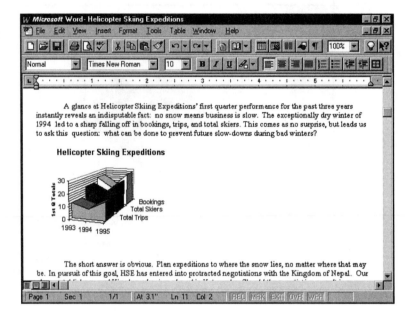

As you can see in figure 23.5, just plopping a chart into the middle of a document may not give you exactly what you want. Existing text gets unceremoniously pushed aside by an inserted object, and the result is as you see. It's easily fixed.

I want text to flow around my chart

Charts look like they really belong in documents when text flows around them. Otherwise, a reader will think you just pasted in the chart any old way (which is exactly what we just did).

To wrap text around an inserted chart:

1 Click the inserted chart in your Word document to select it. Handles pop up around the chart.

2 Click Insert, Frame. If you're in Normal view, Word asks if you want to switch to Page Layout view; click Yes.

3 The Frame border appears around the chart and the chart is moved to the beginning of the paragraph. Just point anywhere inside the frame and drag the chart wherever you want it.

4 By default, text wraps around a frame. If your text isn't wrapping, click Format, Frame for the Frame dialog box. Under the Text Wrapping options, select Around, then click OK. When you're through moving, resizing, and wrapping, your document will look something like figure 23.6.

Fig. 23.6
With text wrapped around it, the chart looks like it belongs here.

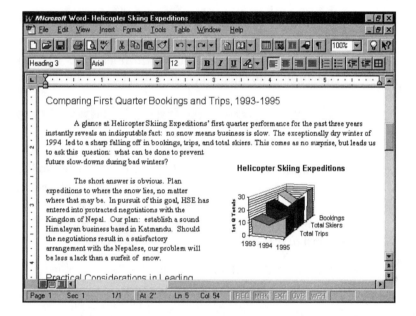

TIP If your chart requires more resizing after you've framed it, it's easier to remove the frame first, resize the chart (just click it and drag a handle), then frame it again. To remove a frame, click the framed chart to select it, then click Format, Frame, Remove Frame, OK.

What if I want to insert an embedded Excel chart?

Charts embedded in Excel worksheets can be inserted into Word documents just as easily as chart sheets. Select the chart in Excel, click the Copy button on the Excel Standard toolbar, then paste the chart in Word.

When you select the embedded chart in Excel, be sure to single-click it. Don't double-click the chart (as though you were going to edit it) to select it. Copying a double-clicked chart leads to trouble when you paste it: if you try to resize the chart in Word, the chart slips out of sight, replaced by Excel worksheet cells.

A single-clicked chart in Excel has a thin border around it; double-clicked charts have a thick border. As long as you copy and paste the former, inserting your embedded chart in Word will be trouble-free.

How do I get rid of this chart?

You've copied and pasted, resized, moved, edited, and wrapped, and you still want to delete your chart in Word? At least this job's uncomplicated. To delete an embedded object in Word, click it, then press Delete.

Can I copy my Excel table to a Word document?

Excel lists and numerical tables are easily copied to Word. Just select the Excel data you want, click the Copy button, and paste it in Word. The data appears at the insertion point, formatted as a Word table. If you want to link the Word copy to the original list or table, use the Paste Special command in Word to paste as a link, just as we did earlier.

Once pasted, treat your copied table like any other pasted object. You can move it, frame it, or use any of Word's table formatting features to format it.

All that clip art in PowerPoint... Can I use it in Word?

Microsoft Office users get a snappy presentations program called PowerPoint. It's used to create slide shows and fancy overhead projection transparencies. PowerPoint comes with an array of image editing tools and a big selection of clip art images. You can alter any of those clip art images in PowerPoint, and then stick them in your Word documents.

To insert PowerPoint clip art in Word:

1 With both Word and PowerPoint running, switch to PowerPoint. If you just want a piece of clip art, choose <u>B</u>lank Presentation in the Power-Point dialog box that pops up when you first run the program.

2 The New Slide dialog box appears next; click the Blank choice under Choose An <u>A</u>utolayout, then click OK.

3 That puts you in the PowerPoint slide editing window. Click the Insert Clip Art button on the PowerPoint Standard toolbar.

4 If you haven't used PowerPoint before, you'll get the Add New Pictures dialog box. Just click <u>A</u>dd All, and sit back and wait a moment or two.

5 Eventually, the Microsoft ClipArt Gallery 2.0 dialog box pops up. Click any of the Categories, and use the right-hand scroll bar to preview the corresponding items in the <u>P</u>ictures box, as shown in figure 23.7.

Fig. 23.7
There's a raft of clip art here. You might even find a picture of a raft.

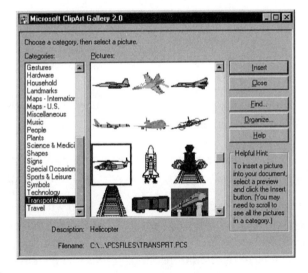

6 When you get to a picture you like, double-click it to pop it onto the slide. Now you can use the PowerPoint tools to edit and resize the clip art image. If you're inserting it in a Word document, you'll want to make it smaller; just drag a corner, as shown in figure 23.8.

7 When you've cut the clip art image down to size and edited it to suit, click the Copy button on the PowerPoint Standard toolbar to copy it to the Windows Clipboard.

Fig. 23.8

PowerPoint lets you do just about anything you want to a clip art image; just click the buttons on the PowerPoint toolbars.

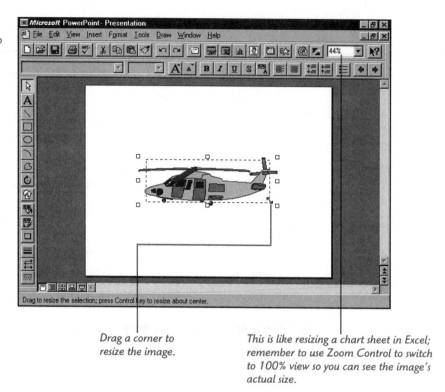

Drag a corner to
resize the image.

This is like resizing a chart sheet in Excel;
remember to use Zoom Control to switch
to 100% view so you can see the image's
actual size.

8 Switch to Word and click the Paste button to pop the image into your Word document at the insertion point.

You can put a frame around the pasted image in Word to wrap text around it and position it exactly where you want it, as I did in figure 23.9.

If you want to edit your clip art image, as I did with the image in figure 23.9, you'll have to do it in PowerPoint before pasting it in Word. Double-clicking the pasted image in Word, unlike double-clicking a pasted chart, doesn't open the image for alterations. It just takes you back to the Microsoft ClipArt Gallery.

I don't care about editing the image. I just want to stick a picture in Word!

You can insert clip art images into Word documents without bothering with PowerPoint at all. That's handy if you don't much care about using Power-Point's tools to edit the image.

Fig. 23.9
I added the shadow effect in PowerPoint before I copied and pasted the image.

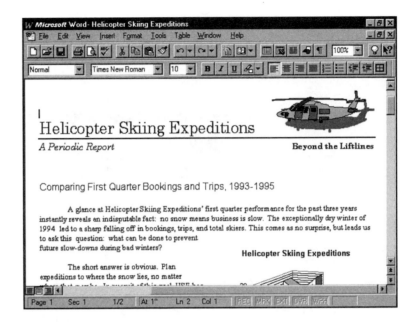

Click Insert, Object for the Object dialog box. On the Object Type list, double-click Microsoft ClipArt Gallery 2.0. The Microsoft ClipArt Gallery 2.0 dialog box pops up; double-click any of the images to pop them into your document. It'll be huge; click the image and drag a handle to resize it.

Word and the rest of the world: faxing and e-mail

Never thought there was any drama in sending mail? Mark Twain described the passing of a Pony Express rider like this: "…a wave of the rider's hand, but no reply, and man and horse burst past our excited faces, and go winging away like a belated fragment of a storm!"

Truth to tell, sending mail isn't very dramatic, at least not when you use Word. If you've set up the Window's fax software and The Microsoft Network, you can send faxes and e-mail right from Word.

Save your document first. In case the transmission goes awry, you don't want to lose any work.

With the document open, click File, Send. The Choose Profile dialog box pops up. Make your choice, then click OK. Microsoft Exchange appears in a few moments, with an icon of the active document displayed, as shown in figure 23.10.

Fig. 23.10

On my system, Microsoft Exchange takes a while to appear, but it's still faster than the Pony Express.

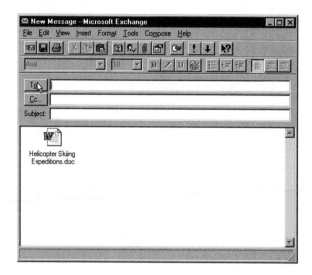

Click the To button and select a recipient from your address book (or add one if you need to). Click the Send button on the Microsoft Exchange toolbar, and your mail is on the way. Depending on your recipient's address in the address book, it goes as either fax or e-mail.

Part VII: Troubleshooting

Troubleshooting Word for Windows 95

Troubleshooting Word for Windows 95

● In this chapter:

- **Tackling the basics, including Help**

- **Editing and formatting text**

- **Working with document files**

- **Solving printing problems**

- **Formatting with styles and templates**

- **Handling columns**

- **Using graphics, frames, WordArt, and more**

- **Working with more challenging features**

Is Word slowing you down? For speedy help, read on. . . . . . ❯

Nothing's more frustrating than wrestling with software that's supposed to make your life easier. If you run into a snag with Word, flip to this chapter to get the help you need. You'll find common questions about Word grouped into easy-to-find categories, for help at your fingertips.

Tackling the basics, including Help

Whether you're learning a sport or a software program, you have to be comfortable with the fundamentals before you can move on to trickier plays. If Word gives you a bad snap or throws you a curveball, the techniques offered in this section can help you recover quickly.

Some of my menus have options that are grayed out, and nothing happens when I click them

They're available in your version of Word. They're just not active because they can't be used at the moment. For example, if you're not working in a table, most of the commands on the Table menu are dormant and therefore grayed out.

These toolbar buttons look awfully tiny on my monitor. Can I make them bigger?

Yes. Choose View, Toolbars from the main menu. Choose Large Buttons at the bottom of the Toolbars dialog box, then click OK.

When I'm using full-screen view, how am I supposed to access my menu?

Even though the main menu disappears, you can open a menu by clicking the top of the screen at the spot where you'd normally find the menu. For instance, if you click in from the upper left-hand corner, the File menu will drop down. You can move from one menu to the next with your arrow keys. The menus are also available from the keyboard; press Alt+F for the File menu, for example.

My Help window takes up most of my screen. How do I keep it from completely overlapping my document?

You can size the Help window any way you want by dragging the borders in and out with the mouse pointer. The new size becomes a permanent part of your Word configuration until you resize it again.

How do I move the Help window?

Click its title bar and drag it to where you want it.

Can I return to my document without closing the Help window?

Yes. Click the Help window's Minimize button, click anywhere in the document window, or press Alt+Tab. The Help window will remain in the background. You can recall it by pressing Alt+Tab.

How do I keep the Help window visible, so I can refer to it while I'm in the document?

Simple. From the Options menu in any Help window, select Keep Help On Top, On Top. Thereafter, you can move between the Help window and your document window by clicking inside one or the other, or by pressing Alt+Tab.

I don't quite understand how the Help files are organized. Does each of the Search dialog boxes have its own Help files?

All of Word's search dialog boxes use the same Help files to get their information; they just give you different ways to search. Choosing "Troubleshooting" and "Troubleshoot Page Breaks and Section Breaks" take you to the same Help screen.

In Help, is it possible to search for entries that include either "page" or "break"?

Yes. In the Find tab of the Help Topics dialog box, choose Options. Then, in the Find Options dialog box, click the option called At Least One Of The Words You Typed.

When I click the Find tab in Help, I get a Find Setup Wizard dialog box that tells me I have to create a database first. What's going on?

Not to worry. Find needs to create a word list from Word's Help files before it can do its job. This is a no-muss, no-fuss procedure. Choose the recommended <u>M</u>inimize Database Size. Word gives you on-screen instructions on what to do next. (You can choose <u>R</u>ebuild from the Find dialog box if you want to choose another option later.) Building a database is a one-time-only deal; you won't have to do it again unless you have to reinstall Word.

Typing and formatting text

The whole point of a word processing program is to make it easy and convenient for you to enter and format text. If you're finding that it isn't as easy as it should be and a problem is hanging you up, check this section first for answers to your questions.

I accidentally pressed some keys that took me out of my document and someplace strange. How do I get back to my document?

If you happened to open a dialog box, click the Cancel button or press the Esc key. If you're in a menu or a text box (such as the ones on the Standard toolbar), press the Esc key.

The keys on the number pad have arrows, but when I press them all I get are numbers. How do I make the arrows work?

Press the Num Lock key. This also activates the keys that have labels such as Home, End, Ins, and Del. Press the Num Lock key again to reactivate the number pad.

Why is there a scroll bar on the bottom of my screen? When would I need to scroll a document horizontally?

You use the horizontal scroll bar for extra-wide documents. For example, you might have a document that you're printing lengthwise whose right margin is out of view. Or if you enlarge your document view with Zoom

Control on your Standard toolbar, your text might become too big to fit in the document window. You use the horizontal scroll bar the same way you do the vertical scroll bar.

Do I have to start each document with 10-point Times New Roman? How do I make a new font and style permanent?

Choose Format, Font from the main menu. Select the font and size you want and click the Default button. Choose Yes when Word asks you if you want to change the default. The next time you quit Word, you'll be asked if you want to change the template. Choose Yes.

Why can't I see my inside border?

If you try to apply an inside border to a single paragraph, you won't see it. That's because it's not there. Inside borders only work in between paragraphs.

How do I break out of a paragraph border box?

When you add a border and press Enter at the end of the paragraph to start a new one, the border also extends to the new paragraph. Right, left, and outside borders expand, and bottom borders get shoved down one line. To avoid that, start the new paragraph first, then apply the border to the previous paragraph. If you've already applied a border and you want a new, borderless paragraph, click the No Border button to clear the border, start the new paragraph, then reapply the border to the previous paragraph.

How do I set tab stops for a list or table I've already typed?

Start by highlighting the text. Click the ruler where you want the tab stop. Of course, you must have tabs at the appropriate places between columns to align the text.

I created a two-column list using tabs. So why doesn't the text in the second column align with the tab stop?

If you used Word's default tab stops to align your second column of text *before* you set your new tab stop, there's a good chance you have extra tabs.

Also, to make your text line up properly, you probably used more tabs in some lines than you did in others. Just delete the extra tabs, and you should be set.

I tried to change a tab stop by dragging it on the ruler. The tab stop changed for only one line! How do I change the tab stops for all the lines?

Select the entire table first, then drag the tab stop. When no text has been selected, dragging a tab stop affects only the line on which your insertion point is positioned.

I've tried creating leaders in my document, but I don't get any. What am I doing wrong?

Have you set tab stops to align your tabular material? Leaders don't work with Word's default tab stops.

I selected a double-spaced paragraph, pressed Ctrl+1, and nothing happened. What did I do wrong?

There's a good chance the person who wrote the document pressed the Enter key after each line (this is a common mistake among inexperienced users). Click the Show/Hide Paragraph Marks button on the Standard toolbar and look for telltale paragraph markers. Delete all but the one that ends the paragraph.

How do I get rid of my bullets? The Delete key doesn't work!

Highlight the list items and click the Numbering or Bullets button. If you want to delete a single bullet or number, the easiest way is to put your insertion point between the bullet or number and the following text and press the Backspace key.

I put my section break in the wrong place. How do I move it?

Select the section break. Click the selected break and hold down the mouse button. A small checkered box appears at the tail of your mouse pointer, and

Word displays the message Move to Where? in the status bar. Drag the section break to where you want it and release the mouse button.

I tried to insert page numbers, but all I get is the word PAGE between two squiggly brackets! Why isn't this feature working?

What you see, {PAGE}, is the name of the field. You can change it to the actual page number in one of two ways. If you're in a header or footer, right-click the field and choose Toggle Field Codes from the shortcut menu. If you're not in the header or footer, choose Tools, Options from the main menu and click the View tab. Under the Show heading, choose Field Codes to remove the check in the check box.

My ruler isn't showing. How do I change column widths?

If your ruler isn't showing, you can change a column's width by dragging the grid line border in the table. Select the column, then touch the right grid line border with the pointer until it changes into two vertical lines between two arrows.

If you'd rather use the ruler, you can make it visible by choosing View, Ruler.

Oops! I accidentally deleted a column. Is it gone forever?

Not if you deleted it recently. If the deletion was your last action, choose Edit from the main menu and choose Undo Delete Columns. The shortcut for Edit, Undo is Ctrl+Z. If you've taken some actions since the delete, click the down arrow next to the Undo button on the Standard toolbar. Find Delete Columns in the selection box and click it. Note, however, that Word also undoes all actions above Delete Columns.

Working with document files

You need to save all your hard work in a document file. When you do so, you can give your document a unique name. This section answers common questions that may arise when you work with documents in Word.

Why should I use Windows 95's Explorer for my file and folder management?

Word's Open and Save As dialog boxes are designed to handle simple, routine file and folder management. Explorer has more functions, and it gives you better options for moving and copying files (for example, the ability to drag and drop). If you're familiar with Explorer and have to do extensive file management tasks, Explorer is probably the better option.

What are long file names?

If you've used computers before, you've probably been frustrated with the fact that you could only use 11 letters in a file name (eight in the base name and three in the extension, such as LTRTOJML.DOC). It was easy to lose track of what was what in Windows 3.1 and its predecessors.

Word's new rules for naming files are much more liberal. Windows 95 allows long file names, and it also allows some characters that other versions of Windows don't.

But with freedom comes added responsibility. If you start typing 50-word file names based on whatever pops into your mind, you're going to have major headaches managing your documents.

How long can my file names be?

Up to 255 characters. It's not likely you'd ever want to create a file name longer than a few dozen characters. However, when you save a file for the first time, Word uses the first characters in the document (if the document contains text) as the default file name. If you simply accept whatever default Word provides, you could end up with a lot of long file names.

I see file names with two periods and other weird characters. Isn't that illegal?

Not in Word for Windows 95. Unlike earlier versions of Windows and MS-DOS, Windows 95 accepts the period as a valid character. Your file name can include letters, numbers, spaces, and all characters except an asterisk (*), forward slash (/), backslash (\), greater-than sign (>), less-than sign (<), question mark (?), quotation mark ("), vertical bar (|), colon (:), or semicolon (;).

Despite Word's willingness to let you use all sorts of character combinations, your best plan is to stick with letters and numbers. Use symbols only if you have a good reason to, such as to separate elements in your file name.

Does it matter if I use upper- or lowercase characters in a file name?

No. MYFILE, myFile, and MyFile are all the same to Word.

Do I have to add a .DOC extension to my file name?

No, Word does it for you. In fact, if you name a file MYFILE.DOC, Word saves it as MYFILE.DOC.DOC.

What if I want to name a file with an extension other than .DOC?

Put the entire file name in quotation marks; for example, "REPORT.PRN."

Do folder names follow the same rules?

Yes.

What happens if I save a file that someone is going to use on a computer that doesn't have Windows 95?

If you share documents with people who use earlier versions of Word and Windows, your long file names will create more confusion than you can imagine. Here's the bottom line:

- You shouldn't use long file names if you share your documents with people who don't run Windows 95 or this version of Word. Other operating systems and word processors won't necessarily recognize the long file names.

- You shouldn't use spaces, periods, plus signs, commas, equal signs, or brackets in your file names.

Can people with other versions of Word use my Word for Windows 95 documents?

People using Word 6 for Windows 3.1 will have no problems; Word for Windows 95 uses the same file format. Also, the WordPad word processor will open your Word for Windows 95 documents. For people using other versions of Word, the answer is, "Definitely maybe." Word for Windows 95 is happy to let you try saving in a format that other versions of Word will recognize, but don't expect miracles.

If you're going to give a file to someone using an earlier version of Word, first make sure you know which version that person is using. (If she says Word 6, find out if it's Word 6 for Windows or Word 6 for DOS; they're different formats.) If you're not sure what version the other person has, save in Word 3.x-5.x for MS-DOS format.

Choose the matching version in the Save File As Type box. Save the file to a file name that's different than the original file name. Also, the file name should not have more than eight characters; earlier versions of Word will not recognize a long file name. Finally, if you have any doubts at all about what word processor the other person uses, provide a plain-text file as well (the Text Only option). The document's special formatting instructions will be removed, but at least your colleague will be able to read the file.

When I create a folder, can I only use it for Word documents?

Word is not actually creating the folder itself; it's instructing Windows 95 to create the folder. Thus, your folder is available to all of your programs. Also, you can manage folders created in Word with Windows Explorer.

I did a content search for a file, and it took more than half an hour! Is there any way I can speed up my searches?

You can take a couple of steps to make your searches go faster. First, don't search the entire drive unless you have to. If you know the file is in a certain tree of folders, search only those folders. And second, avoid using All Files in the Files Of Type text box.

Editing text

Chances are you'll need to make changes to your documents after you create them. If making changes to your document raises questions, this section has answers.

I cut a block of text I didn't want to cut! How do I restore it?

If you haven't moved your insertion point, simply click the Paste button or press Ctrl+V. If you've moved to somewhere else in the document, click the Undo button or press Ctrl+Z to undo the cut. Word restores the cut text to its original location. This second method works only if you haven't made any editing or formatting changes since the cut.

What do I do if I want to delete the highlighted word during a spell check?

Press the Delete key. This deletes the highlighted word in the Change To text box. The Change and Change All buttons turn into Delete and Delete All buttons, respectively. Choose the button you want; Word deletes the word in text and continues with the spell check.

The Add button in my Spelling dialog box is grayed out. Am I missing my Custom dictionary?

Probably not. It's more likely that the dictionary isn't active. To fix the problem, choose Options in your Spelling dialog box. and Custom Dictionaries in the next Spelling dialog box. If CUSTOM.DIC appears in the Custom Dictionaries list box, make sure it has a check in the box and click OK. If CUSTOM.DIC doesn't appear, click the Add button, then choose CUSTOM.DIC from the Add Custom Dictionary dialog box.

Why can't I just add body text in Outline view?

You can. It's just easier to type body text in Normal view because you can see your paragraph formatting.

I just moved my outline heading up, but the body text below it got left behind!

If you move headings around in an outline, you can wind up with orphaned body text, deserted by the parent heading when you moved it up or down. To avoid this, collapse the body text under the heading first, then move the heading. Collapsed body text accompanies a heading wherever you move it.

Printing woes

Printing is not yet a perfect science. If you print and don't get what you expected, try the solutions offered in this section to avoid being put out by output problems.

Word displays a message that there's a problem with the printer

When you install Word, it should detect your printer and make it available to you. But problems inevitably arise. Before you tell Word to retry a print job, confirm that you can answer "Yes" to all of these questions:

Is the printer plugged in and turned on?

Check this first; more often than you'd think, it's the cause of the problem!

Is the printer cable connected snugly to both the printer and the computer?

Printer cables are notorious for loosening at night after the lights are out.

Is the printer on-line?

Usually, there's an on-line button and corresponding light on your printer's control panel. Make sure the light's on or the LED display says Ready.

Does the printer have paper? If the paper is in a tray, is the tray pushed all the way in?

Loose trays are especially common on Macintosh laser printers. Also, if your printer has selectable options such as single-sheet or tractor feeding, make sure the right one's selected.

Does the printer that's hooked up to your computer correspond to the printer Word is set up to use?

If, for example, Word expects a Canon Bubble Jet and finds a daisy-wheel printer, your document won't print as it appears on the screen. Mismatches shouldn't be a concern unless you've got more than one printer available (through a network, for example) or you have reason to believe that someone has changed your setup.

To find out what printer Word expects, choose File, Print. Word shows you the name of the printer in the Print dialog box. If it doesn't match what's connected to your machine, click the Name text box and see if the right printer is listed. A mismatched printer doesn't necessarily mean you won't be able to print. You might have a printer that's compatible with the one you've got listed in your Print dialog box. The only way to find out is by printing some documents.

How do I fix envelope alignment problems?

If your printer chews up your envelope or doesn't print it the way it's supposed to, try putting the envelope in a different way.

Click Feed in the lower right-hand corner of the Envelopes and Labels dialog box, or click the Options button and click the Printing Options tab. Choose the new alignment from the box under Feed Method. Click OK, insert an envelope, and print it.

My text looks white on the screen, but it prints as black. Can't I print white text against a shaded background?

You can. Some printers just need a little help first:

1 Click File, Print. In the Print dialog box, click Properties for the Properties dialog box.

2 Click the Font tab in the Properties dialog box, and select the Print True Type As Graphics option.

3 Click OK in each dialog box, and your document should print with white text against a shaded background.

Formatting with styles and templates

Once you become comfortable with styles, you'll find that they save time and help you produce professional-looking documents. When you need help with styles, look here first.

Why doesn't my new style seem to have all the formatting I added?

When you create a paragraph style, the formatting you use applies to the whole paragraph. You can't, for example, italicize part of a paragraph and save it as a style. You can always go back to the paragraph later and add more formatting, like italics, to particular words or phrases.

I changed the master document's template, and now all the formatting in my subdocuments has changed!

The more you look at a master document, the more inclined you might be to change the way it looks. The Format, Style Gallery command, for example, can give your master document a radically new appearance. That's fine, but the master document's template overrides the subdocuments' formatting. If you change the master's template, the change is also applied to the subdocuments.

Handling columns

Word can automatically create columns in a document, but there's no guarantee that those columns will come out perfectly the first time. If your columns are awry, try the solutions noted here.

Why won't my columns balance?

You've gone through the steps to balance your columns, and they won't balance! Frustrating, but fixable. There are three possible causes:

- Paragraph formatting can prevent columns from balancing. To fix it, click Format, Paragraph, and click the Text Flow tab. Clear all the check boxes in the Pagination group of options, then click OK.

- You might find that the top of the last column begins one line below the top of the column to the left of it. That means you've got a paragraph mark at the bottom of the next-to-last column. Click the Show/Hide Paragraph Marks button on the Standard toolbar and delete the offending paragraph mark.

- If you've converted the document from another word processor or an earlier version of Word, click <u>T</u>ools, <u>O</u>ptions, and click the Compatibility tab. Clear the Don't Balance Columns For Continuous Section Starts check box in the <u>O</u>ptions list, then click OK.

Using graphics, frames, WordArt, and more

If problems crop up when you're working with graphics and frames, check out the solutions in this section.

I don't see the insertion point inside the text box (frame)!

It's there, but it may be hidden within the text box border. Press the spacebar or Tab key to bring it out in the open. Or click the text box border and drag a handle to expand the box. A bigger box might be easier to work with, and it also exposes the insertion point to view.

Why don't I see WordArt in the Object Type list?

WordArt might not have been installed when you installed Word. If you don't see it in the Object Type list in the Object dialog box, close Word, insert your program disk or CD, and run Setup to add WordArt.

I've been experimenting with the Object dialog box, and now Word doesn't respond to the keyboard or the mouse! What do I do?

Get a cup of coffee. Inserting objects can be a slow affair, and Word might just be working on your last command. If nothing happens for more than a minute or two, press Ctrl+Alt+Delete. The Close Program dialog box pops up; select Microsoft Word, and click <u>E</u>nd Task. That shuts Word down, but you lose any unsaved work.

Working with more challenging features

To get the most out of Word, you'll want to use the program's many advanced features. Here's a grab-bag of helpful advice that you can call on when you find yourself in a jam.

Why is the Titles option on the Insert menu grayed out?

You have to select the chart before inserting chart titles. Click the chart, then click Insert, Titles.

I selected my next index entry, but the Mark button in the Mark Index Entry dialog box is still grayed out!

Click the Main Entry edit box. You have to do that for every index entry you select.

How do I get the original toolbars back again?

You might have so much fun dragging buttons around that you wind up with toolbars that are not as functional as you'd like. To restore the toolbars to their original state, click View, Toolbars, Reset. All your button additions and subtractions are erased, and your toolbars are back to where they started.

I'm trying to select text while recording this macro, but I can't seem to do it with the mouse!

That's because you *can't* select text with the mouse when recording a macro. Use the Shift+arrow key combination instead. The mouse does work for toolbar buttons and menu commands during macro recording.

I inserted a merge field I didn't want!

It's easy to click the wrong merge field. Or you might decide you don't want a particular field in a particular spot in your document. Either way, click the merge field to select it. Word shades the merge field to show it's been selected; then press Delete to get rid of it.

Index

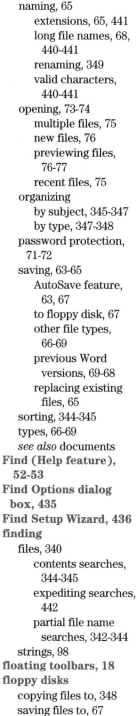

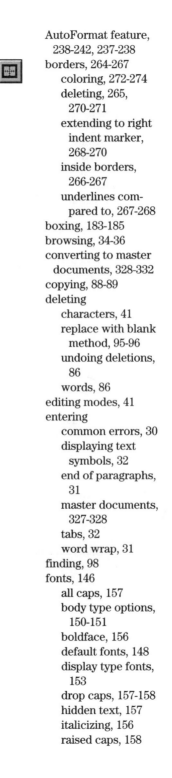

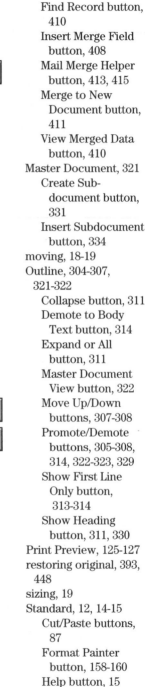

PLUG YOURSELF INTO...

MACMILLAN INFORMATION SUPERLIBRARY™

que · SAMS PUBLISHING · Hayden Books · que COLLEGE · NRP · alpha books · Brady · ADOBE PRESS

THE MACMILLAN INFORMATION SUPERLIBRARY™

Free information and vast computer resources from the world's leading computer book publisher—online!

FIND THE BOOKS THAT ARE RIGHT FOR YOU!

A complete online catalog, plus sample chapters and tables of contents give you an in-depth look at *all* of our books, including hard-to-find titles. It's the best way to find the books you need!

- STAY INFORMED with the latest computer industry news through our online newsletter, press releases, and customized Information SuperLibrary Reports.

- GET FAST ANSWERS to your questions about MCP books and software.

- VISIT our online bookstore for the latest information and editions!

- COMMUNICATE with our expert authors through e-mail and conferences.

- DOWNLOAD SOFTWARE from the immense MCP library:
  - Source code and files from MCP books
  - The best shareware, freeware, and demos

- DISCOVER HOT SPOTS on other parts of the Internet.

- WIN BOOKS in ongoing contests and giveaways!

TO PLUG INTO MCP: ➔

GOPHER: gopher.mcp.com
FTP: ftp.mcp.com

WORLD WIDE WEB: **http://www.mcp.com**

Home Page · What's New · Bookstore · Reference Desk · Software Library · Macmillan Overview · Talk to Us

User-Friendly References for All Your Computing Needs

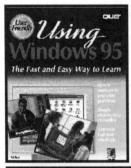

Using Windows 95
0-7897-0092-1, $19.99 USA
Publication Date: 8/95

Using The Microsoft Network
0-7897-0398-X, $19.99 USA
Publication Date: 9/95

Using PowerPoint for Windows 95
0-7897-0365-3, $19.99 USA
Publication Date: 11/95

Using Excel for Windows 95
0-7897-0111-1, $19.99 USA
Publication Date: 9/95

The new *Using* series gives readers just the information they need to perform specific tasks quickly and move on to other things. *Using* books provide bite-sized information for quick and easy reference, along with real-world analogies and examples to explain new concepts.

For more information on these and other Que products, visit your local book retailer or call 1-800-772-0477.